JOURNALS from the EDGE

JOURNALS
from the
EDGE

Bill Boyum

Printed in the United States of America

ISBN 978-1508654193

Designed by Doug Behrens Design - Honolulu
Front cover photo by Don King

The author Bill Boyum and his sister Mimi

To my sister Mimi. We spent many hours laughing and crying together putting the finishing touches on this book. Never would have finished without you.

Contents

25 SEN

REPUBLIK INDONESIA

Commander J.H. Boyum, Patuxent River Test Pilot Training, 1956

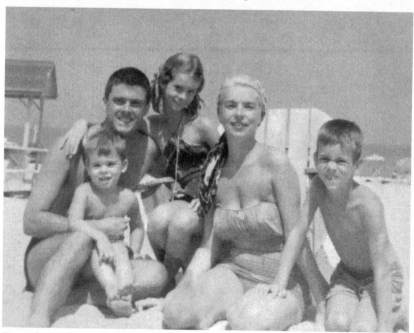

Boyum family, Chesapeake Bay, 1955

Chapter One

Punching Out
PATUXENT RIVER, MARYLAND, 1956

My brother Mikey is four years older than me. He's ten. I like to do what he does. We're searching for sand dollars to skip across the water in front of our house on the Chesapeake Bay, where all the naval officers live with their families. Our dad is a test pilot.

"Mikey," I ask, "where's Lonely Street?"

"What?"

"Mimi keeps playing that record over and over."

"Oh, that. All the girls are going crazy over that guy. He's cool, I guess."

"Is Mimi crazy?"

"No, stupid. It's rock-and-roll."

"She has a new Hound Dog record. I like that one."

He pushes me away.

"You're a goofball."

As Mikey walks towards the surrounding farm fields, I follow him. I'm about to ask if we're going to play in the forts we make inside the piled-up hay when he puts his finger to his lips. A jet fires up, and Mikey starts to run.

"Let's go, Billy," he calls. "It's the air show."

I run behind him towards the runway, where a crowd is gathered.

We squeeze through the crowd to get a better look. Heat waves melt off the tarmac, making the jets on the airstrip look like jelly. The smells of jet fuel and hot dogs fill the air.

Our dirty blue t-shirts have the gold insignia of Naval Aviators. I'm the chubby one with glasses and Mikey is the skinny one.

He's smiling at me, his open hand full of change.

"I got enough for a soda."

I can't help but stare again at his chipped front tooth from the last time Dad went at him.

He pushes me again.

"Quit looking at it."

We make our way to the concession stand on the edge of the crowd for an RC Cola. As soon as Mikey takes his first sip, the sky is ripped apart by the roar of jets, making me cork my ears with my thumbs and cover my eyes.

"Did they crash, Mikey?"

My fingers spread from around my glasses so I can peek just as my brother aims my head up to the sky. I stare, amazed. The jets haven't crashed, and I can see the two pilots pull into a climb, straight up.

I turn to my brother as he points towards the sky.

"You see them now? Those two specks?"

It's only been a second but when I look at the sky again, it's empty.

"Yeah. I see them."

"You lying little four-eyes. You can't see squat."

He rubs my buzz-cut head, just like his. Dad says he cuts our hair like this for speed. It's easy to spot my brother most of the time but in this crowd I'm worried I'll get lost. I reach out to grab his hand, but he pulls it away.

"What happened, Mikey?"

He speeds ahead, fast-walking and fast-talking.

"It's called skinning the cat," he says when I get close enough to hear him. "Those two jets screamed straight at each other, 400 miles an hour, right off the deck of the runway, smoking fast."

"Yeah, Mikey, smoking fast."

He stops suddenly and takes a long swig from his soda. As the bottle lowers from his lips, he grins at me, but I'm careful not to stare this time.

"Boy, those fighter jocks were cool as… Without a blink they snapped their jets into a 90-degree roll a split second before they were about to crash. Looked like inches to me."

"Cool as what?"

"Cool as—nothing. Nothing needs to come after 'cool as.' Those two words say it all. Heard one of Dad's pals say a pilot needs to be at two thousand feet before he can safely punch out. Nothing compares to that cool."

"Punch out?"

"Yank on the ejection handle when there's no hope left. Fires them out of the jet like a rocket."

"Oh. That sounds scary."

"Well, it's the only thing left to do if they want to live but, like I said, they need two thousand feet."

"Two thousand feet? How high can jets go?"

"Jets haven't been into outer space, but it's only a matter of time."

He gives me the soda bottle, and I take a quick sip.

"I really want to fly jets."

Mikey twists his face, shaking his head, and grabs the bottle back.

"Forget it, moron. You're a scaredy-pants and a spaz. Plus, you can't see a thing. You'll never be a pilot."

I look down at my scuffed sneakers.

"Dad has real good eyes, huh?"

"Yep. They're like Superman's X-ray vision. He can see through walls and know what we're up to. Mom says he was one of the first night fighter pilots in WWII so he can see in the dark, too."

I take off my glasses for a moment and squint.

"You dummy. That won't help."

"Why am I the only one with bad eyes?"

"Because you're an orphan. Mom found you on the street and brought you home 'cause we didn't have a pet. She thought you were cute, even though you're a chubby cross-eyed little toad. But now she's too busy to have a pet toad so I have to watch you."

"Uh uh. Mom said."

Mikey shrugs. "Of course she has to say that. She can't tell her friends she found this toad kid on the street. Just look at the facts. You're a blind toad. How can you really be a part of our family?"

"Then how come Dad belts you more than me?"

My brother's face twists into a painful grimace just as he lunges at me with a closed fist. I cringe but he doesn't hit me, just spins away and outruns me once again.

"Wait up, Mikey!" I wail. "I'm sorry!"

Suddenly a boom cracks overhead, stopping my brother in his tracks. I catch up to him and, scared, reach for his hand. He begins to yank away again but then looks into my eyes and lets me hold on.

More cracks and reverberations fill the air as my brother points to the tight formation flying team, which I can see this time.

"Mikey, look! The Blue Angels. F-9 Cougars doing their diamond formation."

He shoves me, playfully this time, smiling.

"Look at the smarty-pants."

An explosion rocks me and my head snaps towards a ball of fire on the runway. Everyone is screaming, except Mikey. He just yanks my arm as a signal to follow him, and soon we're cutting through the crowd towards a gigantic black smoke cloud rising from a nearby field. I bounce off almost everyone we pass as I struggle to keep up. When a fat man with a beer stumbles into me, I fall, scrambling onto the burning tarmac between the legs and shoes of spectators running the other way. Mikey is getting farther away from me. I spot an opening, enough room for me to stand and run to catch up with him, but then black smoke surrounds us and Mikey disappears. I freeze and bend over, grabbing my stomach. A siren screams and my fingers plug my ears. Mikey appears out of nowhere in the dark smoke, grabs my hand, and pulls me with him into the clear air.

My brother's arm hangs over my shoulders as we walk home past the hay bales and our secret hiding places.

"Mikey, whose dad do you think that was?"

He shrugs.

"What happens when you die?"

"They put you in a coffin and bury you."

"And then you go to heaven, right?"

"I dunno. Why you asking me so many questions?"

"'Cause I still want to fly jets."

I rip free of Mikey and take off with my arms spread wide, weaving around the field in my imaginary jet. Mikey chases and tackles me, then tries to stick pieces of straw in my ears, both of us laughing.

Chipped tooth Mikey

Chapter Two

Grunts
CORONADO, CALIFORNIA 1958

Oh boy, my two favorite TV cartoon magpies, Heckle and Jeckle, are getting into trouble again, just like Mikey and I did before Mikey went away to live with our grandmother. One has a British accent, the other talks like a gangster. A bulldog chases them as the magpies run past a ringing phone. They put the brakes on and one bird holds up his hand to stop the dog. The phone is still ringing.

The dog stops and the British-sounding bird answers the phone in three different tones. "You don't say, you don't say, you don't say."

The dog is curious. "What did he say?" The bird answers, "He didn't say." And then the chase starts again. I laugh until there are tears in my eyes.

Lorraine, our landlord, checks in on me. She wears tight leopard-spot pants. A cigarette hangs from her lower lip like it's glued to her bright red lipstick.

"I'm glad you're having fun."

Her voice sounds like a man's. It's gruff but she's nice enough.

I glance at our phone and hope it will ring. I'm used to Dad being away at sea but since we've lived in Coronado, Mom also seems to be gone most of the time. When she's gone, it's just me and Lorraine in this small apartment.

"Where's my mom now?"

Lorraine stares up at the ceiling. Does she have a crystal ball, like the one I saw Popeye use? She starts talking with her cigarette still stuck on her lip.

"Hong Kong? Tokyo? No, this time it's Singapore."

She looks down at me, and I can see her weird eyes surrounded by purple makeup.

"Your mom loves to shop. It's called a junket."

I don't need her to tell me that. Our apartment is already full of junk. There's no room for me to play inside. I love to watch cartoons like

"Popeye" and "Heckle and Jeckle," but Lorraine makes lots of noise with the vacuum cleaner. I don't think she likes watching me while Mom is gone.

"Would you mind if we change to the 'Jack LaLanne Show' while I finish up here?"

I slip out into the alley and shoot everything I can with my slingshot.

~

Everyone in our family is back together now. Mom came back first and immediately got a new house for all the junk she'd bought. She filled our garage to the roof with unopened boxes. There's even boxes inside our house and little room for me to play—so I've been outside exploring every day.

Dad came back next. He'd been away for a long time on his first ship command, the USS Pine Island, a seaplane tender. He took Mom and me onboard for dinner when he first got back into port. Dad wore his white uniform and we were whistled aboard. All the men on the ship saluted and looked as scared of him as I am. I loved the huge crane on the stern that can lift a seaplane out of the water, but the rest of the time on the ship wasn't much fun.

At dinner, Dad spoke to the other officers and no one else talked. I got bored and snuck up on deck to watch movies with the sailors. They threw me up in the air. I liked that but got in trouble. Dad told me it was inappropriate behavior. I don't know what that word means, but I guess it must mean no fun. I asked Mom later and she said we needed to keep our distance from the enlisted men.

Mikey came home after Dad. He'd been living on Maui with Mama Louise, our grandmother from Dad's side, for the past year. I overheard Mom say that Mama Louise thought if she could get Mikey away from Dad, she could inject some love into him. Mom says my brother was too much for our grandmother to handle and that he ran wild. So he's back home now, bunking with me.

I really like the colorful clothes Mikey brought back from Maui, especially his blue and white aloha shirt. I like his hair long, too. It's long enough to part and grease back. Every time I ask Dad if I can grow my hair that long, he sounds like he's going to bite my head off.

Mimi was the last to come home after spending half a year with Mom's relatives in France. Mom says she was well-behaved and is welcome to go back there any time.

I'm happy my brother and sister are home. Dad isn't happy and is always yelling about Mom's clutter of Oriental junk.

But there are times when even Dad is happy. Since I'm Mimi's and Mikey's slave, I have to spy on him to see if the coast is clear. Dad is sitting in his reclining chair, his headphones on, listening to his Big Band music. There's a half-empty drink by his side. His eyes are closed, but his fingers are snapping.

I tiptoe back to the TV room and give Mimi and Mikey the thumbs-up. We jump on our huge Hawaiian *hikie'e* (couch) that our grandmother sent us. It's our island of fun while we watch "Bonanza."

Our new house is right under the approach path for the North Island airstrip.

I'm watching Mom fold laundry in our bedroom. A jet roars over our house and a sonic boom buckles the windows. Mom sees me lurch.

"Billy, you know every air station we live near is going to have loud jets."

She holds up a shirt that's been stained pink in the wash.

"Oh my God. Mikey's new aloha shirt."

Mikey enters our room and stops dead in his tracks when he sees Mom and his shirt. His face turns red.

"Ahh, Mom, how could you?"

"I'm so sorry, Mikey. I know how much that shirt meant to you. Maybe your grandmother can send you another."

"From Maui? That would take forever."

"I'll take you to the PX and we'll find..."

Mom doesn't finish her sentence. I can see why. Dad is standing silently in the doorway behind Mikey. He's hasn't changed out of his work clothes, a starched tan uniform covered with decorations he received from WWII. His face is stern, and I can tell he's listening to Mikey talk. Mikey doesn't know he's there.

"Mom, I wouldn't be seen dead in PX clothes. I'd look like a swabby."

Dad's mouth clenches tight after Mikey uses the word 'swabby.'

I ask Dad so Mikey can hear, "Sir, do you want me to get you a beer?"

Mikey spins and sees Dad glaring at him. Mikey turns back to Mom.

"I'll never live this down at school. Clothes are important. I get teased all the time. The civilian kids at school say they can spot a sailor a mile away."

I exhale when Mikey says 'sailor.'

He turns back to give Dad a quick check-glance, then adds, "I know where to buy cool clothes off base."

I think maybe he's been away too long and forgot Dad doesn't like the word 'cool.'

Mom is just about to reach into her purse to give him some money when Dad steps in and puts his hand over hers.

"Where you'll pay twice as much."

He turns back to glare at Mikey. "When you earn your own money, you can dress any way you want," he says.

"You just want me to look like a grunt."

Dad snaps at the word 'grunt' and begins to slap Mikey and throw him around our room like a rag doll. Mom cries out. Dad shoves Mom and me out of the room, slams the door closed and locks it. But there's no escape from hearing every crack of the belt on the other side of the door.

Mikey screams, "Why? What'd I do?"

Dad yells, "This is a fact of life. When you step out of line, you'll get a beating."

I'm sobbing.

"Mom, why does he always say that? What are facts of life?"

I stare at Mom, but she won't even look at me. She's crying while she pounds on the door.

"He's not one of the sailors on your ship, Jack. You can't break him like some wild horse."

"Mom, all Mikey said was a word. Why? Dad uses words like that all the time."

Mom won't answer me, so I run to Mimi's room. She's a teenager, she'll know why. But her door is locked and I can hear her crying. She's been playing her scratched Elvis forty-five of "Don't Be Cruel" ever since her dog got run over, and the repeating song lines are driving me crazy. I jam my fingers deep into my ears and pound on her door with my head.

"Stop it, Billy."

I run to the TV room and turn on a Popeye cartoon as loud as it will go.

Popeye is getting the crap beat out of him by Bluto. Popeye is lying all bruised up and Bluto is yanking skinny Olive Oyl around by her arm. I'm waiting for Popeye to eat his can of spinach.

Olive Oyl squeaks, "Oh my."

Chapter Three

Shell Shock
1959

We're on the road driving across the country, and Mom's in a bubbly mood.

"Your father has taken trains, airplanes and jets across the country, but we get to have a family adventure all together. Won't this be fun! And on our way to our new home in Virginia we can stop to see your grandparents."

I hear Mimi whisper into Mikey's ear, "She's talking more than I've ever seen her talk around Dad."

"Yeah. And Dad doesn't look too happy about it."

Dad examines his checklist, and Mom jokes that he does the same preflight a test pilot would do for a jet. Dad shoots her an unfriendly glance. But it looks like Mom is right. There's a calculator for figuring miles per gallon and a TripTik map from AAA.

Mom says, "The schedule tells him what's next."

Dad makes a talky gesture towards Mom with his thumb and fingers.

Dad says, "With these new highways Ike built we should make record time."

Mikey whispers to me, "The faster the better. This old Studebaker is a piece of crap."

Dad says, "Each of you will share the responsibility of looking at the road map and being the navigator. Bill, is this our turn?"

"I th-th-think we turn at highway 80."

"God damn it, Bill, open your mouth when you talk."

Mikey grabs my jaw and forces it open and closed, making silly mumbling noises while he does.

"Quit it," I complain.

All of a sudden Dad swings his arm into the back seat and hits all three of us in one motion.

We stop at a gas station somewhere. They all look alike. The attendant leaves a few spots on the windows and Dad leaps out of the car to re-clean the front and back. Mom shakes her head and turns to us.

"God. This is going to be a long trip. He's like Captain Bligh."

The three of us glance at each other.

When Mom turns back away from us, I shove Mikey.

"Mom sounds like she found a can of spinach somewhere."

Mikey twists his face.

"What's with the spinach?"

I flex my bicep and he rolls his eyes.

We're rolling again.

I tell Mikey, "I wish I used the bathroom."

My knees are locked tight together and I bounce to hold it. I tap Mom's shoulder.

"Jack, Billy needs to go."

"Pee stops are at gas-ups. He knows the drill."

My eyeballs are floating and my knees bang against the back of his seat. Dad yanks the car off the empty road.

"There. Are you satisfied? Now get out and make it snappy."

I step out and stare at the endless sagebrush desert. It looks scary out here. I'm not snappy. When I try to force my pee out, it barely dribbles.

I ask Mikey through the window, "Are there snakes out here?"

"Yep. Hurry up. If you're not fast, Dad will ditch you."

I push some more out and zip it. Mikey teases me with a funny look and points to a wet spot on my pants when I get back in the car.

Dad is driving and giving us a lecture on cloud formations. We're staring at the radio. Mimi makes hand gestures to Mom about turning it on. Mom rubs Dad's neck. Dad stops talking.

"The kids want to listen to music."

Dad nods.

Mikey reaches over from the back seat and spins the channel knob. Dad's hand covers Mikey's hand and slows the speed of his spins. I check out the look on Mikey's face. He's scared but I'm amazed how Dad has such sensitive control with his hands. Dad firms his grip over Mikey's and carefully pinpoints the selection to a tune he must enjoy, because we see a rare smile. It's Frank Sinatra's "High Hopes." Mikey slides his hand away and returns to the back seat. Dad snaps his fingers to the song. Inside the car, it seems like the loudest snap I've ever heard.

This radio station keeps playing the songs Dad enjoys. He's singing along to "Kansas City" and is in the greatest mood we've ever seen. Dad even does an enjoyable duet when Marty Robbins sings "El Paso."

He seems carried away by this song and his harmony is so beautiful.

I have goosebumps and glance at Mimi and Mikey. Their faces show they feel the same way.

Pat Boone begins to sing "Moody River" and Dad's duet restarts. We kids make silent gagging signals to this unwanted syrup.

What Mom calls his suicide knob is also putting a smile on Dad's face. Mikey and I watch him crank the steering wheel around whenever a turn comes into view. We notice that the knob has a small picture of a girl with huge boobs.

Mikey whispers to me, "I've seen that in a *Playboy* magazine. Dad likes to get his hands around those boobs every time he drives."

I say out loud, "Playboy?"

Mikey puts one finger to his lips and turns away.

I nudge Mikey.

"What did I do?"

He whispers, "Don't repeat the things I whisper to you. Keep secret stuff inside your head."

"What stuff is secret?"

"Everything I say."

Mimi reaches over and retunes the radio. Dad seems okay with the "Battle of New Orleans."

I tell everyone, "I really like this song."

I belt out the chorus lines I remember.

Mikey tells Mimi, "He sings. Talking, not so good, unless he's talking to himself."

The Kingston Trio comes on with the MTA song. Mimi knows the words by heart and we follow her.

Mikey sings loudest, until he finally stops and whispers in my ear, "It's like we're stuck forever in Captain Bligh's car."

I glance at the rearview mirror. Dad's clenched jaw signals that he's starting to tense up.

Mimi whispers in my ear, "I guess we sang too loud."

Dad slams the radio off.

We stop for gas and, while Dad is out of the car peeing and buying some pickled pigs' feet, we turn the radio back on. Searching quickly, we find Little Anthony singing "Shimmy Shimmy Ko-Ko-Bop." Mom stares at us, concerned.

Mikey tells her, "We know, we know."

Mimi's favorite tune comes on. It's Little Richard singing "Long Tall Sally," and his high piercing ooohs rev her up to a frenzy.

Mom tells Mikey and me, "My God, she's convulsing like a devotee at a Pentecostal church."

I ask Mikey, "What's that?"

"I don't know what Mom's talking about. All I know is that Mimi has a very long neck and it looks like it's about to break."

Dad returns from the restroom and witnesses Mimi's final twitch as Mikey quickly turns the radio down but not off. Dad turns the volume back up to see what she's been listening to and catches the final "have some fun tonight," which I figure we won't be having any of, at least not any time soon.

He clenches his teeth and slams his hand into the off button.

"God-damn jungle bunnies."

Dad offers but I don't want any pickled pigs' feet. Even though I'm hungry, I'm not eating Porky Pig's foot. No food, no radio; I'm bored.

I fly my imaginary WWI bi-plane hand out the window and feel the breeze in my face. If the angle of attack on my hand varies just a little, it results in a quick dive. I supply my own noise for the bi-plane. Captain Bligh spins around and glares at me.

"Shut the god-damn window."

Mom says, "Why? He'll get carsick."

"Open windows increase drag."

"My God, Jack, this Studebaker is as aerodynamic as a brick. No speed records are going to be smashed on this trip. We'll be lucky if we make it to Virginia."

Dad's knuckles whiten on the steering wheel.

I watch in a trance as endless strobe-like crop rows pass.

Mikey tells me, "I gotta get out of this car."

Mimi and I nod.

We stop at a motel. When our parents settle down in the room to go to sleep, we sneak out and huddle together in the car to listen to the radio.

The evening is cool and the radio is magic. All the ways we bugged each other during the boring hot day are gone.

Mimi spins the knob.

"They got rock-and-roll here in Texas?" Mikey asks.

"Come on, Mikey," Mimi says. "Buddy Holly was from Texas. Besides, I think every town in this country has rock-and-roll."

She finds a song and bounces on the seat.

Mimi and Mikey are swaying in the front seat and I'm in the middle. The three of us are singing along with "Johnny B. Goode." Another song comes on with a very loud tom-tom beat. It's about money and the birds and the bees.

Mikey says, "I've never heard this one. Dig it."

Mimi digs it, too. Her neck looks like it's going to break again. And I love the tom-tom drumbeat.

In the morning Dad finds us sacked out in the car, running down its battery with the radio on. Jerry Lee Lewis is belting out "Whole Lotta Shakin' Goin' On."

He yells, "Turn off that screaming-shouting-nigger music."

We lurch awake.

Dad returns to the motel room to investigate why Mom is taking so long to check out.

When we're alone, I ask, "Mikey, what's a nigger?"

"It's a Negro, you dummy; you know, colored people."

Mimi adds, "It's a mean word but I don't know why Dad says that about Jerry Lee. I saw The Killer on 'American Bandstand' last year. He's as white as you can get. That fact of life doesn't seem to matter to Dad."

I ask, "Dad doesn't know colored from white?"

Mimi says, "Strange, huh? We've seen those album covers Dad has of Ella Fitzgerald and Satchmo. They're colored and Dad plays their records all the time. I never heard him use that mean word for them."

I start snapping my fingers.

"I remember Satchmo. Just like Dad's snap. I love that snap."

Mikey says, "That's it. Maybe if The Killer develops a good snap, Dad won't call Jerry Lee a nigger."

The three of us snap our fingers and grin.

Dad returns and the snapping stops.

We're back on the road in Louisiana, but Dad is turning off the highway. I'm scrunching my face. Mom notices and smiles at me.

"We're going to visit a long-lost relative on your Dad's side of the family. She lives near here in Jennings where your father's father, Eric Boyum, moved to from Minnesota in the 1890s. Then he moved on from Jennings to Maui in 1906."

"That's neat, Mom. What happened then, Dad?"

Dad drives on silently.

Mikey elbows me with his you-dummy expression.

Mimi whispers in my ear, "I've never heard him talk about his family."

Mom pushes on with a twinkle in her eye.

"Perhaps since your Dad's branch of the family has been on the move for all these years, we are the long-lost relatives."

Dad's clenched teeth are showing again. Mom is almost smiling.

"Roadrunner, Coyote, kaboom."

Mikey tells Mom, "Billy's talking to himself again."

I look at Mikey and explode my hands apart.

"Fzzzz boom."

"You're weird. I don't think you're my little brother."

I turn and gaze out the window and spot plenty of black faces like the ones I've seen blown up in cartoons.

"Fzzzz boom."

Dad's driving slowly.

Mom asks him, "As long as we're slowing down for these Louisiana speed traps, can't we let the boys open the windows? It's hot, Jack."

Dad looks like he's in another world listening to one of his songs and nods. I see him smile in the rearview mirror. Mikey and I hang our heads out of the window. I see more Negroes and I point them out to Mikey.

He whispers in my ear, "You're half Negro."

"No, I'm not."

"Dad hates them. That's why he hates you—'cause you're half Negro."

"I don't want to be even half of one."

"You can't choose."

I rub the skin on my face and move back into the car. Dad's face is still smiling in the rearview mirror.

"Mom. Is Mikey right? He says I'm half Negro."

Mikey elbows me hard.

Dad is still paying attention to a song he's enjoying.

Mom turns to me and her eyes are wide open. She's smiling.

Mimi whispers to me, "It's trouble when Mom smiles like that."

Mom grabs Dad's arm.

"Jack, your youngest son wants to know if he is half colored."

Dad's face is suddenly angry, but there's a silent gap of time.

Mimi shakes her head and looks at the floor of the car. I don't understand what's happening and shrug to copy Mimi. Mikey sees me and shrugs to make fun of me. I can see Dad's clenched teeth in the rearview mirror. He suddenly turns and hits Mikey very hard in the face with a closed fist. I lean out of the window, making exploding gestures with my hands.

Mom is teary-eyed and no one talks for half an hour.

I whisper sorry in Mikey's ear. He pushes me away.

"You see, that's what I mean. Don't you get it?"

I try to apologize more to Mikey, but he turns away from me.

I lean over to Mimi.

"I hate it when no one talks."

Mimi tells me, "The road signs say we're getting near Jennings. Then we can get out of the car."

I look at Mikey. He has his eyes shut and there are tears on his cheeks.

Mimi tells me, "We better leave him alone for now."

We enter the city of Jennings and I see large white houses decorated with tall white columns.

I tap Mimi.

"Who lives here?"

She shakes her head.

"I've seen white columns like that before in books about ancient Greek gods."

Dad hasn't relaxed at all so I tap on Mom's shoulder.

"Do Greeks live here?"

Dad's head spins towards me for a brief second. His eyes cut through me.

When he turns back, I ask Mimi, "What did I say?"

"I don't know. Maybe he doesn't like Greeks. Right now he doesn't like anything. I think we better keep quiet until we get there."

We look at Mikey, who's been huddled on the edge of the seat since Dad's punch. Mom's trying to talk normal to me, even though Dad's irritated and she's choked up about Mikey. I hear it in her voice.

"No, Billy. This is a sugar plantation town like the village your Dad grew up in."

Dad shoots Mom an exasperated glance and shakes his head. His face turns purple with rage.

Mom turns to Dad in tears.

"You told me you grew up surrounded by sugarcane fields."

Mimi's face looks amazed.

She whispers to me, "This is so good. She's the only one who can get him."

Dad throws up his hands.

"To hell with the facts, on with the story."

Mimi and I exhale when we pull into a long driveway. Mikey holds his face and Dad orders him to stay in the car.

A statue of a black jockey on the front lawn looks like it's frozen in a half run. I bolt from the car.

Our cousin's name is Ione and her house is a fancy one just like so many in this neighborhood. Inside the house it's pretty boring. I drink my lemonade and watch Dad struggle to be pleasant with this distant relative. He does his fake friendly thing where he supplies only enough information to satisfy the need to be polite yet not enough to stimulate more conversation.

After this treatment by Dad, Ione turns her attention towards me and pulls at my cheeks.

"My, look at those dimples."

When Ione turns away, I try to rub off my dimples.

I ask Mimi, "Mikey doesn't have dimples. Why am I stuck with them?"

I notice that Dad is watching me squirm from across the room.

He glances at his watch.

"We really must be going."

As we walk out of the house, I tell Mimi, "I couldn't wait to leave."

"Me, too."

"If Dad hadn't come to our rescue, I would've stared at her cross-eyed. Mikey taught me that trick and it always works. Most grownups only want to be around cute cuddly kids."

"Well, we know you're not one of those."

We laugh until we return to the car and see Mikey's face is swollen and purple.

Mimi whispers to me, "And poor Mikey isn't too cuddly, either."

Mom gives Mikey a light touch with her hand.

We drive out of Jennings and Dad jacks up the car radio to "Rose of San Antonio." He's singing now while he snaps his fingers with that incredible snap.

I snap my fingers and whisper to Mimi.

"Just like that, he's happy?"

Mimi shrugs.

A colored man in a slow-moving car blocks our quick path out of town. We see Dad scowl in the rearview mirror.

"God-damn niggers."

"Now he's mad again. Mimi, why does he hate colored people?"

"I don't know, and I'm not asking. Maybe it's better that he's mad at them and not us."

The colored man pulls into a church. From the church's open windows we can hear beautiful voices singing. I wish we could stop and listen.

As we cross the border into Mississippi, I point at a big entering-the-state sign. We pass the sign and Mimi quizzes me.

"Now how do you spell it?"

"I dunno."

"Well, it goes like this. Miss-iss-ippi. See, sounds like a jingle."

I try the jingle and it works. So I say it over and over again until Dad tells me to shut my trap. I lurch and look at Mikey's face.

Mikey's right. I need to keep silent and secret around Dad. I can say things inside my head.

Mississippi. What a cool word. I enjoy repeating it silently while my head sways. Mikey gives me his you're-a-retard look.

Mimi, Mikey and I watch the rows of peach trees whiz by. We're in a trance while driving through Georgia. Mom's talking about buying some peaches at a roadside stand. I see a huge billboard that says 'Impeach.' The next sign says 'Earl.' And the next, 'Warren.'

"Mom, what kind of peach is an impeach?"

Everyone laughs.

"What's so funny?"

"It's too complicated."

"Why are there bullet holes in those signs?"

No one talks until we leave North Carolina.

Mom cries out, "Oh boy, Virginia! We're almost there."

Dad tells Mom, "But we're two hours off schedule."

"Oh, Jack, it doesn't matter."

I whisper in Mikey's ear, "They aren't going fast."

I point to Negroes sitting with blank looks on their faces in front of broken-down houses with peeling paint.

Mom tells us, "Boys, this is Sandy Bottom, where the Negroes live."

A few miles later we turn off the paved highway and bounce down a dirt road.

"What's that smell, Mom?"

"Cow manure, from the Copeland farm."

At the end of the road I see a red brick and wood house through some tall pines.

Mom says, "It's called 'Sans Souci'—that's French for without a care. They have three acres of waterfront on the Chuckatuck Creek. You'll love it."

Mimi whispers in my ear, "Mom looks happier than I've ever seen her."

After we unload the car I run around inside the house, eager to find something that interests me. There are woodcarvings and art every-where. Mom tells me they're from all the places her parents have lived around the world—strange names like Haiti, Bali and Constantinople. Large Afghan rugs cover hardwood floors throughout the house. Mom tells us the framed pictures of old men with long beards are our ancestors.

"Mom, this house is different."

"Yes it is, Billy."

She's been following me around the house to make sure I don't break anything and finally shows me the library. Mom lets me know that she and her brother and sister grew up with these same books. I open one after another and leaf through to the pictures to explore an exciting fantasy world.

Mikey joins me and checks out one I've put on the floor.

"I read this one. This guy was shipwrecked on a tropical island and made everything himself."

"Neato."

He grabs another book.

"Billy, remember this one?"

There's a smile on his face for the first time since he was punched. He slides *Treasure Island* from the shelf and opens it.

"Remember the movie? That kid got kidnapped by pirates with a map to find buried treasure. Yeah, X marks the spot."

"Yeah, that was so neat."

Mikey shows me pictures that show pirates in smoky taverns and duels on the beach.

Two strong hands pull my shoulders back so that I sit up straight. I'm startled and twist my head to gaze up at a tall, broad-shouldered man with thick eyebrows.

"And you must be my other grandson, William."

Mom tells me, "Billy, this is your grandfather, Admiral William Howard Michael. He would like to have you call him Papa Bace."

When I say it, 'Bace' comes out 'Bus.'

He towers over me and speaks memorized lines from the book, as if he were the one who wrote them:

"I remember him as if it were yesterday, as he came plodding to the door of the Admiral Benbow Inn, his sea-chest following behind him in a handbarrow; a tall, strong, heavy, nut-brown man; his tarry pigtail falling over the shoulders of his soiled blue coat; his hands ragged and scarred, with black, broken nails; and the saber cut across one cheek, a dirty, livid white."

Papa Bace slides his finger across his cheek.

"If you boys care to follow me, I'll show you something that might interest you."

Papa Bace leads us to his study, where we see a sword and a dark picture of a scary-looking man.

"This sword belonged to your ancestor in this painting. Colonel Jacob Michael of the Army of Maryland fought at the battle of Trenton with George Washington during the Revolutionary War."

I look up at my grandfather and he lifts his thick eyebrows high to give me a broad smile. Mikey salutes him so I copy his move, and Papa Bace salutes us back.

Our grandfather leaves the room and Mom continues her tour.

"Papa Bace and Mama Marcelle were married in France after the first World War. 'Bace' was her mispronunciation of his nickname 'The Babe,' from when he played football at Johns Hopkins."

"I like Papa Bus a lot," I say. "He has the same name as me."

"We named you after him. And we named Mimi after Mama Marcelle."

I can hear Mimi and our grandmother in another room, talking French.

Mom goes on, "Mikey, you were named after your dad…"

I see Mikey shake his head and I interrupt. "But Mom, his name is Mikey."

"His full name is John Michael Boyum, which is your dad's first name and my maiden name, Michael."

Mikey pops me in my shoulder.

"That's why I'll always be Mikey. Got it?"

I nod fast.

We move to another room in the house. Mikey points to a framed photograph on the wall behind the door, where most people won't see it,

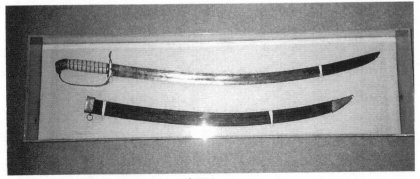

Col. Jacob Michael's Revolutionary war sword 1776

Col. Jacob Michael, Continental Army

of a mustached soldier wearing a helmet. A general is pinning a medal on his chest. Mom sees us admiring the picture.

"That's your grandfather getting the Distinguished Service Cross from 'Black Jack' Pershing for his service in the battle at Belleau Wood."

Mikey elbows me.

"'Black Jack' sounds like a good name for Dad."

"Oh, Mikey."

"Sorry, Mom. Tell us more about Papa Bace."

"Well, in the next war he turned the Officers' Club at Pearl Harbor into a temporary hospital for the wounded during the attack on December 7th, 1941. He got a Bronze Star for that. It also led to my meeting your father for the second time."

W.H. Michael with General Pershing, 1916

I talk to my two fingers, "Mom's had two cans of spinach. Two."

Mikey pushes me.

"No more spinach. You're too old to be talking to yourself. When you want to tell yourself stupid things, stuff it inside your head. No one wants to hear what you're thinking."

Mom is still stuck on her story.

"Your father and I met the first time at a dance when he was at the Naval Academy in 1939. Papa Bace was teaching there, so we lived in Annapolis. I was visiting home from The Packard School for Girls in New York and was invited to the dance."

She has a twinkle in her eye.

"That's where I met your father. He was so handsome and such a great dancer. What was the chance that I would ever see him again? But I did."

Her tone turns serious.

"During his first sea duty after the Academy, your father got lucky when his ship was delayed getting back to Pearl Harbor. They didn't arrive until the day after the attack. He would have been parked in a row next to all the other ships like his. Those ships were all sunk and most of their crews were killed."

Dad storms into the room as she tells us this part of the story.

"God damn it, Jackie, I don't want you talking about that."

He leaves to continue the unpacking.

Mom checks to make sure he's gone.

I ask her, "I don't get it. Why is he so upset about you telling us he was lucky?"

Midshipman J.H.Boyum, 1940

Mom shrugs and continues her story.

"As luck would have it, your dad and I met again after the attack at the medal ceremony in Pearl Harbor for my father. I was a senior at Punahou School. Your Dad proposed to me the night after I graduated. Papa Bace told me not to let a good-looking Naval Officer turn my pretty little head. So I didn't answer then. But before your father went off to some big battle near Hawaii, he wired me and wrote, 'I should be able to attend your wedding in the fall.' Everything was so secret. It was his second proposal, and I said yes. The war was on and we were married in September."

Mom is silent for a moment.

"You know," she says, "my parents were a little worried about me marrying your father. Papa Bace told me, 'there is more to a marriage than good looks and the drama of going off to war.' My parents had waited until after their war to get married."

Mom takes another moment.

"You know, kids, your father used to be really nice."

Mikey says, "No, he wasn't. He was never nice."

Tears well up in Mom's eyes.

She leaves us alone.

I ask Mikey, "Do you know which battle he was in? Mom is telling us neat stuff. It's like she's a new mom. I've never heard these stories before. Have you?"

He shakes his head.

Wedding day, 1942

Today I'm hunting for treasure on the floor of Papa Bace's library, leafing through the pictures.

"Young man, the words are even richer than the illustrations."

I almost jump out of my skin. My grandfather is standing behind me.

"Do you want me to read *Treasure Island* to you?"

I hand him a book. The cover shows a sailor gripping a rope in a small boat with a sailing ship behind him.

"Ah, a Nantucket sleighride."

"Sir, can we read this one? There's pictures of whales in here."

His eyebrows lower and his voice changes tone. Without even glancing at the book, he begins.

"Call me Ishmael. Some years ago—never mind how long precisely—having little or no money in my purse, and nothing particular to interest me on shore, I thought I would sail about a little and see the watery part of the world."

How does he do that? But he must not remember the whole book, because he sits in a rocker and reads. The words and the way they are used are different in this book from the way regular people speak. After every few paragraphs Papa Bace explains what he's just read.

I fall asleep and when I wake, Dad is yelling at Mom in another room about taking her pills. Mom is answering with a strange, baby-talking voice. I don't want to listen to their problems and check to see if my grandfather is still asleep. The low rumble of his breath tells me he is. I'm glad he doesn't have to hear my parents fight. My fingers touch his leathered face and feel the warmth of his skin.

We've been reading *Moby Dick* every night, and when Papa Bace tells me he's going out on the water, I want to join him. It's early morning and there is a mist hanging over the marsh behind our grandparents' home. I'm still thinking about the prime rib feast we ate last night. It was cool when Papa Bace's guest and war buddy, Major Sibley, told the story about how at the end of the Great War our grandfather abandoned the shrine of Mars to worship at the shrine of Venus. Funny words to describe how my grandparents got married.

Now I'm following my grandfather out over a pier that stretches from solid ground over the marsh grass and fiddler crab-filled mud to the deeper water of Chuckatuck Creek.

He's dressed in dirty work coveralls and prepares his rowboat.

"Papa Bus, Mom told me you're an Admiral so that means you'll be the boss of this boat today."

"I suppose I will, but doctors never command ships."

Papa Bace silently rows his old green boat with long, strong strokes out towards the middle of the creek.

"This looks as big as a lake. How can it be just a creek?"

He lowers his thick eyebrows as though to scare me, but I know he's teasing.

"It is. And the shores get much farther apart as this creek joins the James River. When the river opens into the Chesapeake Bay at Hampton Roads, a man can quickly lose sight of land. If you keep going east, the mighty Atlantic Ocean awaits."

"Have you been to that ocean?"

His eyebrows relax.

"Yes, but not in this little boat. It's a dream of mine to someday buy a big enough boat to go out into that ocean and catch a prize fish."

"Like Moby Dick?"

His eyebrows lower again.

Admiral W.H. Michael, 1948

"...as the wind howled on, and the sea leaped, and the ship groaned and dived, and yet steadfastedly shot her red hell further and further into the blackness of the sea and the night, and scornfully champed the white bone in her mouth, and viciously spat round her on all sides; then the rushing Pequod, freighted with savages, and laden with fire, and burning a corpse, and plunging into that blackness of darkness seemed the material counterpart of her monomaniac commander's soul."

This time I am more than a little scared. My eyes are fixed on his eyes and my fingernails dig into the boat's thick layers of paint. He pats my shoulder and I relax.

Admiral W.H. Michael (retired) (Papa Bace) and Marcelle, Chuckatuck, Va., 1959

"Was Ahab nuts?"

"Perhaps, but Ahab was also a great sailor. Even when the compass needles on the Pequod were disturbed, he knew how to determine that they were on the wrong course."

"To kill the whale?"

"Well, yes, that was Ahab's obsessive insanity."

"Obsess...?"

"I'll explain tonight when we read again."

"I like Queequeg."

"Ah, Queequeg. You'd rather sleep with a sober cannibal than a drunken Christian?"

I scrunch my face in confusion.

"I really like his tattoos."

He squeezes me on the shoulder in a comforting way.

I sit next to a chicken-wire crab trap and enjoy the peace while I pick the paint out of my fingernails. I think Papa Bace must have repainted this boat many times. My fingers have a strong fishy smell. I find out why when he removes an eel from a bucket, carves it up and hands a slimy piece to me.

"Put this into the circle of wire in the center of the trap."

I make a tortured face, pretending I don't enjoy the smell. He notices, copies me and we enjoy a laugh together. The smell doesn't really bother me, and I love the feeling of this whole adventure.

"Papa Bus, did you make these traps?"

He nods.

In the middle of the creek, we drop the baited trap into the water, and he hooks the float of another trap baited from the day before with his oar. I want to help and grab the line. He sits back, contented, and watches me slowly pull up the crab pot. It's so comfortable being with him. Dad would never talk to me about war, but I take a chance with Papa Bace. My eyes stay on the crab line.

"Papa Bus, did you see bi-planes in the war?"

"You like those old planes, do you? Or was it the brave pilots inside them?"

I gaze back at him and nod silently to open his treasure chest of memories. He pauses and stares away into his past.

"Yes, well, one night as we were leaving the front for our turn in reserve, we witnessed an extraordinary display. Just far enough to the rear to relax from the stimulation, which makes everyone walk on the heels of the man ahead, we sat down to rest. Shells thudded in the direction of Paris and hundreds of searchlights shot up into the sky. Many-colored star shells illuminated the heavens. From time to time a plane was caught in a ray of light and followed, while shrapnel burst around it. Somehow, at this distance, only the beauty of the thing impressed us, and we sat for an hour drinking in its magnificence."

No one has ever talked to me this way before. I don't want him to stop.

"Papa Bus, did you have to shoot people?"

He takes over the line-pulling for a moment and instructs me silently how to leverage with my legs and back. He hands the line back to me, and I take over the pulling.

"No, I was the battalion surgeon. For a significant time I patched up soldiers at the front."

"Where men died?"

He nods.

"How could you tell if they were all the way dead?"

Papa Bace places two fingers on the side of my neck, where I can feel my pulse push against his pressure.

"They died from bullets?"

"That and many other things, William."

My face flushes when he calls me William—just like his name.

"Last night you saved your good friend Major Sibley when he choked on his prime rib. I would want you to be my friend."

"Well, I'm your grandfather."

"Yes, but the story Major Sibley told about losing his eye in the trenches was really neat. I loved it when he shouted 'Damn the eye' when you wanted to send him away from the front."

"He was a brave man."

I point towards my imaginary war front.

"Damn the eye," I say with my best deep voice.

He gives me an astonished but grinning face.

"I have bad eyes, Papa Bus. That will be my new motto, 'damn the eye.'"

He laughs.

"What other things did you do?"

"Yes. Well, there was also bleeding to attend to, respiratory ailments from gas, burns..."

"Burns?"

"Yes, there is much fire in war. At Pearl Harbor especially, there were many burns."

"Was that the next war?"

"Yes."

"That's a lot of stuff you know how to do, Grandpa Bus. You sure know how to fix people."

The crab pots are near the surface, so he takes the line from me and wedges it into a cleat on the side of the boat. He wags his finger at me.

"I didn't know everything. I just dealt with the things I could see."

I screw up my face and take off my glasses.

"I don't understand. Isn't seeing all there is?"

We switch seats and his strong gloved hands pull the trap into the boat. The crabs rush frantically, looking for an escape. But many of them have their claws locked on each other and look like they're in a crab battle.

"There's an invisible wound soldiers can get called shell shock. I didn't always get that right."

"You mean they were scared."

"More than scared, William, more than scared."

"You mean they were cowards?"

"No, not at all. When people think about battle, they think there is only fear or bravery, right?"

"Yes, sir."

"But when your father and uncles were educated, shell shock was a word that had just entered into the current vocabulary about the effects of combat on men's minds. For their generation the word meant that a man had lost his marbles when the pressure was on. Unspeakable actions, like men running away from battle, resulted from it. But it was something else. A man could appear to be afraid when actually he was severely disoriented. That is shell shock."

"Dis-or...?

It's so wonderful to have Papa Bace be patient enough to explain things and words to me.

"It's when you are lost or not connected to this world."

He studies my continued confusion.

"I'll tell you what I saw. The enemy was made out ahead and we knew we were at the front. We took up positions under the cover of woods. There were only a few shallow trenches. Bombardment became appalling. My medical unit was in a little wood on which a German battery concentrated its full attention. Four or five shells fell in a row at one end, then another row crashed down, and another, until the whole patch was covered. Our artillery had not yet arrived to defend us, so the bombardment went on. We could tell to a second when the shells were going to burst in our part of the woods. Rapidly our trenches became deeper. A marine saw his buddy blown to nothing as the two walked in single file. The boy was shaking like an aspen. He was my first shell shock case. I marched the poor fellow up and down where the shells fell in considerable number, thinking that the fool idea was a good treatment. At every detonation he went into another fit of wild hysteria. I saw the case was demoralizing the other men and I finally sent him out."

I'm scared just listening to him. A man had been blown to bits? It had really happened, not like in a movie where you always know it's just a movie.

Papa Bace is staring at me with a serious face.

"War pushes the limitations of any man."

He sees I'm still confused.

"Let's get these crabs on the table while they're fresh."

I walk into the kitchen with a bushel basket of crabs and tell Mikey, "Look what we got."

We boil them in beer and pepper, put newspaper on the table, set out Mama Marcelle's mayonaise and the whole family cracks crabs for hours. Papa Bace shows me how to dissect the crab and pull out webby tissue on the inside of the main shell.

"Those are the dead man's fingers. Scrape that part off before you crack into the meat. It's no good."

"Will I die if I eat it?"

"It would make you very sick. They're the filters that clean out the grime from the creek."

I smile when I taste a bite and look at Papa Bace.

"I love to eat crab."

He grabs my shoulder and gives me another playful squeeze.

Mama Marcelle points to us and remarks to everyone, "*Maintenant, ils sont comme les deux doigts du main.*" (They are like the two fingers of the hand.)

I crack a shell and blurt out, "We're giving these crabs some real shell shock."

Dad glares at me with a startled expression, and it's easy to see I've stuck my foot in my mouth again. Dad pinches his mouth shut with his fingers and thumb. That signal is obvious, too, but I don't know why I'm getting it.

What I do know is that my grandfather is grinning at me.

Chapter Four

A Bad Seed
1960-1961

Papa Bace's pier is my favorite place in the whole wide world. Today I'm fishing for blue gill and perch. It's low tide and the fiddler crabs are keeping me company out on the mud flats. My rod bends over. It's one of those scary-looking eels that Papa Bace will put in his crab pots. He'll be proud of me.

Mikey and Mimi join me out on the pier to examine my catch and convince me to leave the slimy eel behind to go with them to meet the nearest neighbors who live about a half-mile away.

The Holidays have four kids and Ben is the one my age. He has a neat Southern accent and his voice is friendly. When he speaks to his mother, he's so polite—he's even polite to me.

Ben and I hunt frogs with gigs, fish and run around the forest. The sky grows dark in the afternoon. Crack. I glance at Ben for answers.

"You never heard thunder?"

"No. Sounds like a sonic boom. You ever heard one of those?"

"No. What's a sonic boom?"

"Jets make 'em. They usually scare me, but I'm not scared now. This is fun."

My arms spread out wide and I smile up into a sudden downpour of rain.

"You're crazy. We gotta get outta here. Lightning is dangerous."

We run to his house to get out of the rain but only because Ben is leading me. It's exciting to be outdoors when the lightning strikes.

Staying at my grandparent's house is the greatest. Dad hasn't touched us since we got here.

The storm has cleared and the sun is setting. We hear our grandparents ring their big bell and we all run back to Sans Souci for dinner. Mikey is always the hungriest and runs all the way. Mimi tires first and walks. I give up Mikey's pace and talk to Mimi.

"Is that white lady who serves the food their slave?"

"No, Mrs. Crittenden's their maid. They pay her."

"Why don't we ever have a maid?"

"Dad wouldn't go for it."

"But Mom would, I bet."

"Oh, yes. Mom grew up with house help."

Mimi is older than me and sounds so smart. But at least I can run faster.

Mimi and I arrive at another yummy meal and lots of relatives are there. Dinner includes a Smithfield ham and Mimi lets me know that the town of Smithfield is right across the creek. It's the saltiest meat I've ever tasted, but Papa Bace cuts it paper thin so it combines well with the other ingredients of the meal—like the sweet corn and fresh garden spinach. Dad says you always have to eat your entire main course before dessert. No problem for me—I've seen what spinach does for Popeye.

Dessert is our grandmother's eight-layer cake. It's outrageous, but we only get one thin slice and that drives Mikey and me crazy. I've got my mouth open in frustration about not getting another slice when I glance at Mikey giving me his mouth-open signal. It's too late. Dad reaches over and slaps me across the face—right in front of everyone. I fall out of my chair. When I get back up, I see Mama Marcelle storm away from the table and Papa Bace glare at Dad. Didn't they know about him?

Papa Bace tells me, "Go to the kitchen and have Mrs. Crittenden give you some ice. Take some time, William."

The ice makes the pain go away, and I talk Mrs. Crittenden into another piece of cake. When I leave the kitchen, dinner is over and everyone is seated in the living room, enjoying drinks while the sunset casts a golden glow through the large picture window overlooking the creek. If I hadn't seen and felt what just happened at dinner, I would think the name Sans Souci feels perfect in this moment. But I don't understand how the adults can suddenly sweep everything away and pretend like nothing happened. Mikey has told me that alcohol drinks make people forget bad stuff. I guess it's working, but no one is talking to each other.

The grownups are listening to the radio and seem to be paying close attention. Even Mimi and Mikey are listening. No one is laughing. TV makes me laugh with all the goof-off stuff Popeye and Heckle and Jeckle get into.

My hand slides over the carvings on the front of the radio's tall wood case. Mama Marcelle breaks the silence and touches my face gently.

"William, radio was our link to the world when we were younger."

I sit down next to Papa Bace and try to pay attention like everyone else in the room. Eric Severeid is reporting. The words are too big for me to understand. Papa Bace sees me scrunch my face and explains what the words 'doubts' and 'conviction' mean.

"Young man, I think he's trying to tell us not to ever fool ourselves into thinking we have all the right answers. A closer study can always reveal something we didn't know. Don't stop asking questions."

I've got a question in my head and glance over at Dad. He's holding his drink and staring at nothing. Is he thinking about what just happened at dinner? I look down at the floor in silence and listen to Eric Severeid.

The news from overseas is about Laos and Vietnam. I love to hear the names of faraway places around the world and have never heard these names before. Our grandparents have a wonderful picture atlas and Papa Bace shows me where those two countries are. But as he drags his finger across the Pacific Ocean, Mikey points to the Hawaiian Islands.

"I've been to Maui."

Maybe the word Maui will make Dad smile. Mom has told me many times that Dad was born on Maui and lived there until he was seventeen, when he shipped off to the Naval Academy. Living seventeen years in one place sounds great to me, especially if that place is an island in Hawaii. If I were Dad, I would smile. But when I glance at him, he still looks blank.

Mom sees my look and touches my arm.

"Eric Severeid used to be a war correspondent during WWII and is Norwegian like your dad," she says.

I wonder if Eric Severeid smiles.

"Mom, what's a war correspondent?"

"They write about soldiers when they fight."

"Oh. But all the wars are over, right?"

"Yes, but there are plenty of other things to report. No one is going to listen to the radio in the future. If you're a correspondent, then you'll be on TV."

Mikey gives me a playful headlock.

"A correspondent? Right. Mr. Magoo with buck teeth."

Mom is serving Mikey and me breakfast before we charge out for another day of running around in the forest.

"Hey, Billy," Mikey says as he waits for his scrambled eggs. "The grownups have a plan to yank your teeth out."

"Mikey, that's cruel," Mom says. "Billy, corrective dental surgery will improve your bite."

"Will they yank my teeth out, Mom?"

"In order to allow room for your front teeth to move back, your bicuspids will need to be extracted, not yanked."

"I don't want anybody pulling my teeth out."

"Papa Bace says it will help."

Papa Bace enters the room and lays his hand on my shoulder.

"It will be good for you, young man."

His gentle eyebrows are comforting.

"I guess so."

I tell Mikey, "I could be a corres... uh, newsman."

Mikey pulls me aside and whispers in my ear.

"They just don't want to watch Dad slap you anymore. They think your extra teeth are making your mouth hang open."

My grandparents offer to pay for having my teeth yanked out. Their dentist in Suffolk is named Reginald Holland, and he's ready to start right away.

Dr. Holland is a drunk. I can smell it on his breath. He says the X-rays show I have very strong teeth with multiple roots—Mom says from all the milk I drink. The dentist wrestles my teeth for hours before they begin to budge. When he pulls away for a momentary break, he arches his back, wild-eyed, and hoots like a madman while he plays loud hillbilly music on his radio. At that moment I can't help but notice that his teeth are yellowed and decayed. Dr. Holland scares the crap out of me. On the way back for Sans Souci, I threaten to jump out of our moving car if Mom ever tries to take me back to him again.

It's high tide and our family is waterskiing down on the creek. Mom and Dad know how to slalom ski and the three of us kids are picking it up quickly. Dad is an expert at towing us out of the water gradually. He calls it easing out.

I tell Mikey, "Something fun with Dad? I can't believe it."

"It'd be more fun if I was driving."

Dad wants to take a beer break, and Mikey talks Dad into letting him drive the boat. Dad says OK but gives Mikey a long briefing on all the procedures involved in operating an advanced piece of machinery.

Mikey is nervous standing there with Dad and is nodding fast. Dad must think he's finally ready and allows the two of us to take off on our own.

The boat idles away from the pier.

Mikey says, "Words. He says so many damn words. It's simple."

He pushes the red gear shifter forward and then taps the green throttle forward like we've seen Dad do as we move into the deeper part of the creek. But then Mikey stands up, even though I heard Dad tell him to always sit. He grips the steering wheel and slams the throttle all the way forward. The wind is blowing his hair back, and there's a huge smile on his face. Mikey carves the ski boat into a high-speed turn. This is so exciting and dangerous. Both of my hands are squeezing the side of the boat.

Mikey slows to a stop. I'm still squeezing.

"You can let go now. You're up."

I put on my float ring—one of Dad's orders.

"Come on, hurry up."

The eel I caught yesterday had such sharp little teeth. I know this creek is full of them.

"You going or not?"

I jump in and put on my skies.

The tow rope tightens and Mikey slams the throttle all the way forward. The boat leaps to full speed and my arms feel like they're going to yank out of my sockets. When Dad tows me, I enjoy looking down at the skis skimming across the water to see how fast I'm going, but this time the two skis are wobbling. Mikey is driving the boat too fast for me. Dad has taught us hand signals to speed up or slow down and I'm signaling like crazy. But Mikey isn't looking back. The boat swings into a sudden turn, and I whip away from where I was feeling safe in the middle of the wake. My skis cross up on the wake's wave and catapult me out of the bindings. I'm bouncing across the creek like a skipping stone until I hit the muddy water.

Mikey pulls up next to me with the boat.

"Come on, no crying. Just stuff it in. You don't want anyone to think you're a baby, do you?"

Mikey grabs me by the float ring and rolls me into the boat.

"Man, you looked like the human cannonball. Shoulda seen it. Kaboom."

He's laughing. The human cannonball is our favorite act at the circus. I think about it and start laughing.

We're still laughing when we pull up to the pier. But Dad is standing there wearing his sunglasses. He removes them as we tie up, and it's easy to see his mood. I spot the binoculars around his neck and know this won't be good.

We return to the house and Mimi tells us that our grandparents and Mom are in Suffolk to buy groceries. Mikey and I retreat to our room, feeling safe inside Papa Bace's house. But Dad enters our room.

"Bill, you need to leave."

I do and know what's next.

Mimi tells me, "Dad must think he can get away with stuff he isn't supposed to do when no other grownups are around."

I'm in the living room with Mimi when my grandparents and Mom return home to Mikey's screams.

Mama Marcelle puts her hand over her mouth. "*Mon Dieu,*" she says as we hear Dad yell at and beat Mikey inside our room.

"You just don't listen," he's yelling. "When you cross the line, you will get the belt. It's a fact of life."

I mouth Dad's last sentence to myself and cringe. Dad uses that expression, fact of life, every time he beats us, but I still don't know what it means.

We hear a crack of the belt, but there is another noise that is even scarier. I think Dad sounds like a wild animal. Mom clutches Papa Bace and her fear-filled eyes are locked on his.

It's weird to watch our grandparents witness the sound of Dad beating Mikey. They saw him slap me at the dinner table the other night when I had my mouth open. I saw how shocked Mama Marcelle and Papa Bace were then. But that was nothing compared to how crazy Dad gets when he belts us. I've heard these scary sounds many times, and it feels better now that Mom, Mimi and I aren't the only ones who know what's going on.

Papa Bace makes a fist and pounds one time on the door.

"Commander Boyum."

The belting and screams on the other side stop.

My eyes snap up to Papa Bace's face. His voice has sent shivers through me.

Later I overhear Mama Marcelle tell Mom, "Jack isn't around enough to supply the consistency to give the discipline the boys need. His attempts are sporadic and overdone to make up for it. It's good Mikey is staying with us when you leave."

This is the first I've heard about this plan and it feels like a punch to my stomach. Good for Mikey, but what about me? This is the second time Mikey will get to live with grandparents and escape from Dad. Did they forget about me? Mikey does get beat more than me, but I think he's the strong one. Leave me behind, too. If Dad doesn't have Mikey, he'll probably beat on me more than he already does. I wish I had the guts to speak up for myself.

Our parents are driving Mimi and me north on Route 1, back to our home in Alexandria. I start choking and coughing when we drive by a dusty farm field. Dad's voice is playful.

"It's not the cough that carries you off, it's the coffin they carry you off in."

Mom says, "Jack. Please."

"That used to make you laugh."

"It lightened things up twenty years ago when you were at war. He's just a boy."

Dad stops to pee at an Esso station in Richmond.

I tell Mom, "I miss Mikey already."

Mimi says, "Me, too."

Mom bursts into tears.

"We'll go back to see him real soon. Don't worry."

Dad comes back from the restroom and glances at Mom.

"What the hell is the matter now?"

"Oh, Jack," she pouts.

"Oh, Jack," he mocks with an absurdly high voice.

Things are getting tense, and I want to put Dad back in a better mood. I've overheard conversations about another ship command.

"Are you going to have another boat, Dad?"

He looks at me with that don't-say-stupid-stuff look.

Mom butts in.

"Yes, Billy, it's the Titanic."

Dad glares at Mom.

Mom looks away from Dad but says, "What year did that boat sink, Jack? Was it the year you were born?"

Mimi whispers in my ear, "I think Dad just hit Mom's iceberg."

Mom turns to Mimi and me and puts her hand over her mouth.

"Oh, whoops. I mean ship. According to your father only an ignoramus calls a ship a boat."

Dad's lips are pressed tight. His eyes are locked straight ahead on the road and his knuckles whiten on the steering wheel.

No one has spoken since Richmond but when we drive through Fredericksburg, I point at a statue of a Confederate soldier with a tattered Stars and Bars flag flying over him. Dad surprises me by speaking.

"Route 1 was the battlefield road of the Civil War."

"Are there any soldiers left from that war?"

"No. It's all history now. I believe the last ones died around ten years ago. It's been ninety-five years since that war ended."

"That soldier looks rusty. He'll probably fall down soon."

"It's not rust, Bill. That's bronze, and all it takes is a good shine for it to be new again."

Mikey has been living with our grandparents for the past year. It's Christmas vacation and we've driven down from Alexandria for the holidays. I'm excited to be back at Sans Souci so I can finally finish the whale story with Papa Bace.

It's evening and the radio broadcast is over. We all laughed at the strange way President Kennedy said the word Laos—Lay-os. Papa Bace is in his rocking chair. I've found the book and he's reading to me. A sailor on the lookout for Moby Dick has fallen into the ocean. The life-buoy on the ship was thrown over to save him but the sailor disappeared and the cask that served as the life-buoy sank, too. It's the last one, and the ship's crew is worried... until Queequeg offers the coffin he'd had made for himself when he thought he was going to die. Papa Bace speaks as the carpenter.

"Let me see. Nail down the lid; caulk the seams; pay over the same with pitch; batten them down tight; and hang it with the snap-spring over the ship's stern. Were ever such things done before with a coffin?"

I interrupt, "Why did they do that?"

"Well, to turn the coffin into a life raft."

"Neato."

"Yes, William, but it was disturbing for those superstitious seafaring men to be using a coffin in this way."

"You mean they were scared?"

Papa Bace lowers his eyebrows like he does when he's trying to spook me, but he also has a slight smile and a twinkle in his eye.

I'm sharing the same room with my brother and it feels great to be back with him again.

"Mikey, I keep all my secrets now. Nobody knows what I'm thinking, but I'll tell you if you want to know."

"Then you're in with me."

Mikey shows me his new favorite western on TV, "The Rebel." He tells me the main character, Johnny Yuma, was a Confederate soldier and is now a bitter young man wandering the West, trying to find inner peace. But when trouble comes his way, he has a sawed-off shotgun that solves the problem. "The Rebel" is OK, but I'm anchored to my chair and love to watch the beginning of the show, when Johnny Cash sings the theme song.

Mikey tells me he really likes the shotgun and wishes he had one.

The TV show is over.

Mikey whispers, "Follow me."

We sneak off deep into the forest surrounding our grandparents' home, and I notice Mikey is carrying something wrapped in a rag.

"What's that?"

"You remember the picture behind the front door of Papa Bace getting the medal from General Pershing?"

I nod.

Mikey grins.

"That wasn't the only thing General Pershing gave to Papa Bace. He also gave him this."

Mikey unfolds the rag.

"A pearl-handled nickel-plated Colt .45."

"Oh no. Mikey, you're going to get it if they find out."

"But they're not going to find out, are they? I just want to shoot it once. Then we'll put it back."

"Remember when Dad whipped both of us for stealing purple gumballs? He's briefed us lots of times about stealing. And this is a gun, Papa Bus's gun. I don't want to do anything to get Papa Bus mad. He even yelled at Dad."

"I'll shoot it once and then I'll let you try it. Don't you want to find out what happens when you pull the trigger? No one needs to know."

I'm shaking my head and want to run away, but I'm interested as Mikey loads the chamber. Mikey lifts the gun up to his eye level. It's too late for me to run away, so I rush behind him for safety.

He pulls the trigger and the gun sounds like thunder. Bark explodes from a nearby tree as Mikey is thrown back onto the ground, still holding the gun, knocking me down with him. My ears hurt. Is Mikey dead?

No. He's looking at me and laughing in a weird way.

It seems so strange. I know I would be crying. I need to stay on the forest ground. It feels good but still not safe.

There's a sound of steady footsteps through the pine needles.

Papa Bace steps on Mikey's arm and removes the gun from his hand.

Without a word he drags both of us by our shirt collars back to the house. Papa Bace's face is beet red.

He drags us out by his pier. His grip on my arm feels like steel.

"Did you have a hand in this?"

His voice is as loud as when he yelled at Dad.

Mikey says, "It was only me."

I'm frozen in fear.

He points me to the house.

I enter and Mama Marcelle orders me to our room. From there I overhear her voice break as she tells my parents how Papa Bace's blood pressure is high and he can't take this aggravation. According to her, Mikey has been misbehaving like a wild animal since he's been living with them, getting into fights at school and being forward with girls. She feels that they're too old to control Mikey, and this incident with the gun is the last straw. She says Mikey should return with us to Alexandria at the end of our visit.

I stare out of my window at the pier, where Mikey is scraping the paint off Papa Bace's rowboat.

It's been a week since my brother shot our grandfather's gun, and I'm the only one who isn't still giving Mikey the look. I follow him out the door.

"Where we going to play?"

"I just wanna run away. I wish I could sail to some remote island, like Robinson Crusoe."

"Hey, we can make a pretend island and a cool fort where no one can boss us around."

"Nope. Right now I'm hitting it out of here for the Holidays' house. They shoot guns and no one gets mad. Wanna come?"

I think about how loud the gun was and how much trouble it caused.

I stare at Mikey and shake my head.

"No more guns. I'm gonna stay here with Papa Bus. He's almost finished reading me the whale book."

Mikey walks down the quiet dirt road by himself, and I go back to the house.

The Pequod was near the equator and Papa Bace is reading how Captain Ahab had changed course in the middle of the night because he smelled something in the air. At dawn the sea has a long, smooth streak and the sailors are on alert. I feel tense and know that Moby Dick must be near. Who will die? The Captain or the whale?

My grandfather is explaining the gold doubloon and Ahab's harpoon forged with the blood of his sailors. I'd never be able to understand this story on my own.

Mom interrupts us to say that she and Papa Bace need to drive to Suffolk. Town errands are usualy boring, but I'm jumping in the car because my grandfather is still in the mood to explain the strange English in *Moby Dick*. I don't want to miss out on anything.

Mom is in the front seat and I'm in the back. Papa Bace drives out on the bumpy dirt road from Sans Souci. Before we start talking about events in the book, I spot a man plowing his field with a tractor next to the road.

"Papa Bus, I like tractors. Who's that?"

"Sam Copeland. He's one of our neighbors on this road. One of his legs was torn up in the war. He limps now but can still drive that old tractor."

"What does he grow?"

"William, he grows peanuts."

The first three words of his sentence are clear, but the word 'peanuts' comes out of his mouth kind of mumbly. He speaks so clearly all of the time. Why is 'peanuts' hard for him?

The car slips into the drainage ditch on the side of the road. Mom screams like she's hurt, and I think she must be hurt bad. But that can't be because we were going so slowly and didn't even get knocked around.

Why is she screaming about the car crashing? It wasn't scary for me at all. Then I see that Papa Bace is slumped over the steering wheel. Is he hurt, or has he gone to sleep again just like when we've both fallen asleep together reading a book? Why is Mom still screaming so loud?

I touch his cheek. His skin is warm. I place my fingers next to his neck just as he showed me how he did it as a medic in two wars.

Mom begs me for an answer with her eyes.

I'm confused. Can't find his pulse. Keep searching. Probably not good at it. Dad says I'm not good at anything. Mom's sobs are constant and deep. Her fear is making me worry. Could Papa Bace really die? No. I won't let it happen. But I'm just a kid. I need a guy like my grandfather right now to show me what to do. I feel helpless. This isn't his normal sleep. Is this death? What does death mean?

I begin to tremble.

Sam Copeland has limped to the car. He reaches in and touches the side of Papa Bace's neck. Then he looks at Mom.

"I'm sorry, Ma'am."

Today Dad tells Mikey and me, "You know, boys, the world isn't fair. Death is a fact of life."

Mikey and I escape the indoor sadness and run through the woods near the house.

Mikey tells me, "I don't need him to tell me what's not fair."

"Yeah. We lost Papa Bus, and I'll never find out if Ahab killed the white whale."

Mikey looks at me like I'm crazy.

"Who's Ahab? What are you talking about?"

"A crazy mean captain in the book he was reading to me. Ahab lost his leg, and now he's chasing the white whale that bit it off."

"Can't you just read the rest by yourself?"

"Nah. Only Papa Bus knows how to read it, and now he's dead."

Mikey spots the tree he shot with the gun.

"Yeah, Papa Bace is a great man."

Mikey is still staring at the tree. I finger the huge hole.

"He stuck up for you when Dad was going at you with the belt."

Mikey yanks my hand from the hole.

"I know."

Tears roll down his cheeks.

"Mikey, he told me how he saw a soldier get blown to bits in France."

"What?"

"Yeah, they were getting pounded by artillery and had to dig their trenches deeper to escape the shells."

"Papa Bace told you war stories?"

"Yeah, when we were crabbing. He knew tons of stuff about war and fixing soldiers."

"Yep, Papa Bace knew everything."

"Nope. He told me there were some things he couldn't figure out."

"Like what?"

"Something invisible that soldiers get."

"Invisible? No, you're either shot and killed, or you're shot and wounded. What's invisible?"

"I just know it's something really bad and I'm glad no one we know has it."

I stare at our family as we drive north to our home in Alexandria. Mikey is with us again and has run out of grandparents. No one speaks for the entire drive, and Dad doesn't allow anyone to turn on the radio. Is it because they're sad about Papa Bace or because Dad is still angry with Mikey?

When we arrive at our home, Dad shoves Mikey and points to his room.

"Just because your grandfather died doesn't mean I've forgotten about your theft."

"But Dad," I say, "Papa Bace punished Mikey for that."

He slaps me.

"Which reminds me, you never were. You followed your brother, and it's time you found out what that means."

Dad directs me with finger stabs in my back.

I'm crying. Of course I followed him. He's my brother, and now I'm following him to our belting—together.

Mikey whispers in my ear, "Try to not cry—just stuff it in."

Mikey and I stare at each other while Dad gives both of us the business. This is not the first time Dad has beat us together. It hurts so bad, but I manage not to cry. Mikey isn't crying, either. Instead, he yells.

"It doesn't even hurt. You can't hurt me."

Dad turns all his attention to Mikey. He's shaking Mikey like he wants to rip him apart. I can't stand to look at Dad's scary face.

Dad screams, "You god-damn thief. In parts of the world they would chop your hand off so everyone knows what you are."

His voice sounds like Papa Bace's when he read how Ahab roared at his men.

Running from the room, I hear Dad slam the door behind me. From just outside I listen. There's a moment of silence.

Now Mikey is screaming in pain. Is Dad killing him? I run to get Mom. She rushes through the door and charges into the bedroom to cover Mikey. Dad's eyes are closed as he whips Mikey with a coat hanger. There's blood. Now Mom is in the way and she gets hit with the coat hanger.

"Oh my God, Jack!"

Mom's staring at Dad as if he were a stranger.

Dad opens his eyes and rushes from the room.

I've been watching Mom put iodine on Mikey's back for the last ten minutes. The three of us are sobbing together. Mimi is still in her room with pillows over her head.

We hear Dad yell to us from the kitchen in a cheerful voice.

"Who wants strawberry shortcake?"

His voice sounds friendly.

I'm squeezing my temples while I stare at the welts on Mikey's back. He's still crying.

"I'm stuck with Dad forever."

We've been home for a few weeks and Dad never allows Mikey any free time. Mikey finishes one chore and Dad immediately has another for him. I go to the kitchen for a glass of milk. Mikey is polishing Mom's silver and Mom and Dad are preparing pot roast.

Mikey asks Dad, "Is this good enough?"

"No. Not for a white glove inspection."

Mom has red teary eyes. Dad has red angry eyes.

I escape outside with a plastic tray I've found in the garage that I use as a sled. We live on a steep hill and there's eight inches of snow on the road. It's fun to go fast, even though I know a car might hit me on the cross street at the bottom.

My legs are tired and cold from walking up the hill. Sneaking back into our house, I feel dizzy from the sudden warmth. My eyesight is blurry and I stumble into a hallway table, sending a porcelain Buddha crashing to the floor.

Dad yells from the kitchen, "God damn it, Bill. Pick up your feet."

Why is Dad getting so upset? He hates all those statues Mom brings back from the Orient.

I hear Mom say, "Oh, Jack. It's his depth perception."

It's Mom's Buddha and yet she's defending me. But now I'm scared because Mom is talking about my eyes. If Dad sees that I'm not wearing my glasses, he'll belt me. I always leave them behind when I play so I won't get creamed for losing or breaking them. Besides, Mikey teases me about them all the time. Tiptoeing back to my room, I grab the ugly things and report to the kitchen looking like a four-eyed toad.

Mikey is chopping carrots. Dad barks at him.

"Smaller."

I grab a piece of carrot. Mom tells me, "If you eat carrots, your vision will improve."

"My God, Jackie. The kid has bad eyes. It's a fact of life."

Mom ignores Dad.

"Don't you want to be a fighter pilot like your father?"

Dad glares at Mom.

Mikey says to Mom, "You fixed his teeth. Can't you fix his eyes?"

"Maybe we can," says Mom.

Mikey laughs at me.

"You'll be our special project, like Frankenstein."

"I don't want to be a project."

"Yes, you do. You'll look just like Boris Karloff, not dead but almost dead."

Dad glares at Mikey.

"Less talking, more chopping. Keep your eyes on the action."

He starts chopping the carrots very fast.

Mom cries to Dad, "Jack, he's going to chop his fingers off."

Mikey screams, "It doesn't matter. I'm a thief."

Dad throws up his hands and walks away, shaking his head.

I'm not too excited about getting my eyes fixed after my experience with the crazy dentist. When Mimi gets home, I tell her about the big idea. She gives me her smarty-pants look.

"Mom thinks there's hope for you so she can keep her dream of having at least one son become something exciting, like when she first met Dad. She knows Mikey is bitter and couldn't care less about being a pilot."

"Do you think I should be one?"

"Maybe. You know, Billy, all the astronauts are fighter pilots. Remember all those handsome guys who used to come to our house for dinner?"

"Sure. I thought they were cool."

"Well, they're the ones going into the space program. Space is the future."

"Dad says my bad eyes are a fact of life."

"Oh, come on. You think Mom is going to be stopped by one of Dad's facts of life?"

A 1961 calendar hangs on the wall. I twist my head sideways to imagine the numbers upside down. It's still 1961. Mom and I are at the Naval Hospital in Bethesda, Maryland, waiting in the hallway for my appointment to have an eye exam and pre-surgery analysis.

Mom is reading a fashion magazine. I'm startled and look up from the *Boy's Life* in my lap. A white security cop is going berserk. He's yelling at someone and his voice sounds like Dad's the last time he was beating Mikey. The cop pulls a gun from his holster. My hand grips Mom's leg.

"Mom, look."

But I don't need to tell her. We hear the gun fire. The man next to the cop falls to the floor. Mom screams, pushes me down and lies on top of me while the cop continues to shoot. The gunshots are not as loud as Papa Bace's .45, but they're sharp and crisp. I hear a whiz through the air. What will it feel like if we're hit?

I know Mom sometimes feels powerless with Dad, but that cop has a gun. So it's incredible how she's protecting me now. I can hear screams and moans from people who are hurt. The cop keeps shooting. How long can this go on before Mom gets hit? I've lost Papa Bace. I can't lose my mother.

Another cop shoots the crazy cop. Just as suddenly as it started, it's over.

When I look around the hallway, there are four people on the floor with blood all over them. Is this what Papa Bace felt like in WWI? It looks real, but I can't believe it. We're in a hospital where people are supposed to get fixed. I start to ask Mom, but she has her hand over her mouth and is sobbing. She just shakes her head at me.

It's been two months since my eye surgery. After what happened the first time I saw the eye doctors, I was afraid to go back to the hospital for the operation. But Mom told me, "People don't just start shooting other people for no reason. That will never happen again." What she said made sense, and I gave in to having the operation.

It was horrible. No one got shot but when I came to, I felt very sick and threw up. Mom said it was from the ether. I asked her what ether was and she told me it was something to make me sleep.

I hate sleep now. Before this operation I was always excited to wake up in the morning, but now I have to wear patches over both eyes to protect them. I can't tell if I'm daydreaming or awake, but when I hear Dad yell at Mikey, I remember the pain on Mikey's face when we were being belted together and cry. Mom comes into my room and touches the tears on my cheeks.

"Don't be sad. You'll get one patch off in a few more weeks. Just a little longer."

Dad's gone.

Mikey tells me, "Thank God for the Navy. Mom says Dad's away at the War College in Rhode Island, and now I can watch TV all I want."

"What about me?"

"Well, you're blind as a bat but don't worry. I'll tell you what's going on."

"Can we watch 'Lassie?'"

"No. 'Gunsmoke.'"

Mikey talks me through 'Gunsmoke,' but when I hear Marshall Dillon's gun, I tremble.

"Billy, what's wrong with you?"

"Can we watch something else?"

"Yeah, sure. How about this? It's called 'Hawaiian Eye.' It's black and white, but that won't matter to you, I guess."

"Not funny, Mikey."

"OK, OK. Hey, I've been to Maui. I can tell you what everything looks like."

Mikey describes the beautiful blue and green water, the palm trees and white sand beaches. The 'Hawaiian Eye' show begins and someone is singing about Hawaiian Eye.

"What is it, Mikey? Is there a big eye on the TV?"

"No, dummy. Guys are riding surfboards on waves. I'd like to do that."

"I want to be an astronaut like Commander Shepard. Mom says my eyes might be good enough to be a pilot after these patches come off."

"Yeah, right. You want to be cooped up inside that little Coke-bottle capsule, clicking switches? You call that fun?"

"Yeah, it's so free. I'd like to fly around in outer space. Isn't a hundred miles above earth outer space?"

"Who cares?"

"What do you think is fun?"

"Eating a mango on Maui."

"Maui is fun?"

"Maui is paradise."

I don't know what mangoes are or what paradise is, and even space exploration isn't going to keep me happy until I get these patches off my eyes.

We're back at Sans Souci to visit our grandmother.

Everyone is off doing other things this afternoon, and I'm alone with Mama Marcelle. The doctors told Mom my eye operation was a success, but one eye still has a patch and I'm not supposed to play outside until I can see with both eyes. I get comfortable on the big Haitian couch under the picture window that overlooks Chuckatuck Creek. It brings back all the great crabbing times I had with Papa Bace. My grandmother is listening to her phonograph play a talking book about some mystery that is as hard to understand as *Moby Dick*. But the sound of the narrator's voice and the creak of my grandmother's rocking chair put me into a trance that breaks when she stops rocking. This is the first time I've seen her without her glasses. Without them her face looks sad. I can tell she still misses Papa Bace.

She notices my stare and lifts the needle off the record.

"William, you must do well in school so you don't have to be a garbage man when you grow up."

I'm surprised by the way she has switched her attention to me.

"I'll be a fighter pilot, I guess."

She shakes her head.

"Military men are men without imaginations. The military is like a welfare state that fosters violent drunks."

I don't know what a welfare state is, but I know what violence is.

"But Papa Bus?"

"Ah, but he was a doctor, my young man, and that's a distinguishing difference."

Mom is always talking about my future, and it makes me squirm. Talking about my future with Mama Marcelle also starts to feel uncomfortable. I want to change the subject. I know so much about Papa Bace and so little about her.

"Where in France are you from?"

"My family came from the Vosges, in the east. In my lifetime the Boche have invaded three times."

"The Boche?"

"The pig-headed Germans. The Huns."

She leaves the room momentarily and returns with some photographs.

"These are my nephews who were in the Resistance fighting the Nazis. They were put in concentration camps after they were captured."

She points out numbers on their wrists. They're so skinny that they look like bags of bones.

"Didn't the Boche feed them?"

She purses her lips together and her eyes water.

"They ignored the Geneva Convention."

She points to one nephew's picture.

"The Germans killed him. My sister Germaine died of grief soon after his death."

My grandmother teaches me that the Nazis were more than just opposing blue-colored toy soldiers in my war games. Aside from the shooting between soldiers, there was also horrible cruelty to civilians during the war. She's angry when she talks about Germans and teaches me a new word, 'atrocity.'

I realize Mama Marcelle isn't only thinking about losing Papa Bace but many people in her family, even from a time before I was born. I didn't know them but if they were anything like my grandfather, I can understand why she's so bitter.

Mikey is back from the neighbors and he and I are in another room when we overhear a tense conversation between Mom and Mama Marcelle.

"Mikey killed him. He gave my Bace high blood pressure. The boy is a bad seed."

"Oh, Mum," our mom cries.

Mikey runs upstairs.

I overhear Mama Marcelle tell Mom, "Jacqueline, I don't know if you and Jack should ever have had children."

Tears flood my eyes and my throat feels tight. I bolt upstairs to our room to join Mikey, but the door is locked.

"Let me in."

"Go away."

I sit against the door and cry.

"Go away."

I pound my fist on the door.

"Come on, let me in."

"Is anyone else there?"

"No."

The door opens. I slip in and he locks it behind me. Then he sits on his bed, fingering Papa Bace's Colt .45. The sight of the gun scares me.

"Mikey, you got in big trouble the last time you stole that. Give it to me and I'll p-p-put it back."

Mikey raises the gun to his temple.

"This time I'm going to kill myself. You heard them. I'm worthless."

"No, no, please, no. Don't leave me alone."

Mikey drops the gun back down to his lap. His face looks up at me like it's melting. I feel so sad and helpless looking at him. I'm scared and get up to go.

"I'm going to tell Mom."

"Remember what I told you about secrets?"

"OK, OK."

I stay and sob. Finally I calm down enough to talk.

"Let's make a vow, Mikey. We'll be brothers forever and watch over each other."

I hold my two hands out toward Mikey, like the offering plate at church. He nods and lays the Colt in my hands.

"Don't ever tell anyone about this. It's our secret."

"OK, Mikey."

I sneak into the study. The case for the gun is right where Mikey told me it would be. The felt lining feels smooth and rich. The gun must have meant so much to Papa Bace. I place the revolver into its case, lock it and hide the key where Mikey told me he found it.

Mike and Bill Boyum, Patuxent River, Maryland, 1953

Chapter Five

Cool Stuff
1962-1964

Tap tap tap. I can tell we're off the smooth surface of the highway. Mikey's head bounces off the window with every bump in this road. In a split second Dad's irritated face whips around but he sees what I see and turns away. There are tear tracks on Mikey's cheeks. His eyes stare blankly out the car window and his mouth hangs open. I'm worried about what Dad might do next and whisper in Mikey's ear to lean away from the window, but Mikey doesn't do or say anything. He hasn't said a word since we left Alexandria. Seconds and minutes go by and Dad does nothing. I know the tapping noise bugs Dad but guess even he knows there isn't anything more he can do to make things worse for Mikey. Dad shrugs.

Mom says, "He's never been this upset about moving before."

I'm the only one who saw him with Papa Bace's gun to his head and know that moving isn't making Mikey sad. Mama Marcelle calling Mikey a bad seed keeps repeating inside my head when I look at Mikey's face.

Dad has new orders. We're moving again and driving all the way across the country. Mom told me where but I didn't listen. All I can think about is my brother—this long drive must be the worst torture for him.

We're in San Francisco. Mom tells us Dad has shipped out with the command of a helicopter carrier, the USS Princeton.

Mikey's suddenly excited and friendly with me. We escape our small apartment and jump on trolleys and buses to Kezar Stadium for a football game. The 49ers' great quarterback, John Brodie, has a great game. We love the roar of a packed stadium and mostly I love running with Mikey.

The game is over and I grab his arm.

"Mikey, are you happy now?"

He rips his arm loose.

"What are you talking about? I'm fine."

"Well, you know, the gun."

Mikey points his finger at me.

"Forget about that. Stuff it inside and never talk about it again, not even with me."

He smiles at me.

"Now come on, let's go."

Mikey moves fast and it's hard to keep up with him. But I don't care as long as he's happy.

~

We didn't stay long in San Francisco and now we're back living in Coronado in our old house on Pine Court.

I wander the two blocks to the beach. There's the Hotel Del Coronado at the far south end. The last time we lived here, the hotel was the first thing that made me want to check out what was down here by the ocean. It looked like the Disneyland castle I saw when I snuck on top of the church roof with Mikey. We got the belt for climbing up there, but it was worth it.

After I discovered the ocean, I played at the beach every moment I could. The hours and days spent looking at starfish in the tide pools in front of the hotel made me happy back then, but I won't be doing that anymore. That's what little kids do.

There's the fence for the Naval Air Station and the edge of the runway. I also used to play war with the Navy jet shadows as they landed and took off. There was a rusted battle helmet I found in the boxes of junk in our garage. The leather chin straps were rotten and looked like one that was used in WWI. Maybe it was Papa Bace's. Back then, I played imaginary war games and could scream as loud as I wanted when the jets rocketed just over my head. I won't be doing that anymore. Besides, it's crazy loud right now. The takeoffs are non-stop and sound like thunder. I don't remember this much action when we lived here before.

I run back to our house to see what Mikey's up to. He sees me but is yelling at his transistor radio.

"Cube-er, Cube-er. No one is playing any music—they should just launch the missiles and get it over with."

"Why don't you put on that record you like so much?"

Dad is at sea and since he's been gone, Mikey has been playing Mimi's old forty-five record player. He's only got one record, and he plays it over and over again. The one about money and the birds.

"I dig it."

The great tom-tom beat begins.

"Mikey, Dad would never go for this record, would he?"

"Nope. But I got plans. Want to come?"

Today there are tons of people buying food and stuff at the PX commissary. We push ladies' shopping carts and load their cars for quarters. Mikey is pushing so fast. I try to copy him, and my cart almost tips over. When we reach a lady's car, Mikey sounds like Eddie Haskell on "Leave It To Beaver," telling her how nice she looks.

"Here's some extra for you and your little brother."

We're running like crazy for the next cart, Mikey waving the dollar bill at my face.

"Man, it's like it's raining money today. Just leave the talking to me."

At the end of the day I'm real tired, but Mikey gets other jobs pushing peoples' lawn mowers.

"Why are you working so hard?"

"'Cause money is all you need to be free."

Mikey buys some barbells with all the money he's been making. He's also been drinking those Vic Tanny muscle shakes they sell on TV. When he's lifting, he's serious so I don't bug him.

Mimi is home from her freshman year at San Diego State across the bay. Dad's still out at sea. Mom says he's off in the Pacific for a few months. That means Mikey and I can relax.

I hear Mimi tell Mom, "Oh my God, Mom, I got to see President Kennedy. It's true what they say about him. He does have charisma."

"You know, Mimi, your father and I were Jack and Jackie long before they were."

I ask Mimi, "What's charisma, anyway?"

"It's magnetism, the kind I need from one of Mom's great silk dresses she bought in Hong Kong. Where are they, Mom?"

"Out in the garage."

I follow Mimi and Mom into the garage because Mikey is always nicer when Mimi comes home. Mikey is lifting weights on a bench press in a small area he has cleared. Mom's still-unopened boxes from her many trips to Hong Kong and Singapore are packed to the garage roof. Mimi laughs.

"Mom, we still have all this junk from the last time we lived here four years ago?"

"It's not junk, Mimi. I have some Noritake China in there. They're expensive items. The Navy pays for my trips. It's one of the good things about being a Navy wife."

I say, "If I ever become a grownup, I won't have a garage full of unopened junk. I know Dad will be screaming about this clutter when he gets back from sea, just like he always does."

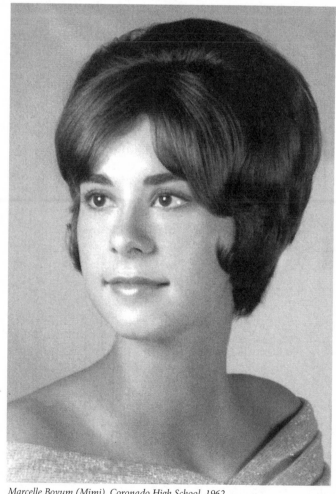

Marcelle Boyum (Mimi), Coronado High School, 1962

Mikey ignores me.

"Hey, Mom," I continue, "remember my pal Jimmy Orland? He told his mom about some of these Chink statues you've brought home, and his mom said she thought some of that expensive stuff was illegal to bring back here. Is it, Mom?"

"You tell Jimmy to mind his own business. Besides, they're civilians."

Mom has that devilish twinkle in her eyes we all know so well.

"Between you and me," she continues, "I get great deals on those things. They're only expensive here."

"So you could sell them here and make money if you wanted."

"Yes, if I wanted."

Mikey sits up from the bench press and taps me in the chest with the back of his hand.

"You see, Billy, that's why Mom has this junk. She gets some pretty cool extras from Dad's job as a Naval officer."

"Just because he's in the Navy?"

"Yep, when you fly jets, you don't have to live like the rest of the jerks in the world."

Mom puts her finger to her lips, turns and leaves us kids to talk.

Mikey says, "Hey, Meems, you must have a date. Back here to rip off another one of Mom's dresses?"

"Keep lifting those weights, big boy."

She looks at her watch.

"In ten minutes you'll see what a real man looks like."

"UDT?"

She nods.

Mikey waves her off.

"They're kinda cool, but it's still the Navy."

"Well, whatever you do, you better get your grades up. Money to live on isn't just going to fall out of the sky."

"I've been making money."

"Come on. Pushing shopping carts at the PX?"

"What about those UDT guys you date? How much do they make?"

Mimi's eyes open wide. She smiles and flexes her biceps.

"Who cares?"

I've heard these letters so many times.

"What's UDT?"

Mimi tells me, "It stands for Underwater Demolition Team. You know, frogmen. They're trained at the amphib base."

"Down by the Silver Strand?"

"Yeah. Mom's always driving that way to buy cheap booze in Mexico."

Mikey interrupts, "How cheap?"

Mimi shrugs.

I say, "Mikey. Who cares about booze? I wanna hear the cool stuff about frogmen."

Mimi says, "I've got to get ready. See you boys later."

I'm alone with Mikey.

"I'd like to be a frogman."

"So?"

"I'm only telling you. Mom is always asking me what I'm going to do when I grow up and then she latches onto it like it's my decision forever."

"Like being a pilot?"

"Yeah, like that. It sounds cool, but I just don't know if I want to do the same thing Dad does."

"Well, I hate the Navy. But whatever you do, you should keep it to yourself. Telling Mom ruins anything. I keep all my plans secret."

"Will you tell me?"

"No."

"Why?"

"'Cause you're a project and I can't have a project slowing me down. You gotta start finding your own friends."

These past months Mom keeps telling me Mikey's friends are hoodlums and he's been in tons of fights at school. It's true. I've seen a few of his fights, and it scares me to see how mean he can be. Mikey always wins and has blood on his shirt.

Dad came home for a short time, but Mom didn't tell him about Mikey. She's worried what's going to happen when Dad returns from sea and starts asking questions about why Mikey was suspended from school. I worry, too. It's so fun when Dad is gone, but we never know when he's coming home. Mom doesn't even know.

Mikey still does some things with me. He takes me to the movies and we go on all the scary rides when the circus is in town. But when he meets up with his pals, it's time for me to split. That's OK; I have friends, too.

All my new pals are Navy kids and their fathers are also out at sea. No one tells us what to do. They're going places fast on skateboards. If I want to hang out with them, I need one, too.

The word is that the best wheels are off of skates from the roller rink in San Diego. My friends tell me to take the ferry across the bay, get on the bus to the rink and slip out with the skates when no one is looking.

I broke several of Dad's drill bits removing the wheels from the skates, but I'm proud of what I've made. A skateboard means I can go fast just like everyone else.

I've been straightlining the only steep hill in Coronado, near Glorietta Bay, for the last month and have crashed a few times. One day when I get home, I can hear Mom and Dad talking. Oh, man, Dad's back.

I overhear Mom from another room.

"That Billy, it's a wonder he doesn't kill himself. I took him to the hospital several times while you were gone."

God, is Mom trying to get sympathy from Dad? I told her not to tell him stuff. Maybe she's trying to make him feel guilty for being gone so long. She's told me it bothers her.

"Oh? From what?" Dad says.

"Skateboarding."

Mom just doesn't get it.

"And where did he get this skateboard?"

"He made it with your tools."

I know Mom's proud of me, but now I'm screwed.

Dad marches into the garage and finds the mess I left of broken drill bits and tattered sandpaper.

"Bill," he yells, "in my room immediately."

In the privacy of our room, Mikey stares at me after my belting. He looks pissed off and I flinch when he lifts his hand towards my face.

"Are you mad at me, too, Mikey?"

"No. Fuck no. Relax. You've been hit enough."

Mikey is shaking his head and I let him touch my bleeding ear.

"You're still a kid. Fuck."

Dad leaves for work and Mikey screams at Mom.

"You can't just let Dad do this anymore."

"What can I do?"

"Divorce the son of a bitch."

Mom looks shocked and it's not about Mikey's swearing. He swears all the time.

"Mikey, that would ruin his career."

"I don't care about him, Mom."

"You don't mean that, Mikey. Maybe the juvenile authorities can help."

"Don't you remember those idiots? They're worthless."

Mikey storms off and I'm left gazing at Mom, feeling bad. Divorce shocks me, too. There are many divorced parents in Coronado, but the idea terrifies me. Mikey's pals talk about divorced women in the worst way, like they're easy. I think I know what that means. Mimi says Mom has health problems. I don't want her to be divorced.

What would divorce mean to me? Having no dad would be different, and I'm scared of different. We're moving around all the time and this kind of change might even bring worse problems. Every kid in Coronado I've heard talk about his father says he's been belted. I'm not the only one. It's like one of Dad's facts of life. Let's just keep things the same. I know what that is.

I feel bad that I'm causing so many problems, but I don't know about Mom's idea, either. I guess Mikey stormed out because he knows what the juvenile authorities do. I've heard about the juvie home for kids. Tough kids are trapped in a prison and pound on kids who aren't so tough, like me. The idea of ending up there scares the crap out of me. Mikey has been to one a few times, but he can fight. He's almost old enough to live on his own now and then I won't have anyone to protect me. This whole thing is making me feel sick to my stomach. I run all the way to the beach.

Boss. That looks really neat. Young kids like me are skimming on round pieces of plywood coated with resin along the wide area of one-inch deep foam before the waves finally meet dry sand. This isn't skateboarding, but it does look like fun and I'm sure Dad won't want me doing it.

Dad's car is in the driveway. He's back from work. Mom catches me when I try to sneak in the back door.

"We're going to dinner at the Greys' home. Dad will be leaving again in a few days for sea duty and it will be good for us to have some family time together."

"Are we related to them?"

"No. No. Of course not. But Captain Grey is a fighter pilot. He flew with your father off the same aircraft carrier during the war. They're close friends, and Mikey is pals with their son, Duke. It'll be fun."

I see Dad enter the room and feel the cut on my ear.

"Oh, that's neat, Mom."

I go cross-eyed so only she can see me and then walk away.

Mom says after me, "Apparently Captain Grey helped sink a ship during the war."

I turn back to her.

"Really?"

I blow up my toy model ships with firecrackers but can't imagine what a real ship would look like when it explodes.

Dad says from behind us, "It wasn't just a ship. It was one of the two biggest Japanese battleships, and he dropped a bomb right down its stack."

How does he sneak up on me like that? Does Dad remember belting me this morning? What he's saying does sound interesting, but all of a sudden he's friendly? Maybe this get-together could be fun, but I'm still shook up from my skateboard beating.

What was Mom thinking? This isn't family time. There are many other Navy pilots and wives drinking at the Greys' home. Chubby Checker's "Limbo" song is playing on Captain Grey's Akai tape deck. Mikey elbows me. One of the wives is leaning back to get under the limbo bar Captain Grey has set up in his living room. Her big boobs are about to pop out of her low-cut sequined dress. Some of the men are howling.

I point Mikey towards Dad, who's in a circle of men. One of them lays his hand on Dad's shoulder.

"And then Smilin' Jack here…"

When one of the other pilots points towards us, the storyteller lowers his voice and the hum of the room muffles the rest of his story. Mikey and I can see a huge grin on Dad's face.

Mom approaches us, grabs my arm and turns me towards another man.

"Billy, this is Captain Grey."

"Sir."

Captain Grey booms, "*My* name is Bill. Have you earned the right to call yourself by the same name?"

His spooky eyes turn my excitement into fear. My hand is locked in his and I'm worried he's the same as Dad. Even with a clean shave, his beard is dark. And although he's smiling, he looks even more like Bluto than Dad does.

"You're a lucky boy to have a father like yours."

"Yes, sir."

Silent moments pass. I turn to bolt, but my hand is still locked inside his. Mikey is giggling off to the side. He must have already learned this the hard way.

Chubby Checker begins to howl. Some couples are twisting. A woman hands Mikey two drinks to hold, slides in between Captain Grey and me, and begins shaking her hips. He releases my hand and grabs the woman's waist. She motions for Mikey to bring their drinks and then leans towards me and rubs my back.

"I'm Duke's mother, he's out in the garage."

As we bolt from the room, I hear one of the men address Captain Grey as 'Stud.'

I follow Mikey into the open garage. We have to step carefully around a huge mess. This must be where Duke sleeps, because among all the

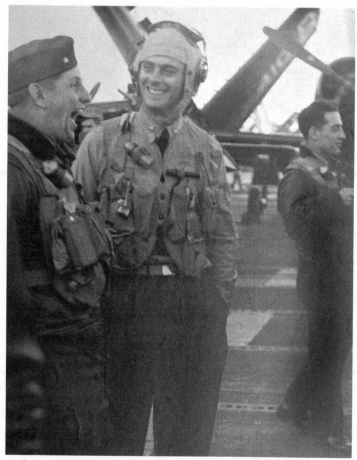

Lt. Commander J.H. Boyum (Smilin' Jack), flight deck of USS Wasp, 1944

surf clutter is an unmade bed. The surf posters and pictures taped to the wall are cool, but I have a question that needs answering from when Mikey took me to see the Paul Newman movie "Hud" last week.

"Hey," I say, "I thought Hud was the stud. Why did that man call Captain Grey 'Stud?'"

Mikey leers at Duke and mouths a line from the movie.

"The only question I ever ask any woman is..."

Duke yells the finish, "What time is your husband coming home?"

They both echo, "Hud has a barbed-wire soul."

"What are you guys talking about? I thought it was because he dive-bombed a Jap battleship."

Duke tells me, "He did."

"I heard another man call our dad 'Smilin' Jack.' I didn't know our dads had different names. Did you, Mikey?"

"Yeah, and yours will be 'Retard.'"

"Ah, come on, what's with all this stuff about women?"

Mikey stiff-arms me and chuckles with Duke.

"We're not telling you. Now don't bug us."

I'll just eavesdrop on their conversation and try to pick up what I can—but I'm distracted right away.

"Check it out, Mikey! Bitchin', huh?"

Duke nods towards a new surfboard in the back of his room. Mikey runs his fingers over the edge. My eyes are popping out of my head.

"Nice rails," says Mikey.

"It's a Yater. Still need to pay for it."

"Soon."

They nod at each other. I wonder why but my attention shifts again and I pick up some odd footwear by his bed. It's a strapped leather sandal with a piece of car tire stapled to the bottom. Duke answers my questioning eyes while he grins at Mikey.

"Huaraches. I got 'em in TJ."

I know that's Tijuana.

The tire sole seems to be loose, and I peel it back from the leather. It's been hollowed out underneath.

"Mikey, look at this cheap Mexican shit. They can't even make a tire right."

He smacks me on the side of the head.

"Why you got to go and touch everything, dork?"

Duke laughs and carefully takes them from me.

"It's OK, they've served their purpose."

I figure he means that since they're cheap and made in Mexico, they aren't expected to last long. But maybe I'm wrong because Mikey nods again to Duke. I can tell there's a ton of stuff I don't know that they know. But I do know that Duke's dressed like a surfer because I've seen his same look at the surf movies and recognize his freckles and sun-bleached hair. His nose is peeling and he's barefoot. His Pendleton shirt and faded blue jeans are grungy. I'm curious about the board.

"You surf?"

My brother slaps me again on the side of my head.

"Why you hafta say that stupid shit? Of course he surfs. Everyone knows he's the meanest hot dogger at the beach."

Duke's smiling at Mikey.

"The little scurve. They all say shit like that."

He lifts his chin at Mikey with recognition and changes the subject.

"Who ratted on you for working on that reject?"

I saw the fight and know what Duke's talking about. Mikey was scary mean.

"Don't know, but he had it coming, saying all that shit that was nowhere. So I had to straighten him out."

Mikey points to a rusty VW bug with broken-down surf racks on top, parked out by the curb.

"Your wheels are toast."

Duke waves it off.

"That'll change soon. How 'bout you?"

"Got a Vespa."

The motor scooter belongs to my sister's UDT boyfriend, who leaves it at our house when he's off training. Mikey steals it sometimes and now he glares at me not to blow his story. He turns to Duke, who seems unimpressed.

"But I got my eyes on something with four wheels."

Duke pops Mikey with a playful shoulder shove.

"Oh yeah, man. Get a car, get a board and start surfing. Chicks don't dig hoods. And man, you gotta have a back seat."

Mikey nods at Duke's wisdom.

"Yeah, set me up. I can get the bread from my mom till we…"

When Duke rolls his eyes towards me, Mikey stops in the middle of his sentence and then says, "Where do I get a board?"

They're keeping secrets from me. I know it, but I don't care. A surfboard? Bitchin'.

~

Mom never gives me a list of chores whenever Dad goes to sea. She lets me do what I want. I don't think she has any chores, either, because she's always driving to TJ. Mikey and Duke have been riding down there with her, but Mexico sounds boring to me.

The beach is my favorite hangout. Ever since Dad left two weeks ago, I can come here any time I want to watch other kids skimboard. There aren't any grownups here to snitch me out when Dad returns. And I can make a skimboard.

The skimboard is much easier to make than a skateboard. I can run fast, throw the board and jump on for a long ride, kick the board and jump on again. I'm doing this every day. Afterwards I hide the evidence in the caves of huge boulders along Ocean Boulevard. Now I have a secret.

Skimboarding is pretty tiring and when I stop to rest, I watch surfers ride waves. I wish I could make a surfboard.

Dad is still at sea. Mikey jingles Mom and Dad's car keys in front of my face.

"Wanna go for a drive?"

"Where?"

"The Gordon and Smith shop in La Jolla. Mom gave me some dough to buy a board."

"For you?"

He's ginning at me.

"You see, I'm a troubled teen and Mom heard I was hanging out with hoods. She wants me to be a good boy like Duke. Thinks surfing is a wholesome activity."

"What about me?"

"Like I said, you can come along if you like."

"Mikey, that's not what I meant."

"You coming or not?"

We arrive at the shop and Mikey's talking to the salesman. I'm admiring a blue and white board with a half-moon laminated skeg that I know from my pals on the beach is a very cool thing. Mikey comes over to check it out.

"Is this the one, Billy?"

Mikey mounts surf racks on the car and drives to school every day with the board on top. I ask him about the board and he keeps telling me he's going to try it, but he never does.

Mom has been very generous with his use of the family car while Dad's gone, but tomorrow Dad comes home. That's Mikey's problem. All I care about is the board that's still on top of the car. It doesn't have a scratch on it. He's concentrating on popping zits in the rearview mirror but I know that's how he makes his plans.

"Got a date tonight, with Shirley, can you believe it? Guess this surf deal really works."

Mikey is cleaning out his trash from inside the car and spots me rubbing my hands down the rails until I pick at some light scratches around the gutter tracks on the car. He checks out what I'm checking out.

"Dad's going to flip out if he sees that. Shit."

I smirk.

"Don't sweat it, Mikey. Dad's a bodysurfer and loves the waves. Yeah, he'll understand."

"Real funny, wiseass. Someone's gotta take those racks off and buff out those scratches before he gets back."

He pops his head out and grabs my arm.

"Listen, scurve. You gotta do it. I got to get ready."

"Scurve? Just 'cause you talk like Duke doesn't make you a surfer."

"You gonna help me out or not?"

"The board. I want to try it."

"Deal."

~

Dad's home from sea but it doesn't matter. He can only corner me at meals so I skip many and escape to the beach. I've been surfing, and that's all I care about. Today I'm skipping school. Nobody cares about me today anyway. Everyone is watching TV.

It's foggy on the beach. I drag Mikey's board towards the water and see a surfer standing at the water's edge, checking out the waves. It's Duke Grey.

I stop a little behind Duke because every time I get too close, he whacks the back of my head.

"Hey, Duke."

His eyes remain fixed forward towards the ocean. The tail of Duke's wet suit hangs down loose so he looks like a beaver, but I don't tell him that. Still focused on his surf-check, he doesn't turn towards me when he speaks.

"Bitchin' waves, gremlin. You going out?"

"Yeah, sure."

I try to sound enthusiastic even though I'm already feeling how my bones will ache from the icy water. The ocean is so cold I know I won't last long out there. Each wave that hits my face will feel like screwdrivers are poking into my eardrums. I wish I had all that frogman stuff and a wetsuit like Duke's. He even got one for Mikey. Maybe I should ask him for one.

"Where's your brother?"

"Watching TV, about the president."

"Nothing he can do. When you're dead, you're dead."

Staring at the back of Duke's head, I know I don't understand everything that has happened today. He steps towards the water and I follow.

I've caught a good one and step back quickly to crank a turn. I love this rush of speed when I take off on a wave.

Back on the beach, my blue lips quiver over my chattering teeth. I'm burying myself in warm sand but it's not enough.

The older surfers my brother's age are also fresh out of the water and huddled around a fire they've made inside an oil drum. They're not shaking. From forty feet away, I can see heat waves rise from their drum. I wish I could get closer, but I'm afraid of them. These guys are tough and don't let anyone outside their group hang out near them. I think they only let me this close because I'm Mikey's little brother. Maybe some of their heat will drift in my direction.

Mikey has shown up and is talking with Duke. The surfers shoot the shit and take turns punching their fists into a useless board they call a surf sacrifice to make the waves get bigger. I've seen this before, but today the surf is good. Why are they still pissed off? They look my way every so often. Are they making sure I don't come too close? I'm freezing, but forty feet away is as close as I dare to get.

The surfers quit punching the board. They're talking and smiling. They sound so cool to me as they use their hands to describe their maneuvers, just like the fighter pilots do at our parents' parties.

"I cut back and did an el-rollo and pulled into the curl," says one.

Another stretches his foot out in front of him.

"Hung five out there. Felt so cool."

I smile and snap my fingers over and over again.

I yell, "I think we're Jets."

"Jets? You're a little dweeb," says Duke.

"Oh yeah?"

"Hey, Mikey. You're little brother thinks he's cool."

I keep snapping my fingers.

"Chukes are definitely Sharks. Those greaser car guys are nowhere."

All the surfers crack up.

"Correctamundo, you little gremlin. They need to stay in Chula Vista where they belong."

I'm burying myself with sand to keep warm.

Duke yells, "Hey, you little turd, come here."

His voice seems edgy and I stay where I am. He keeps waving me over to them. The heat from their fire is too much to resist. I edge towards the drum, scared because I finally see Duke close up. He usually has a friendly grin, but today there are bruises all over his face. Someone has beaten him up real bad. He waits until I'm close, then grabs and lifts me stretched out over the fire drum.

"I'm gonna bar-b-cue me a gremmey."

I panic at the thought of getting cooked. The flames make me remember a picture on the cover of Dad's *Time* magazine of a Buddhist monk from Vietnam lighting himself on fire. Why would someone burn himself up? Is Duke just teasing me? Maybe not. Papa Bace had told me about how horrible those wounds were. Burning to death has to be the worst way to die.

I struggle in Duke's arms when I feel the heat. Mikey says OK and Duke lets me down. Up close I can see that Duke is also missing a tooth.

The surfers each punch and shove me.

Duke tells me, "You can hang out here from now on."

The surfers are laughing and the punches don't hurt for very long. Even though these guys are rough, I like being adopted by this gang.

I go over and punch at the surf sacrifice board.

Mikey tells me, "You punch like a sissy. Use your hips."

He demonstrates and I copy him.

Duke talks to another surfer and I pull Mikey aside.

"Who worked over Duke's face?"

Mikey brushes me off.

"Probably some Chukes. Surfers fight greasers whenever they meet. Duke is always going through Chula Vista on his way to Baja. He's lucky 'cause those hodads use knives."

I shudder. I love the surf rebel image, but the rumble scene scared me when Mikey took me to the movie "West Side Story." The stabbing deaths of Riff and Bernardo looked real. That was only a movie, but I've heard other stories about surfers fighting greasers in real-life rumbles.

Duke's face is proof.

"Do you drive that way when you go to TJ with Mom?"

Mikey looks at me for a second, like he's trying to figure out what I'm talking about.

"Oh yeah, with Mom, for her booze runs, right? Uh, no. We drive down the Strand."

Mikey seems distant. I wonder if he's worried about knives.

Today Mikey and I are walking home from the beach when Duke yells us over to his rusted VW. I examine the ropes he has put through his windows to tie down his dinged-up surfboard. Duke is rifling through the trash in his car.

"If I can't find the keys, you gotta help me jump-start this piece of crap."

He pulls out a pamphlet called the Fallout Shelter Handbook from the car's trash heap.

"I heisted this. Check it out."

Duke flings the manual to Mikey.

I look over Mikey's shoulder. The page shows a cut-away of a small concrete cubicle with a happy-looking family inside it. A husband with a contented look on his face sits with his smoking jacket and pipe listening to his phonograph. The wife bakes cupcakes with a proper apron and two kids happily play cards, just like in a scene from the "Ozzie and Harriet" show.

Mikey says, "Can you believe this? An A-bomb has blown the whole world to smithereens and they're listening to records?"

"That's a fallout shelter?"

Mikey ignores me and reads the table of contents, which includes How You Can Survive a Nuclear War, Build a Shelter Now, Stock up Now, While You're In a Shelter, and finally Guerrilla War. His finger immediately jumps back to While You're In a Shelter.

"Hey, Mikey, I was snooping around Dad's room the other day when he was gone. Knocked over a stack of quarters and dimes he had on his dresser. Was real careful to stack them back perfect just the way he had them."

"So?"

"So I found pictures of mushroom clouds. That's A-bombs, right?"

"Yeah, that's A-bombs. You see anything else?"

"One picture showed a small island. The other was just a hole, no island."

"The old man was taking pictures of A-bombs? How do you have the balls to take pictures of an A-bomb? They blow the crap out of everything. Nothing lives. Hey Duke, you think anyone has a shelter here in Coronado?"

Duke is still searching for his keys and ignores us.

I turn back to the picture in the manual.

"Mikey, whose family is that? Our family doesn't look like that."

Mikey laughs.

"Our family isn't even close. I know there's no way in hell I could ever be cooped up in that small of a space with Dad. Driving across the country is bad enough."

"This is it, Mikey. We'll just surf until the bomb drops. It's the only way."

I hold my arms wide apart and imagine it just like the thunderstorms I loved at Sans Souci. The heat from the blast will be a fantastic moment of relief from the bone-chilling ocean. At least it would be quick if I got vaporized, like getting struck by a bolt of Virginia lightning.

"We all gotta go sometime," says Mikey.

I know he's copying what I've heard from many surfers. If he's talking like them, then I will, too.

"Correctamundo."

"So you're a surfer now?"

"Yeah, Mikey. I'm gonna surf forever. I'll never be afraid of the end of the world."

Duke pulls his key from under the seat and presents it to us like it's the key to a bank safe.

"I'm not worried about the end of the world—just what's gonna happen after I graduate."

Duke looks like the Thinker on the "Dobie Gillis" TV show.

"Shit, I dig it here on the beach. My parents can have their martinis—I'll take the surf any day."

I nod.

"But Duke," I ask, "how will you get food? Our dad always reminds us that he feeds us and we'll have to work someday to feed ourselves. What kind of work will you do?"

Mikey slaps me on the side of my head.

"Moron, any kind of steady job is a walk away from the surf."

Duke says, "Yeah, work is a four-letter word. We all know what Maynard would say."

I scratch my head. They don't seem serious. I want to be serious.

"I might join the UDT."

Duke throws his forearm into my back, looks at Mikey and points at me with the back of his thumb.

"Hey Mikey, your little brother wants to be a frogman."

They're both cracking up and it bothers me.

"What's so funny? You guys don't even have a plan."

Duke puts my head in an arm lock and scrubs it hard with his knuckle.

"We have a plan, gremmy. Don't you worry about that."

He releases the headlock.

"But down the line? I don't know. There's this thing called the draft."

Mikey stops laughing.

"Oh, man. You got that right."

Duke also sounds more serious.

"My dad says I need to stop wasting my time at the beach. He thinks the Marines will straighten me out and I should sign up before I get drafted into the Army."

I ask Duke, "Why not the Navy?"

Mikey pops me in the shoulder and answers for Duke.

"And be a swabby? No, thank you. That's what you'll be, Billy, if you become a frogman. Besides, swabbies don't surf."

Duke rubs his huge surf knots, proof of too much knee paddling.

Mikey tells him, "That's enough to fail your draft physical."

"Yeah, I might be able to get out but screw it, I'll just go. What can happen? There's no war. I'll just do my two years and hit it back to the surf. Baja or maybe even Hawaii, where the water is warm."

Duke elbows me, knowing I can dig that.

"You see that's the trick, gremlin. Two years. You don't want to be a lifer like our dads. You think you'll just be swimming underwater for your whole time in the Navy? Get used to it, gremmey, you're a surfer, not one of these robots that go to work and salute everyone."

Duke is shaking his head.

"My dad's too old to fly now, so he just spends his time kicking my ass. I guess jets are cool for a while, but I'll have my fun on the waves."

So it wasn't the Chukes that worked over Duke's face.

Mikey snickers and Duke snaps at him, "Don't act so tough, Boyum. You've hidden in my room for days after your dad beat the crap out of you. Only he just used a belt, you pussy."

This is the first time I've heard Mikey and Duke talk about their family stuff like this but from the way they are talking, I can tell something is bugging them. They seem edgy with each other right now, even though I know they're best pals because they spend almost all their time together. Mikey says Duke has been paddling surfboards with him to get in shape.

"Hey, I know what you mean," Mikey says. "Our dads are pricks."

"I'm not blaming my dad, Boyum. Screw you. I don't have to explain anything to anybody."

I'm amazed how things can go from fun to tense so quickly.

Mikey quickly pulls me behind his back.

"Billy, you better beat feet."

"What?"

"The fuzz, the truant officer, you dummy. Get going."

I skip school any time the surf's up. But Mikey and Duke are seniors, and their high school years are already done. If I get caught, it's the board of education on my backside. Dad gave the principal of the school the thumbs up to go harder with me. But there's nothing that can keep me away from the beach.

It's been about two months since President Kennedy was shot, but I still hear many people talking about it. Not me, but Mikey always does. He uses this big word, 'conspiracy.' He told me it meant that a bunch of guys got together and pulled something off. Not that I care—I just like listening to him.

Dad was home when it happened last November and said he wasn't going to start liking the son of a bitch just because he'd been killed. I thought Dad might like JFK because he was a Naval officer, but Dad didn't have one kind word to say about him. He must be the only one in the world who feels that way. Everyone else I've heard talk about Kennedy is sad. Even though Mikey thought the president was a good guy, he knew better than to ask Dad about any conspiracy.

Mikey and I have our own conspiracy today. The Beatles are about to go on the "Ed Sullivan Show," and we're not telling Dad. I just checked up on him in the living room where he's half asleep, snapping his fingers, a beer at his side, his headphones playing what I'm sure is some Big Band favorite. Mikey has a huge grin when I give him the thumbs-up signal. He shuts the door and cranks up the volume.

The last song finishes and we hear a sound. Mikey turns the volume down low during the commercial. Dad peeks in, checks us out and closes the door.

Mikey whispers, "That was close."

"Hey, Mikey," I say, "you think those guys look like girls?"

"Don't be stupid. They're from England. It's different over there."

"Well, surfers don't look like girls."

"So?"

"So who do you think is better? Corky Carroll or Phil Edwards?"

"Another dumb question. Is this what you and all your gremmie friends talk about?"

"Yeah."

John Michael Boyum (Mike), Coronado High School, 1964

"I'll tell you something. Doesn't matter how long your hair is. If you talk about dumb shit like that, you sound like an old lady."

"What do you talk about with your buddies?"

"Whether Clay can handle Liston. I think he can. You see, that's a fight. The winner knocks the other guy out and makes a ton of money. That's important shit."

"Winning or money?"

"You're hopeless."

The fight was fantastic. I listened to it on the radio with my friends after I told them they sounded like old ladies when they talked about surfers. Just like Mikey predicted the younger, skinnier Clay knocked out the older powerhouse, Liston.

I'm home and want to ask Mikey what he thinks about the fight, but he's gone off with Duke somewhere. It seems like he's gone all the time these days.

~

The beach is the only place for me. I'm running there right now and it's almost dark. Dad is away again and I told Mom there's supposed to be a grunion run tonight. She let me go. She always lets me go when Dad's gone, but I don't really care about smelly little fish.

There's a full moon and I'm sitting in the dark on the edge of a surf party by a fire, watching guys make out with girls. They have a transistor radio playing rock-and-roll and I slowly fall asleep on the sand.

In the middle of the night I have to pee, and in a half-sleep I drift towards the sound of the waves. Some frogmen emerge from the ocean wearing full-length wet suits and hoods. They're lugging big plastic-covered bundles out of the surf. I wonder if their boat sank. Good thing they have their surfboards with them.

One of them spots me and points. I hear another laugh and realize they're watching me pee. Beats me why they're in such a good mood.

~

Dad's a good detective, better than any of those guys on TV. He's been back home for the last few weeks so I can't skip school when the surf is up. But summer vacation starts tomorrow and I'll be able to surf every day.

I'm at the beach now. Duke shows up in a new ride—a snazzy funeral wagon with his new Yater surfboard sticking out the back. I slide my hand across his hearse.

"Whata boss machine. How...?"

He interrupts me.

"Someday you'll go to Baja, you little turd. It's so bitchin'. The waves are cleaner and there's cool stuff."

"Like what?"

Duke whacks the side of my head.

"Cool stuff, that's all."

I'm so stoked walking home from the beach with my board. That's right, Mikey has given me his Gordon and Smith for keeps.

As I get close to our house, I can see Dad is packing our car with a look that tells me to steer clear. Mom stands next to him and I can see she's been crying again. His face is red and he's obviously pissed off.

Are Mom and Dad finally getting a divorce? A lot of my friends here in Coronado tell me their parents are divorcing. The front door slams and interrupts my attempt to hear what they're saying. Mikey races out of the house with a small travel bag. He sees me.

"Hey," he says, "I'll spot you in a few."

I stare at him while he throws his bag in the back of his friend's car that's just pulled up. The car burns rubber. Dad jerks his head towards the squealing car and I see his clenched teeth.

"Mom, what's going on?"

"Your brother is flying to the Bahamas and is going to miss his graduation ceremony today. He has his diploma and he says that's all he needs."

"Bahamas? Where's that?"

"Off Florida, in the Atlantic. It's nice."

"Did you give him the money to travel?"

"No, he made his own money."

Before I can figure out how mowing lawns and pushing shopping carts would make enough for Mikey to travel across the country to an island in the Atlantic Ocean, Dad demands Mom's attention.

"Jackie, how many blenders do we need to keep? Damn, this should be simple."

"Jack, just let the movers take care of it."

I yank on Mom's arm.

"Movers?"

"Yes. I'm sorry, Billy. I haven't told you, there's been so much going on. The orders just came out of the blue. Your father has been trans- ferred to the Pentagon."

"We're driving across the country again?"

"Well, you and your Dad are. I'm flying to Virginia to look after your grandmother. Billy, she's very sick."

"So Mimi's transferring to UCLA, Mikey's going somewhere with his pals and I'm going to drive across the country alone with Dad?"

"Yes. I'll see you at Sans Souci."

I stare at Mom and feel sick.

Dad yells, "Bill, pack what you need for two days and get in the car."

On the ferry crossing over to San Diego, Dad and I get out of the car for some air. It's June, but the air feels cool here on the foggy bay. Dad stares at the three anchored carriers. I see one of them is the Princeton, his last command. He's relaxed now that we're on our way.

"Have you thought about what you're going to do when you fin- ish school?"

The end of school is still a ways off in my mind, but what surprises me more is his interest in me. Maybe he's bored. Does he actually want to talk to me? I certainly don't want to bring up Duke's grim outlook for a Naval aviator, so I go for the easy out and kiss ass.

"I want to be like you, Dad, and fly jets."

The first part is a lie and who knows about the second.

"I guess you're learning young what it means to move around a little. That's life in the military."

I'm surprised his tone seems so understanding, but notice he hasn't accepted the part about my being a pilot and only gives me the hazy military routine, which I know can mean many different things.

As far as moving around goes, a little is an understatement. As soon as I make a new friend, we move. Finding pals and fitting in has always been hard, but now it's especially painful to be alone. I hate moving and he has no idea how much—but I don't trust him with any of that.

"Yes, sir, I know what it means."

I had found a path I enjoyed in Coronado and was looking forward to figuring out mysteries like Duke's surf haven in Baja. I loved my life in Coronado. "It" means we're moving far away from all that.

D.C.? We're going back there? Why? I never had fun there like I have in Coronado. We've already been to D.C. Once was enough.

But only Mom asks me about my future. Dad never does. Does he really care? I feel uncomfortable telling him anything. He'll start prying like he always does when I'm in trouble. I'm not going to be fooled by this mellow mood. Instead I'll turn things around and ask him about his future to keep him friendly.

"Will you have another ship command in Washington?"

I know there's no port in D.C. so it's a stupid question, but I don't know where else to start.

Dad scratches his neck.

"I'll be working at the Pentagon."

Sounds like a place, not a ship. He doesn't seem very happy. A ship would have made him smile.

"Where does the Princeton go without you?"

There's a long pause.

He's still staring at the ship and seems to be talking to the coastal fog.

"Da Nang."

"Where's that?"

When he realizes I'm listening, his tone changes.

"Um, nowhere, Bill."

"Will you fly the new Phantoms?"

"No. Not anymore."

His last words seem gloomy and I know it's time to shut up. I've failed at faking my interest and bumped into the limit of what we can talk about. I go back to the comfort of the stuff I keep safe inside my head. Mimi's still in college and now my brother is gone. Mikey has had his friends but we've still done so much together. It's been great to have a brother with his reputation as a fighter to scare off any guys who might pick on me. Will he forget about me now? I'm going to be on my own with Mom and Dad until I finish high school in another unknown place on the East Coast.

We drive off the ferry and head east. I want to take a nap after the ferry ride and close my eyes, but my mind is still churning.

Something has happened to me in Coronado that's finally great—surfing. It satisfies every need I have to be happy.

Before surfing, kids used to tease me about being a weakling. I knew my lack of balance and eyesight were issues that could result in my not making the cut for flight school or even the UDT program. It's easy to see that those pilots and divers are a tough bunch who won't hesitate when they need to make a decision, like the way Duke's father Captain Grey dropped a bomb on a Japanese battlewagon when he was a young pilot in the war.

Surfing has toughened me up—out in the water and back on the beach. There's no room for hesitation when you take off on a wave. As far as I can tell, there isn't much difference between the boldness of surfers and Navy heroes. In my book surfing is the best training for my dream of becoming one.

But I've heard the older surfers say that the East Coast has little surf and the water is colder than California.

Dad's singing along with Mitch Miller on the radio and I feel myself drift off into sleep.

Chapter Six

Vietnam
1964-1965

I wake from my nap in a pool of sweat. It's blazing hot and Dad is glancing at his AAA TripTik dated June 1964. We're driving into the mountains east of San Diego. He hands the map to me.

"Fifty hours."

"Huh?"

"We should make it to Virginia in fifty hours. Looks like you're the navigator on this trip."

There he goes putting the pressure on me right from the beginning. Fifty hours is a little over two full days to cross this huge country. I stare at Dad and wonder why we're always in such a hurry. Is this a fighter pilot thing? Does he feel he can hurry faster because he's alone with me? Fast means Dad will be more edgy in order to stay on his schedule. I shut my eyes and feel like my eyeballs are going to pop out of my head. This is nuts—I'm driving across the country, alone with Dad.

The heat hasn't let up and Dad hasn't turned on the air conditioner, but he does tell me I can open the window. He's smiling at me. This is unexpected and I enjoy it.

"Can I open a beer for you, sir?"

"Yes, son."

It's so strange to hear him say "son" in such a gentle way. I can't even remember his ever using the word. But the relaxed feeling continues.

Dad's a weather expert, no doubt about it—he's an expert at everything. He's pointing out some of the incredible lenticular cloud formations over the mountains. Information of any kind coming from him feels great because then I have a good idea what his mood is. Is it because I keep popping beers for him? I like the way this is going, so I keep them coming.

It's flat after we leave the mountains and we're on our way to Yuma. Johnny Yuma? Who knows? We don't see another car for what seems like forever. Who would want to come out here to this desert? I figure only people like us, Navy families crossing the country, and it doesn't look like there are many of them.

Dad glances at me.

"Sir, did I do something wrong?"

"No. I'm just noticing that you're looking fit. Here. I want you to try something."

Dad places my hand on the wheel.

"Just a light touch. You see?"

He takes his hand off the wheel for a moment and then guides the car to the center of the road when I drift.

"Think you can do it, Bill?"

He has always called me Bill, not "Billy" like Mom, Mimi and Mikey call me. Saying my name has often meant he was pissed off or I was about to get a belting. This time my name sounds different. He's asking me if I want to put our safety in my hands. His confidence fills me with pride. It does look easy and I nod. We pull over and switch places.

The car lurches with my first taps to the gas pedal.

"Easy, Bill."

His tone is still gentle.

The car eases up to speed. I can do this. The road is straight for many miles. After a few minutes I'm relaxing and glance at the speedometer. We're racing at 50 mph and the wind is rushing in our windows. Was Dad driving this fast? Am I staying on the right part of the road? I guess he could reach across and grab the wheel if he needs to, but the way he has put his faith in me is beyond my understanding. He has spent my whole childhood telling me how I can't do things and now this?

"Slow down before we get into Gila Bend, and watch out for police cars."

This is so neat. There's wind in my face and Dad trusts me. But even with the wind it's hot. I glance at Dad again to see how I'm doing and he's sacked out. Gila Bend comes and goes and I'm pushing the gas a little harder.

I see signs for Phoenix and tap Dad. He's alert right away.

"Isn't this a big city, Dad? You better take over till we get past Tucson."

"Yes. Good idea. Did you know I flew into Tucson during the war when we flew across the country? It was one of five stops on our way to San Diego, where we loaded our planes onto jeep-carriers to sail to Pearl Harbor."

Was he dreaming about that?

"No, sir."

He's never told me anything about his past.

"That was February 1944. Damn, it's been twenty years. I had received my wings less than a year earlier. This was after a few months of night fighter training at Quonset Point, and we were flying our new radar-equipped Hellcats across this same part of the country we're driving through now, only in the opposite direction. I was put in command of a squadron of young pilots and it was a big responsibility to keep an eighteen-plane formation together."

"Sir, I'm glad I'm just driving a car."

"Well, you done good."

In the past he's always hammered me for using the wrong pronoun or verb tense and I know what he just said isn't good grammar. I'll take the compliment and the fun that goes with it. Jeez, he's talking to me like a regular person and letting me drive even though I don't have a license. Maybe the world has turned upside down.

He lets me drive again after Tucson and I'd like to ask if the town of Tombstone we're driving through is the one with the OK Corral. But he's napping again. How did cowboys in the Wild West live in a place like this? It's too hot. I sure wouldn't want to get stuck here. The heat is making me sleepy and I wake him to take over.

He's driving and it's a good thing. The cops pull us over for doing 20 in a 15 mph zone just outside of Bisbee.

As we pull away, Dad says, "God-damn rednecks. It's our out-of-state plates."

I'm thinking that Dad's old green Hawaii license plates are always going to call attention to our car.

I'm right. It happens again in Lordsburg and Deming, New Mexico. I figure we'll be broke by the time we make it across the country. Even though the driving is easy, Dad decides to remain behind the wheel.

He must have forgotten about having Hawaiian plates because he's smiling and singing again.

"Nothing could be finer, than to be a *kama'aina* in Hawayyyeee."

He explains to me that a *kama'aina* is someone born and raised in Hawaii. That sounds great for him, but I wish I were from one place I could call home.

It feels like I've just drifted off when Dad starts shaking me awake at the crack of dawn in a motel in El Paso. The room is dark and I'm disoriented until he turns on a light.

We ate some spicy Mexican food last night and my stomach hurts, plus our motel was noisy and I had a hard time falling asleep. We stop at a pharmacy to get me some Pepto-Bismol. That fixes my stomach and once again we're on the road. Dad is singing again, a fun song about Texas. Texas is about three states wide, plenty of time for him to teach me the chorus lines. He even lets me pound the beat on the dashboard.

"Deep in the heart of Texas!"

After our song he tells me about another airfield he'd landed on in one of these Texas towns, but I'm too tired to know where we are. Our early start has me fading off to sleep with the sound of his voice. It's comforting to hear him talk.

I'm awake and Dad's excited to buy some hot peppers when we get to Shreveport, Louisiana. He offers me one and says it'll wake me up. I'm done with hot food and shake my head. Dad says he has a cast iron stomach.

I see lots of Negroes walking around the towns we drive through in Louisiana. But this time Dad isn't barking out the mean remarks he used to make.

Driving across the country is a pretty regular thing for me now. I'm getting to be an expert. All you have to do is follow the map. U.S. 80 all the way. We cross a huge river. There's that big "Entering Mississippi" sign with the beautiful flower on it. I remember Dad's reaction to my repeated words when I was little, so inside my head I repeat the Mississippi jingle of the big word. It's fun even when I hide it.

Driving through Vicksburg, Dad tells me there was a pivotal battle here during the Civil War. Up in the northeast part of the state is Shiloh, where his mother's father fought and was wounded as a Union soldier. Dad inherited his middle name, Hoag, from this same grandfather.

He's so different from what I'm used to. I wonder if Mom told him to be nice to me.

Dad lifts his eyebrows, puts his finger to his lips and turns his ear towards the radio. I hear the words "invasion" and a "search for boys."

I'm almost fourteen but I guess I'm still a boy even though I can drive this car. Maybe those boys are lost. The talking on the radio is in an accent that's so thick I can't understand much of what they're saying. Maybe Dad doesn't, either, because he pushes the off button.

Without the radio on, I stare out the window. People are walking around like normal, but they're all white. I know there's as many Negroes in Mississippi as there are in Louisiana. Where are they?

Dad wants to show me how to wiggle my ears. Holy cow, I can't believe this. It's really hard to do when I try. He laughs at the faces I'm making and makes funny faces of his own.

"Dad, did you ever live around here?"

"I went to flight school in Pensacola, just south of here."

"When you learned to fly helicopters, right?"

"No, long before that, during the war, for airplanes."

I slipped up when I called him 'Dad' instead of 'sir,' but we're talking just like pals and he doesn't seem to mind. Signs for Meridian get him talking again.

"There's a Naval Air Station in Meridian. The airfield is named after Admiral McCain. He was our Task Force CO on the Wasp during the war. Our night operations were secret and I reported directly to the Admiral and not to the ship's captain. The old man had an odd hat he would wear and false teeth that whistled when he spoke."

It's amazing that some of these towns can dig up his memories like they do. This area doesn't seem like a place for a Naval Air Station. Pensacola is by the water, where I think a Navy base should be. I wish we could go there and swim in that blue water I remember from when he was stationed there a few years ago.

But Dad's not thinking about swimming in Pensacola.

"I'll always be indebted to Admiral McCain for the night he allowed me to land on the Wasp with enemy aircraft in the area," he says. "I only had twenty gallons left in my tank. Bill, that's fumes for a two thousand-horsepower engine, so it was a high-risk decision. If there had been any mishap on landing where a fire resulted, it would've been a catastrophe not only for the ship but for the Admiral's Task Force Command."

I try to imagine what landing in the ocean would have been like at night if Dad had run out of gas.

"How long before your plane would have sunk?"

"Bill, with sunlight a pilot might be lucky enough to pull off a splash landing. If he did, he'd have about a minute to get out. In the dark..."

He doesn't finish and abruptly changes his tone.

"God damn it."

Here we go again. Did I bring up a bad subject? That good mood was so bitchin'.

I follow his eyes. He's not pissed at me. There's a roadblock up ahead. I bet Dad is going to say the word hick again.

"Aw, Dad. Another speeding ticket?"

"No, Bill. This is different."

I know Dad hates unscheduled stops. He sounds upset so I'll just shut up and watch.

A fat policeman studies the back of our car. I can see his holster at his hip. Dad sticks his head out of the window.

"Is there a problem, officer?"

The cop sticks his face into our car and Dad has to move his head back to make room for him. The cop stinks and he's chewing something fast. His rotten teeth remind me of the drunken dentist who pulled out my teeth in Suffolk.

"No problem. No problem at all. I need your license and eye-den-tification."

Dad hands him his military ID and license.

Right now I'm sure glad I'm not driving.

The cop studies Dad's stuff.

"Mister military man, Captain USN. I have a question for you. Is Hawaii a nigger state?"

My whole life I have learned to recognize intimidation, mostly from Dad. This cop is showing me all the signs. He has just used the mean word I've only heard Dad use in private—and this man is a policeman.

I look at Dad. How is he taking this? Maybe they think alike.

But this isn't the way it is. I can tell when Dad despises someone and right now he's fuming. He doesn't answer the cop's question, but the set of his jaw gets his point across.

The cop pulls his face out of the window and another cop talks with him. Other men, without police uniforms, are carrying rifles. The sun is setting and the idea of nighttime is spooking me. Even though this man is a policeman, I don't trust him. The combination of his manner and Dad's reaction is scaring the crap out of me.

I'm nervous about guns. The memory of the crazy cop at the Naval Hospital is still in my mind. Just because a man is a cop doesn't mean he's a good guy. In a whisper I start the Mississippi jingle while he questions Dad.

"What's yo' business heah in Mississippi? We have sailors out heah pokin' around from that base in Meridian. You with them?"

"We won't be staying in Mississippi."

The word 'won't' booms out like thunder and I see the cop flinch.

"Better yet," the cop says as he backs up a few paces.

He stares in my direction and strains to listen to my whispering Mississippi jingle.

"You may move on through, sir."

He says the words 'may' and 'sir' in a disrespectful tone. Dad's face is beet red.

As we drive away in silence, Dad checks the bright headlights behind us in the rearview mirror. The road map is in my lap and I stop whispering my jingle, but I'm still nervous.

"Dad, if we take this back road just past Meridian, we can drive south to Mobile and then over to Pensacola. We could spend the night there and go for a swim tomorrow. Doesn't that sound good?"

"It does sound very good, but I don't want to go on any back roads, Bill. I'm sorry but there aren't any good roads here. It isn't as simple as what you see on the map."

The headlights behind us stop when we cross the border into Alabama. I see signs for Tuscaloosa to the north. That seems like another funny name to play with, but since we left Meridian I don't feel like playing with words anymore. Besides, we're going east to Selma and Montgomery and it feels good to be out of Mississippi.

Dad informs me the police back in Meridian are searching for three young men who are missing. When I ask him what he thinks happened, he shakes his head silently. I tell him I was scared and he squeezes my knee in a reassuring way. He's giving me his fake smiles I've seen him use at parties.

Has he shaken the incident and returned to the good mood we were having? Maybe he hasn't, but if he's pretending to make me feel good, then that feels even better. This trip with Dad is incredible. I don't know what to think. It felt great when he gave that redneck cop the Dad treatment. If I'm going to run into bad people outside my family, I want Dad at my side.

We're in Virginia and before I know it Dad turns onto the same bumpy dirt road where Papa Bace had his stroke. Sam Copeland isn't on his tractor today, tilling the soil for his peanuts. Our car stops in front of Sans Souci. Dad turns to me, smiles and glances at his watch.

"Fifty seven hours but we did have a few glitches, didn't we?"

"We sure did, Dad."

We stare at each other longer than we ever have.

"Well, let's see how your mother's doing."

When she sees us her eyes flood with tears as she tells us my grandmother is so sick that she's going to have to move to a nursing home.

Today Mrs. Crittenden will watch Mama Marcelle because Dad has decided to drive us to Virginia Beach. He loves the water and knows it'll help Mom. It always works for me, and I know I won't get to do much surfing in Alexandria. Seeing Dad sensitive to Mom's feelings after our trip together makes me feel even better about him.

Virginia Beach smells like the ocean and I love it. Mom and I watch Dad stride out into the waves and bodysurf.

I tell her, "Dad says he won't be flying anymore."

"Well, he's forty-five. He's too old to be a pilot."

I'm watching Dad. He does look a little older. I haven't seen him with his shirt off since we were here four years ago. His hair is gray above his ears and this is the first time I've seen a little flab around his waist.

"I bet he could still fly pretty good if they let him."

I can feel Mom looking at me while I watch Dad.

"You had a good trip together?"

I smile and nod. Though it bothers me that she might have influenced him to behave the way he did with me, it's hard for me to imagine Dad being forced to do anything, even by Mom.

When we get back to Sans Souci, Mom tells me the house is going to be sold since Mama Marcelle has to move into a nursing home.

Mom and Dad start supervising the packaging of family heirlooms. Mom says the Revolutionary War sword from our ancestor Jacob Michael is going to her brother. She looks at me admiring it, disappears and returns with *Moby Dick*.

"Mama Marcelle told me your grandfather would have wanted you to have this book, Billy. Maybe you'll read it to your kids someday."

She hands it to me and all the great memories I have of Papa Bace come flooding back. I can't imagine having kids, but I'll be satisfied if someday I'm able to understand the old English.

I give the book to the movers and see them place Papa Bace's pearl-handled .45 on the table to be wrapped.

The gun brings up bad memories and I escape out to the pier that Papa Bace built. This will be our last time at Sans Souci. I need to think about my grandfather again, even though it has been four years since his death. Walking down his pier makes me feel like he only died yesterday. His home represents his life to me and knowing I will never see it again, I've come to say goodbye.

The sunset lights up the marsh shoreline and soon a blanket of stars rests over me. Their light reminds me of Papa Bace's memories of the multi-winged airplane illuminated by star shells over Paris in his war. Dad calls and I immediately get up to run back to the house.

"Coming, sir."

"No, it's OK. I'll join you out here for a moment."

He sits silently next to me for quite some time and then points to the stars.

"That's the Big Dipper and at that end is Polaris, which will always show you true north. On the under side of the world you have the Southern Cross."

"Have you been there?"

Dad remains fixed on the stars.

"Well, mostly just north of the equator, so during the war I could see the heavens in both hemispheres. I used those stars many times to navigate my way home at night."

"You mean your carrier?"

"Bill, at that moment in time the Wasp was my home."

"Oh."

I assume Mom lived somewhere else, but I don't bring that up.

"So you could find it with just stars?"

I love these war memories from Dad. His mood is so gentle—like it was when he told me about his cross-country-town-hopping with an airplane on the same route we had just driven. I sense that something peaceful surfaces in him when he reminisces, like when he relaxes while listening to Big Band music with his headphones.

"Yes, stars and other pointers. You have to realize that usually the Wasp wasn't in the same place where I had left it when I launched. So finding the way home was sometimes tricky. I knew I was getting close when I found the phosphorescent trails that are created in the ship's wake. I used those once I got close and followed their path as they grew brighter."

I try to imagine a home that moves away from where it was when I left it.

Mom rings the bell for dinner.

Since Papa Bace's death, the pier has gone into disrepair and there are gaps between the boards you could fall into now that it's dark.

"Walk behind my steps."

I wonder if Dad really can see in the dark just because he's a night fighter pilot.

~

Mom, Dad and I are living in our new home in Northern Virginia. I like this TV show. The sound of machine gun fire brings Mom into the living room.

"What are you watching?"

"'Combat.' It's about fighting the Germans in WWII."

Mom has a pained expression on her face.

"Why don't you go do something fun outside and get the hang of this place before school starts?" she asks. "You only have one more week. Billy, you're going to be in high school."

It's hard for me to be as excited about school as Mom is.

"I was hoping I could do something fun with Dad."

"It makes me feel very happy to hear you say that, but he's wrapped up with work at the Pentagon."

"What do they do at the Pentagon anyway?"

"The military makes all their decisions there."

"Boy, Dad's gone all the time. I thought this new job was supposed to be different."

"It is different and he was supposed to get August off to move us in here, but something important happened and they canceled his leave. The Navy comes first."

"I know what Dad would say, 'It's a fact of life.' But I wish it wasn't."

Mom gives me a long hug.

It's Sunday morning and we're eating breakfast. Dad's finally home for the day and is reading the *Washington Post* Sunday comics while he eats. Mom places a stack of newspapers at his side.

"These are from this last week."

Dad checks through the stack and pulls out Wednesday's paper. I glance at the headline because it has the word planes on it. "American Planes Hit North Vietnam After Second Attack on Our Destroyers; Move Taken to Halt New Aggression."

His face scowls for a moment before he puts that newspaper aside and returns to the Sunday funny section.

"Dad? What's the matter?"

Mom interrupts.

"Billy, did you know that we're only a few miles north of George Washington's home, Mount Vernon?"

I glance at Dad.

"Neat, Mom."

"Yes. Our house is just a few miles south of Alexandria. Fairfax County is a wealthy neighborhood."

"Oh."

George Washington is sort of interesting but I don't care if this area is wealthy. That headline looked interesting. I start to search the pile of newspapers. Mom walks over and removes the stack.

"These are your father's."

She returns with more food.

"Would you like to see Mt. Vernon on the map?"

"I already saw the map when we drove up from Sans Souci. Dad, wasn't there a big river near here?"

If there aren't any waves, at least I could go for a swim. Even a river will do.

I'm waiting for Dad to answer, but his eyes are locked on the newspaper. He looks kind of edgy.

"Look at this, honey. We'll be damned if the future is like Dick Tracy and his two-way wrist radio. I'd never get away from work."

Oh, good. Dad isn't really mad. It's just about something in the comic strip. Mom sees Dad isn't paying attention to me.

"Yes, Billy, it's the Potomac."

I walk up behind him and jump on his back, excited about an idea that has popped into my head. I throw my arms around him.

"Can we swim in the Potomac River?"

Dad lurches, grabs my arm and flips me off his back onto the floor.

He yells, "Don't you ever sneak up on me again."

He fixes me with a brutal look until Mom gets his attention.

"Jack."

I'm still on the floor on my back, my hands close to my face.

"I'm sorry, sir."

He tries to shake his anger to explain, but his tone is still gruff.

"Get up, Bill. The answer to your question is no. That river is polluted. There's a pool at Quantico Marine Base just south of here. I have to go there this weekend but you'll need to do some chores around here to deserve a trip to the pool."

I didn't mean to sneak up on him. Sudden things always surprise me, too, so if I surprised him I understand why he's mad. But I did mean to hug him. Sometimes I do stuff without thinking. There must be some way I can get on his good side again.

"Can I mow the lawn?"

"Yes, after I brief you on the mower."

Dad checks me out on the mower procedures and I'm excited to go out and get some cutting done, but it's raining for the rest of Sunday. He informs me that wet grass doesn't cut well and I'll have to wait until it dries out.

It's Monday morning and Dad has driven off to work. I vow to give the lawn a buzz cut before he returns tonight. The grass is still very wet, though, and I have to wait. When the sun comes out in the afternoon, I can't contain myself. Pulling the start rope doesn't work for me as well and easily as it did for Dad. The mower starts, but the long wet grass clogs the chute and the engine sputters out. It's hard to restart. I lift the wheels up to let it unclog before moving forward but the going is slow. Dad could arrive at any moment and I want to be finished.

The grass in this one spot is still very wet. The chute is clogged and I'm going to have to shut the engine down. When I do, I don't let the blade completely stop spinning before sticking my hand inside to clean the chute. The blade cuts the tip of my right index finger to the bone. I yell for a moment and then it's numb. Sinew is hanging out of my finger and I don't even cry.

Dad rolls into the driveway and I'm squeezing my finger at the base, but blood is still seeping out the tip. Mom has heard me and runs out of the house. She screams.

"It's OK. Just a little cut."

Dad is examining my bloody finger and looks very angry.

"You didn't follow my orders, did you? The rotors were still spinning, weren't they? Now I'll have to drive you to the hospital."

"I'll drive him, Jack. You go relax."

Dad storms away.

"God dammit."

On the way to the hospital I'm in tears and not because of my finger.

"Mom, I feel so bad about goofing up. I was hurrying for him."

"It's just his work."

"Why did he call them rotors?"

Mom glances at me.

"He mentioned helicopters to me once but he doesn't tell me much. Just don't bug him about a word. Your father is under a lot of pressure right now. I thought he was mad at me, too, but he finally told me many of our troops are going to be sent to Vietnam. It looks like there will be another war, Billy, and he's very frustrated with his current job. But please, please don't bring this up with him. When he gets home he just wants to escape from his work."

It's hard for me to think about war right now. My finger is beginning to throb and blood is still oozing from the paper towel Mom wrapped around it.

Mom's right. Something bad is bugging Dad. He comes home from work and goes right to his easy chair for his headphones and a Manhattan. It's hard to believe he's my same dad that I enjoyed those great feelings with when we were crossing the country. Any question I ask is met with silence or a very limited, disinterested response.

Mom yells "Mikey" at the front door and I mouth to Dad that Mikey's here. He removes his headphones and gives me a blank look. I'm thinking that he will get up and join me to greet Mikey at the door, but he doesn't even get out of his chair. I'm not going to wait to figure Dad out. I run to the door.

Mom is already hugging my brother, but I wouldn't know from looking at him that he's Mikey. He's got a tan and his hair is long and bleached out. Mikey has his shirt off and I notice he's bigger, with well-defined muscles. He gives me a strong hug. When he speaks to me his voice sounds sleepy but very happy.

"Where's Dad?"

I point towards the living room. Mikey drops his bags at the door.

"Hey, Mikey, are you going to live with us?"

With everything that has happened with Mama Marcelle, Mom hasn't told me what Mikey's plans are except that he's going to attend George Washington University in D.C. I follow him to see how it goes with Dad. Maybe seeing Mikey will snap Dad back into a good mood.

Dad is out of his chair when Mikey enters the living room and has a look on his face that is difficult to read. Not mad but not happy, either. He's studying Mikey and seems confused. Mikey doesn't hesitate and hugs Dad. Dad pulls back slightly.

"You're back."

"Yes, sir. Great to see you."

Mikey smiles and pats Dad on his stomach.

"Flying a desk, huh, Dad?"

I notice Dad's gut has grown even more since I noticed it at the beach.

Right now, Dad's face is easy to read.

Mom grabs Mikey and I follow.

"Let me show you your own room. You'll love this house. You won't have to share with Billy anymore."

Dad shoots Mom an angry glance as we leave him and I know he's getting blindsided again.

Mom leaves us in Mikey's room, closes the door and returns to Dad. Mikey and I can hear a loud angry discussion. I can't pick out the exact words, but I have a pretty good idea that it's about Mikey living with us. I don't care and want to pry Mikey for all the details about his trip to the Bahamas.

Mikey tells me about diving, water-skiing and picking up chicks. Man, that sounds like fun.

"But you know, Billy, I can't tell you what it's like to be there. You'll just have to go yourself someday, then you'll know."

I'm trying to figure out what's different about my brother. I want to experience what he has. He pops me on the shoulder.

"So tell me how you survived that trip across the country with Dad."

Everyone and everything is changing, and telling Mikey about Dad is complicated. I don't even understand it myself, especially now that he's changed back.

"You know, it wasn't bad."

Mikey rolls his eyes.

"No, Mikey, he was different on the trip. It was cool. But since we've moved in here, he's..."

Mikey lifts his eyebrows at me.

"The same old Dad?"

"Mom says..."

"Mom's always making excuses for him. But hey, it's all cool, man. It doesn't matter what the old man thinks. That's his world. There's a different world out there that is fun and happy."

I kind of get what he's talking about, although I've seen a different world out there with Dad and it isn't fun or happy.

My brother has picked up another accent from his travels—the most noticeable part of it is a smooth, slow-talking raspy voice. He sounds like he's not going to let Dad get him down, which is different from the Mikey I used to know. No matter how he talks, I'm stoked he's home.

~

It's been two months since Mikey returned from the Bahamas. He's living at home while going to GWU. I'm on the other side of the door and overhear Mom and Mikey talking in his room.

"Mikey, there's some things I'd like to talk with you about before your father gets home."

"What's up, Mom?"

"I just wanted to remind you that it's important for you to do well in school so you can keep your draft exemption."

"Jeeesus, Mom, why are you bugging me about that? You don't think I hear about the government upping draft quotas at school? That's all anyone talks about."

"OK, sweetie, but I'm also concerned about the agreement I made with your father about your grades if you're to get free room and board."

"Gee, Mom, thanks for reminding me about that. Makes me feel real wanted."

"I'm trying hard, Mikey."

Mom's crying. She opens the door and rushes by me.

Mikey sees me standing in the doorway with a black eye.

"Did you get this from school?"

I shake my head.

"That bastard. I'll figure something out, Billy. I'll get you outta here."

He touches my face and shakes his head.

"Go get something to eat. I'll check you before I roll out."

I'm in the kitchen staring into the refrigerator when Dad gets home. He shoves aside a box of stuff Mom has left in the middle of the kitchen floor.

"Clutter, god-damn clutter. Can't we at least keep our pathways clear?"

His face has that menacing look the way it did when he slapped me two days ago. I still have the fridge door open, but my attention is frozen on Dad. He grabs my arm and yanks me away as he slams the fridge door. He's shaking my arm and my whole body.

"Think first. Then open the door and get what you need."

His head spins in every direction around the kitchen and he finally releases my arm. Mom has left dishes, drinking glasses and fresh food sitting out on the counters. Dad begins jamming everything into its proper place in the cabinets.

Not looking at me, he yells, "Clutter everywhere."

I escape to my room but a minute later Dad throws my door open.

"This place is a pigsty. You need it ready for a white glove before you eat again."

Dad is silent for a moment and I can tell he's listening to Mikey say goodbye to Mom in the living room. He charges away from me. I hear him open and slam Mikey's bedroom door. What's going to happen? I follow to find out.

Dad steps in front of Mikey before he gets to the front door.

"Where the hell do you think you're going?"

Dad's fingers push Mikey in the chest in order to prevent his escape as he does his usual clenched-teeth intimidation.

"This isn't your flop house where you can use your mother as a servant. Get back in there and clean your room."

Mikey swipes Dad's finger away and glares at him with the look I've seen before when he's fought other guys. He's eighteen and strong from lifting weights. Mikey's smooth voice and tan have faded since his return from the Bahamas. Right now he could be meaner than Dad.

"You going to hit me, old man? Are you? 'Cause if you are, I'm going to hit you back. I've had enough bullying from you, you son of a bitch."

Mikey's words stun me.

Dad steps aside and in a low voice says, "Leave now."

Mikey stands firm and I watch them stare at each other for seconds that seem like hours. Mikey's face finally breaks into a smirk.

"OK, old man."

Mikey yanks the front door open and slams it shut behind him.

It's been two weeks since the blow-up with Dad and Mikey. I guess Dad is OK with Mikey's living on the street or wherever he ends up. For me, things are worse than ever. Every time Dad locks his eyes on me, I wonder if he's thinking that I saw him back down.

I've been avoiding any eye contact with Dad. He's home for the weekend with instructions for Mom and me not to answer the phone, period. With this new war in Vietnam, the Pentagon has problems that can never wait until Monday. He told us he's tired of getting called into work on weekends, but I'm pretty sure he's trying to keep Mom from getting a call from Mikey.

I'm staring at the back of Dad's head. He's anchored in his new reclining chair, with his new Akai tape deck by his side and his stereo headphones wrapped around his ears. Everything is new and improved. Ten years ago he had a record player and his easy chair didn't recline like this one. His old headphones looked like something he'd saved from WWII.

Back then, because I was the youngest, I was Mimi's and Mikey's slave. It was my job to check in on Dad to see if he was on cloud nine with Cole Porter. If he was, and his Tom Collins drink was at his side, half empty, then I could report back to my sister and brother that the coast was clear for us to turn up the TV and laugh and scratch, Dad's term for our making too much fun noise. Sometimes we'd forget to check on him and then hear his headphones smash against the wall.

"Uh oh," Mimi would warn.

Dad would enter the room with angry red eyes. All three of us would go stiff on the *hikie'e* like dead outlaws. Eventually we would all cave in and point our fingers at each other. That worked when we were together. He'd point to our rooms and slam the off button, but no one got hit. Spying was key. If his eyes were closed and his fingers were snapping, we could have fun.

I miss watching "Bonanza" and "Gunsmoke" on that large Hawaiian-print *hikie'e*. Those Bonanza brothers felt as comforting to me as being on that huge couch with my brother and sister. Right now Dad's eyes are closed and it reminds me of those good old days—but more than Mimi and Mikey being gone, there's something else missing. Is he happy? I can imagine that he would sure like to be one of those astronauts sitting on top of an Atlas rocket, counting down to launch into orbit around the world. But the Navy says he's even too old to fly a jet. Is that why he's pissed off all the time? Mikey isn't around to bug him anymore, so what else could be bothering him?

I tried to watch the news with him yesterday. The Marines were wading through good-size surf, landing at Da Nang. That's the name Dad had let slip out when we left Coronado. Now I know it's a place in Vietnam. I asked him if there were always good waves there and he just glared at me as if I were a moron.

Maybe the election has pissed him off. LBJ just beat Goldwater who, like Dad, was a military pilot and a Republican. This is the second time in a row Dad has voted for the loser. He says we'll have a redneck running our country for four more years.

Four more years and I'll be done with high school. I think my best plan is to avoid Dad whenever I can. Avoiding him isn't hard when he's anchored to his chair as he is now. A half-empty mug of cold draft beer rests at his side.

I go to the kitchen for a drink. Mom's whispering on the phone.

"Come home tomorrow morning. No, your Dad won't be here. I can help you out. I know you're working. Please, Mikey, don't be so angry."

Mom's on the phone and Dad's listening to his music, so I'm going to sneak into the downstairs rec room and turn on "American Bandstand." A skinny kid is snapping his fingers to the beat of "My Guy."

That's what's missing. Dad used to snap his fingers, even when he had his eyes closed in his easy chair. Now his fingers are still.

Chapter Seven

Dope?
1966-1967

This week's *Newsweek* says that the North Vietnamese Army has escaped to hide in Cambodia after the battle in the Ia Drang Valley, where many of our soldiers were killed. Dad will be real pissed off when he sees this, but at least I don't have to be around him.

I'm in a private school in Silver Springs, Maryland, a suburb of D.C. Of all the schools we checked out, I picked this particular one because they send many students to the Naval Academy.

Mikey convinced Mom to send me to boarding school in order to get me away from Dad. Our grandmother on her deathbed was so concerned about my living around Dad that she gave Mom the money to pay for this school. It's neat living away from home for the first time, but I'm still getting used to it. The library is where I read all the magazines about current events. Most of the news these days has to do with the war in Vietnam.

The dinner bell rings and I leave my sanctuary, but it's hard to get excited about eating. Dorm food is horrible. Even though it's tense at home with Dad, at least Mom feeds me well. What I'd give for some of her chicken and dumplings.

~

I've been away from home for a few months and I think my family has forgotten about me. This weekend I'm watching other kids leave for an overnight away and I'm feeling lonely.

Mom and Dad live forty-five minutes away so theoretically I'm permitted to leave on Saturday morning and return Sunday afternoon. But when I try to contact my parents the phone just rings and rings.

At the end of summer, before school started, Mikey scooped me out of the house and we sped up to New York City in Mimi's Porsche to see the Beatles. The concert was great, but I haven't heard from Mikey since then even though he has an apartment in Georgetown.

I have the freedom to leave but nowhere to go.

A student answers the hall phone, then yells at me.

"Hey, Boyum, get ready. Someone's picking you up."

Couldn't be Mom and Dad. They aren't spontaneous. If it is them, I'm a little worried. Many of the students who have no weekend privileges make catcalls from the windows when parents arrive to pick up their kid.

I've heard them yell, "Steve has been a real good boy. He beats his meat every night."

I'm still getting ready when a roar goes up among the boarders. "Check out the Porsche and the babe out front."

I finish stuffing a weekend bag and bolt to see why the guys are so jacked up, but I stop at the dorm's front door when I realize it's my brother, revving the Porsche Mimi brought back after her recent travels through Central Asia and Europe. She's working at TWA here in D.C. and Mikey has talked her into letting him use her car again.

A beautiful blonde opens the door and steps out. Mikey impatiently waves me over. I'm a bit confused but run when the chick also waves to me. She directs me into the front passenger seat, and then sits on my lap. The dorm rats go wild when she turns and waves to the windows.

The radio is cranked up to top volume playing Smokey's "Going to a Go Go" as we speed off well over the speed limit on these side streets. I grin and hold onto the blonde's waist.

When Mikey drops her off at her place, she raises her hand to her pursed lips with her thumb and point finger pinched.

Mikey shakes his head.

"Later, baby."

I think that's a strange response for what I figure is the signal to keep your mouth shut.

We're racing around the streets of D.C. and I ask about the girl.

"Last night's date," he says with a smirk.

I'm checking out my brother at the wheel. He's wearing a jacket and button-down shirt. Nothing appears out of place except his tie, which is blowing in the wind. But the girl, this car—he's like a preppy James Bond.

Mikey's apartment in Georgetown is a mess and is covered with more rock concert posters than I have. I don't see any textbooks.

"Hey, Mikey, you still in school?"

He shoves me playfully.

"You're my dad now? Like I could even consider dropping out."

He says it in a fun way and is still smiling with a wide grin, almost like a drunk's, but I don't smell booze on him. His speech has the same sound that it had when he got back from the Bahamas. Nothing can change Mikey's good mood.

"Hey, don't get me wrong, Mikey, that was so cool for you to come. It's just that after the Beatles concert I figured... well, I figured you'd forget about me now that I'm away from home."

Mikey lays his hand on my shoulder.

"Hey, we made a vow, didn't we? Wanna beer?"

"Naw. Beer makes me sick."

He wiggles my tie.

"Me, too. Hey, drop the Mikey routine, OK? It's Mike from now on."

"And I'm Bill?"

"Yeah, Bill. How you doing at school?"

"It's OK, I guess, but no one likes me. Some upperclassman tried to haze me with a paddle. I grabbed it and hit him in the face with it. Sent him to the infirmary."

Mike slaps me on the shoulder.

"Way to go."

"Yeah, well, they gave me detention for a month and since then everyone thinks I'm crazy. Now I hide in the library and read. It's pretty lonely."

"It'll change. Don't worry. What are we going to do to loosen you up?"

I yank off my blazer and tie.

"Cool. What's next?"

"Well, first of all, I bought you some new threads."

"Mikey, whoops, I mean Mike, how can you afford it? Mom told me you were selling vacuum cleaners and were tight on money."

"Man, everything has changed. Don't sweat it."

Is Mom sneaking him money? I push that thought out of my mind as I try on these snappy Ivy League clothes.

Mike inspects my new look.

"Nice duds."

I'm happy to be getting a break away from school and excited my brother has not forgotten about me. He was so pissed off the few times I saw him after Dad kicked him out of the house, I figured I wouldn't be seeing him much. But here we are. He's happy and that makes me happy. Mike is the only person I can relate to in my lonely world.

We're more comfortable with each other outside the tension of our parents' home. I can finally enjoy all the good things I have ever remembered about being brothers. Making new pals has been a strikeout and it's bitchin' that Mike wants to hang out with me.

Checking myself out in the mirror, I tighten up my tie. From my Gant shirt to my Bass Weejun loafers, I look pretty damn good.

"Bitchin'."

"Maybe it's time to lose the bitchin' and that sloppy surfer style you've hung onto since Coronado."

"Guess you're right. Yeah, easy on the eyes, huh?"

"Yeah, now you're lookin' tight."

"Tight, huh?"

"Yeah, that's how it is."

When I'm showered and re-dressed, Mike magically flashes two tickets. He grins with bloodshot eyes. I point to the tickets in his hand with a silent question. He explodes with a spin dance move.

"Howard Theater. James Brown and the Fabulous Flames, baby."

"Another concert?"

Mike's face changes by the second in a single burst of words. He's having fun just talking to me.

I've heard James Brown on the radio. He's the godfather of soul.

We enter the Howard Theater in the black part of town. The first thing I notice is a strong, unfamiliar smell. The next thing is that we are the only white kids in this place. If there are others, I don't see them.

Mike points towards the crowd and whispers in my ears.

"Soul brothers."

I'm amazed he knows many of the sharp-dressed, cool-speaking black guys. One nods with a smile when he runs into Mike.

"Say what?"

He has the same tone of voice that I've just noticed in my brother. I remember how Mike copied Duke's surf slang. He has a chameleon's ability to pick up accents, and now he's showing me how he fits in at the Howard.

The black guy is lit up.

"Sure right, it's the milkman."

I immediately try to translate this to myself; milkman, white guys, I think I get it.

"Slap me some skin, brutha."

Mike gives him a complicated handshake and smiles a bright toothy grin. His return is smooth. Each syllable is separated and crisp.

"Co-pa-se-tic, man."

Mike glides through the crowd and engages other guys. His eyes lock on each soul brother and his free hand covers his handshakes. Mike's manner is so intimate and intense. It's too much for me to try to understand and I turn away to watch the show.

Another black guy lays his hand on my shoulder.

"Need to meet my friend MJ?"

The music is very loud and I don't understand so I gesture with my hands and shoulders to say that. The guy waves me off in a disgusted manner and struts away.

Mixed into the loud music I hear words like 'hooch' and 'babysitter' in conversations around me.

It's a strange new language with familiar words that have become unfamiliar in their current context. Even though I don't know what's going on, I do know that it's comforting to have friends here since we stick out so bad. It's a fact of life that people are reluctant to let outsiders into their crowd. These cool black cats are sure making an exception in our case, especially when I think about all that tough treatment black people get in places like Mississippi and Alabama. They're being so friendly to us here. I would say it's bitchin' being here, but now I have to come up with a new hip word.

Every note from the Fabulous Flames is well timed and sharp. So is James Brown. He's a fabulous showman alright, dancing to "Papa's Got a Brand New Bag." If our papa could see us now, he'd flip watching this entertainer move to "I Feel Good." With this war in Vietnam, I know Dad sure doesn't feel as good as James Brown. The godfather is outta sight. Wow, what a great word.

~

Mike got in touch with Mom and told her I'd like to come home every once in a while.

This weekend I'm home watching TV. Dad walks by and scowls when he sees me watching "The Addams Family." "McHale's Navy" is on next. Dad marches back in while I'm laughing and chowing leftovers from dinner. He slams the off button.

"You don't need to waste your time watching a family full of freaks and Navy screw-ups. There's more to life than watching the boob tube for hours and stuffing your face."

Now I realize how great it was to have escaped to boarding school. Dad is so uptight. But even though he's given me a hard time, I need to bring myself down to earth by connecting with him in some way. Maybe with my new happier, confident attitude I can groove when I talk to him.

Dad turns on the news. There's a strange aircraft with a saucer on top taking off from Tan Son Nhut Air Base in Vietnam. The newscaster says these planes can monitor all air traffic in a combat area, including missiles. The operation is named Big Eye, which sounds very funny to me and I attempt to make the most of it.

"Hey, Dad, that plane looks like a UFO."

He gives me his you're-an-idiot look so I leave.

I always flop when I blurt things out, and joking around with my uptight old man is useless.

In the other room, Mom whispers to me, "It's his. That plane is his. Now that our country's at war, your father's new job at the Pentagon is overseeing its development. Getting Congress to pay for it hasn't been easy. In September one of his good friends, you remember Jim Stockdale, got shot down. Your father is pretty upset."

"Is Captain Stockdale still alive?"

"Yes, but they captured him. God knows what's happening to him now."

Mom's information makes me proud of Dad's efforts. Maybe I should try again to connect?

I go back to the TV room but stop and stand in the doorway. Dad's still watching the broadcast. Another pilot has been shot down. It scares me to see him clench his teeth like he did when he belted us, and I decide not to sit down. The bad news about the war is never-ending. At least McHale and his Navy screw-ups make me laugh. I don't want to waste my life being bummed out.

Dad rises from his chair and doesn't even glance at me. I hear the front door shut and see him from the window, staring into the star-covered sky.

I've learned that the night sky is a safe place for him to think. Maybe I should join him the way he joined me on the pier at Sans Souci. But so much has changed. I'd be faking it to act like we're great pals. Walking around on eggshells is a drag and I always blow it when I try to talk to him. His job is obviously important and I'm impressed that this plane is really capable of helping our pilots avoid missiles. I feel bad for those POWs, but hanging around Dad is a bummer. School is easier to handle than being at home, especially when I can cruise around with Mike on weekends.

∼

It's another Saturday morning and Mike is revving Mimi's Porsche. I fly out of the dorm and jump in.

"Man, I'm starving."

"The chow's that bad here?"

"Yeah, it's bad but I didn't eat anything at all yesterday."

"Why?"

"One of my classmate's father is a POW. He's a fighter pilot."

"That's why?"

"Yeah. Dad is always on me for stuffing my face and I figured I could go a day with no food. My friend's old man isn't getting much, so we go without eating one day a week. Just want to think about him and the other pilots stuck over there."

"That's cool. You trying to be some kind of monk?"

"No, asshole. And right now I want two burgers and a shake."

The weekend fun seems like it will never end with Mike. We've seen every soul group that has come to the Howard and when the Redskins have a home game, we're there. At the games Mike has to pee all the time. I know I enjoy it when I pee, but Mike's happier than anyone when he gets back to our seats.

Mike is parked illegally with Mimi's Porsche in front of the dorm entrance. My weekend bag is already packed. Outta sight.

But when I open the door to the car, Mike looks bummed and shakes his head.

"Sorry, Bill, no dice. Just came by to say adios. I enlisted in the Naval Reserve."

My thoughts flood with shock. Everything was so perfect.

"Why? You have a student deferment. What happened?"

"Yeah, well, not anymore, I flunked out of GW. If I didn't enlist I'd get drafted and that would've meant I'd be a grunt instead of a swabby."

I remember the lack of books around his apartment.

"Oh."

I move on to the next option.

"The Naval Reserve? Why not go to flight school?"

He chuckles and looks away.

"You still think that's your bag?"

"Yeah, maybe. A lot of guys go to Annapolis from our school."

"Well, it's not for me, pal. I just want to stay away from the shooting and get done with it as fast as possible."

"Man. Shit," is all I can say.

I'm blown away. Why does life always catch up and ruin the good times? I know the military is a fact of life. I'll have to go someday. But now just isn't the right time to have this happen to either of us.

Mike is still smiling.

"We had a great time, didn't we?"

"Maybe too good, huh?"

He hugs me.

"Take it easy, Bill, and don't worry about me."

I'm home in Alexandria for summer vacation.

Mom's a little more drunk than she is when Dad is home.

"Your father is on some carrier off Vietnam."

"Doing what?"

"Telling pilots what to do. What else?"

I had forgotten how it's impossible to get details from Mom, even when she's sober.

She's still rambling.

"I suppose he's swapping stories…"

Her voice slurs.

The phone rings and I answer. It's Mike, calling me from boot camp.

"It's horrible here. They're all rednecks."

I try to be the upbeat one.

"Aw, man, just hang in there. It'll change. Isn't that what you always tell me?"

"I told you that when I was…"

He fades off, then starts again.

"Bill, these guys have no dreams. They just want to be swabbies. I'd rather be getting shot at than hanging out with these idiots."

It scares me that he's so upset. He sounds like a caged animal.

"I should have known about the Navy. We had enough of this shit from the old man."

My gut aches for him.

"What happens next?"

"We're shipping out of Norfolk next week on the Roosevelt. To Vietnam. Don't know what I'm going to do but I'll try anything to get out."

My heart skips a beat. *Newsweek* had a picture of the Franklin Roosevelt with a flight deck full of Phantoms and I know that won't be a turn-on for Mike.

Mike sounds desperate—just like he did when he threatened suicide after being blamed for our grandfather's death.

"Bill, don't tell Mom anything. I'll keep you posted."

I like it that he's still calling me Bill instead of Billy, but when the phone clicks off I feel sick.

Dad's back home from his short visit to the war. He's a little happier than the last time I saw him. I ask about his trip and he only tells me about the fine young men he worked with and the teamwork they're establishing to keep everybody safe.

"But, sir, one of my friends told me there's a lot of people who don't think we should be over there."

"No. They're wrong. Ike was right when he was president. If one of those countries falls, there will be hell to pay."

Summer vacation is almost over and I join Dad to watch the news. Some kids are evading the draft by going to Canada. There goes his good mood. He's swearing at the TV when Mom answers a call.

She appears upset after she hangs up.

"That was the Navy. An anchor chain crushed the bones on Mikey's ankle and he's in the hospital."

I've seen those anchor chains. They're as big around as my arm. No way I could pick up even one link. I'm squirming.

I see Dad is shaking his head.

Mom asks him, "What's the matter?"

"There are procedures. This doesn't make sense."

~

School has started again and the cafeteria food is as bad as ever. I've figured out the bus schedules to Alexandria and without Mike around I'm more motivated to go home for weekends.

Mom is whispering to me in the kitchen.

"What's wrong with Mikey? He went into Virginia Beach and someone broke a wine bottle over his head and now he's getting a psychiatric evaluation from the Navy doctors. I'm afraid to tell your father. He'll be furious."

"Mom, can you wait until I go back to school before you tell him?"

Even though it has meant missing some great meals from Mom, I've stayed in the dorm the last few weekends. The library and the world of news magazines is where I hang out. The war in Vietnam isn't going well for U.S. soldiers.

The horrible dorm food has made me forget how miserable Dad is and I'm back home.

Mom is whispering to me again. Her whispers never mean good news.

"The Navy has given Mikey a general discharge for being insane."

"Insane, Mom?"

"Well, mentally ill. The only thing your father has said since I told him is, 'A general discharge is no better than a dishonorable discharge.' I just don't know what to do now, Billy. Your father has been sitting in his recliner, staring away at nothing."

"He always stares away at nothing in that chair."

"But he's not wearing his headphones, Billy."

I tiptoe around the house and manage not to run into Dad for the rest of the weekend.

It's been three months and Mike hasn't kept me posted at all. Mom's worried, too, especially after the Navy gave him such an ominous psychological evaluation.

Finally, Mike calls me at school.

"What's shakin' for Christmas vacation?" he asks as if I have some busy schedule and we've been speaking regularly.

"Mike, Mom's worried sick."

"It's all cool, man. I'll call her."

"Where the hell are you?"

"In Aspen, diggin' the snow. Wanna go skiing?"

Mike sounds fine, like he's my same old fun-loving brother. If that's insane, sign me up.

"Are you crazy?! Hell yeah, I do."

Dad doesn't care about Christmas and doesn't care about my trip as long as he isn't paying. He does sound disappointed that I want to hang around with my screw-up brother, but he gives me an unenthusiastic OK to go. Mike sends me money for airfare and tells me he'll pay for everything.

He instructs me to get a 12-21 student youth fare card from United Airlines. I'm supposed to go standby for a seat on a flight to Denver.

I'm at Washington National Airport checking out the destination board, feeling confident that from now until I'm twenty-one I can go to any airport and jump on a cheap flight—anywhere. Other young guys and girls with backpacks wander around the airport. But right now I'm going to fly on a real jet for the first time, to Denver, right over all those troubled Southern states I drove through with Dad. I'm jazzed. From now on flying is for me.

My small Rocky Mountains Airline plane lands in Aspen and Mike picks me up. I point to other guys on the street of this small town as we make a few stops on the way to his pad on Hyman Avenue.

"Is everyone a hippie here?"

"Yeaah, man."

He stretches out his words to make fun of me.

Hippies have been a constant topic of conversation around school and all I know is that they have long hair and dress weird. Mike is having fun with my naïve generalizations.

"It's free love, man. The girls will make it with anyone."

That sounds great even though I know he's teasing me. From where I'm coming from, all I can think about is girls. And there are many young ones my age walking around the streets of Aspen.

"Can you be serious?"

"Listen, Bill, I don't know what you've heard, but these hippies are athletes. If you live here, you ski. Just because their hair is long doesn't mean jack."

"A stereotype?"

"Hey, check out who's the smartass."

"Everyone in this town has long hair except me. You'd never know you were a swabby three months ago."

"Changes, Bill."

We arrive at Mike's cabin. I've never been in a log cabin before. After I've settled in, Mike dresses with a coat and tie.

"I'm off to work."

I give him a quizzical look.

What can he do that brings in enough money to pay for my trip?

"I'm a waiter at the Refectory Steak House at this new ski hill called Snowmass."

Wow, I guess waiters make a heap of money.

Mike sets me up to sleep out in the living room where I listen to the Butterfield Blues Band when he goes off to work. But it's hard to relax. His place smells like my school roommate's dirty socks. I've learned how to do my own laundry at school. Maybe I can do a load for him and be a good houseguest since he's been so generous. Now where are his dirty clothes?

I open one of his closets and discover the smell comes from two large duffle bags.

Mike gets home and the first words out of my mouth are, "What's with all the rotten hay in your closet?"

He laughs.

"Jesus, Bill, you're not ten anymore."

I squint my eyes.

It bothers me to be slow to figure things out, but it's obvious that I have been.

"Dope?"

"Yeah, dope. That hay paid for your ticket."

I'm confused and a little tense. Mike searches through his record collection and pulls out a Beatles album.

"And you were smoking dope in D.C., weren't you?"

Instead of denying it or playing it down like I thought he would, his answer catches me off guard. He's grinning at me while he drops the needle onto a song and cranks up the volume. The Beatles pound out "Money." Mike bobs his head and almost sings what he says next.

"Yeah. Smokin' the shit and movin' it, too. Remember the Milkman and the handshakes at the Howard? That was me. Guess I did a good job of keeping it from *you*."

He accentuates the word 'you' as he pounds on an imaginary drum. Incredible. He has just turned the table and made it about me. How did he do that? He sounds proud and hip. I feel out to lunch and shake my head in disbelief.

"Can you turn that down?"

He does and I continue.

"I just never thought you would."

This last year the school has been showing us movies to scare us about smoking pot. Their arguments and presentation were pretty much over the top, but the message had worked its way into my head. Dope to me was like something only shady heroin deadbeat types would do—or like guys who go to a Bob Dylan concert and complain about Vietnam and A-bombs.

But I remember the sharp-talking, finger-snapping soul brothers who were Mike's connection at the Howard. They didn't look like hippies. The stereotype didn't fit everyone.

"Why do you do it?"

Mike gets very serious for a moment and takes the needle off the record.

"You know how heavy things got living at home."

"Yeah."

"Well, I was pissed at a lot of things and just didn't know how to control myself. You can blame yourself for just about anything if you think about it long enough. That's what was happening to me and it was eating me up. So I tried some weed in the Bahamas right after I got out of high school, and it made me feel good. Then when I came back to Alexandria, things blew up with Dad. After that I was out on my own selling vacuums and encyclopedias and going to college. Just got so pissed about everything. It was a bad scene, man."

I nod.

"Yeah, I know. I remember those times."

"Sorry, but that's the part I'm scared of."

I've never had this kind of conversation with anyone. It makes me feel really good, especially since it's with my brother. He's so open with me. The old way we were brothers is changing into something I never imagined.

"Anyway, I started drinking heavy at the Georgetown University Club and getting into more fights. This black bartender enlightened me to the fact that I needed to mellow out and gave me a joint. It worked, so I started slipping out of drinking parties to sneak a hit. When I slipped back in I would be loose and hit it off with the chicks much better than when I had been drinking, plus I stopped fighting. Later on that bartender took me to the Howard. All those brothers you saw asked me if I wanted to meet their friend MJ. Didn't hesitate and said, 'Shit, yeah,' and that was that. Started to sell weed for some extra scratch."

"Scratch?"

"Dough. We had fun with it, didn't we?"

His memories remind me of all the money we spent in D.C. So Mom hadn't been bankrolling him.

"And you made lots of... scratch?"

"Way more than from encyclopedias, Bill. You can hate me if you want, but this is who I am."

"I don't hate you. I'm just confused."

"Just dig it, Bill. Just dig it."

Mike places the record needle on "Money" again.

"Hey," I say, "I remember that song. Barrett Strong, right?"

"Yeah, now the Beatles are doing it. Different guys, same song."

Mike sacks out. I stare at the ceiling, trying to sleep, but keep thinking about what he has just told me.

Dope isn't on my mind this morning. Mike has laid out all my ski clothes and equipment. I'm amped to get dressed—except for the tights. The only thing left is to learn how to ski.

"You'll learn from the legendary Jack Heath."

Ski lessons? This is fantastic.

The lifts are only a few blocks from Mike's house. A crystal blue sky adds to my anticipation with each step. I don't know if I've ever seen or breathed air this clean. Every exhale sends out a cloud of steamy vapor.

The streets are full of people marching to the chairlifts in their bulky boots. They have their skis over their shoulders, like soldiers carrying rifles. The dry snow squeaks as I march along with them.

Unlike any soldiers or ROTC I've ever seen, many of the skiers are smoking pot as they make their way to the lifts. The sweet aroma spreads in the windless cold dry mountain air.

One of the pot-smoking skiers near me pinches his fingers to his lips and raises his eyes in question. It dawns on me that he's inviting me to share his joint with him. This gesture brings a smile to my face when I remember how it had always meant to keep my mouth shut when Dad gestured that way. Old things have new meanings.

When these long-haired ski bums offer me pot or grass or whatever they call it, I shake my head no. But I think it's amazing. What an incredibly friendly place Aspen is.

I go to the prearranged meeting spot and soon a thin athletic man of around forty-five approaches and introduces himself as Jack Heath. Jack wears a cool straight-brimmed Navaho hat with a colorful beaded head-band and aviator-style Ray Ban shades. Whenever he takes his hat off I notice a Marine buzz cut that's noticeably different from everyone else's long hairstyles. His tanned clean-shaven face has a Piz Buin shine like a oiled broken-in baseball glove. He speaks clearly and concisely like a military man, but he's friendly and a great instructor.

When Jack Heath floats down the mountain, his knees are locked tight enough to hold a penny between them and his hat never moves. Everyone gives him obvious respect. I love skiing immediately and learn quickly from Jack.

My first day on the slopes is over and I'm so tired that I can barely walk back to Mike's empty cabin.

A note on the fridge says he's gone to work again. After a long shower I put the Chambers Brothers album on the record player and bundle up on the couch. Muscles I didn't know I had ache. What a day I've just had.

I jump up when I hear a knock on the door, imagining Mike's hands must be full of food. He's promised to bring home some lobster from the restaurant since his refrigerator is empty. I could eat a horse.

"Hi, I'm Betty."

The most beautiful girl I've ever seen stands in front of me. Betty has long raven black hair and wears black pants and a tight black fuzzy sweater.

"Is Mike here?"

She shivers and wraps her arms around her chest.

I gape.

"Yeah, no, come on in and get out of the cold."

She does and smiles at me.

"You're his brother, Bill, aren't you?"

"Yeah."

"He told me he had a brother my age. I was hoping you'd come."

All the warm air in the cabin escaped when I opened the door. The temperature now is just as cold inside as out. But that's only one part of my shivers. Her smile is intense. My heart is pounding and I'm shaking from what I think must be the cold.

"Yep, I'm here."

I sound so dumb to myself.

She glances at the couch and pokes me in the ribs.

"You cold? Get back under your blankie and I'll roll the doobie."

"Do you know...?"

"Yeah, I know."

She goes into the closet and reaches into the duffle bag.

"It's Oaxacan, isn't it?"

"Uh, I don't know. Smelled like dirty socks to me."

She laughs.

"Well, even if it's not, it'll do."

I'm overwhelmed in so many ways as I watch her.

"Does everyone smoke pot in this town?"

"Just about. Even the mayor smokes it. Why?"

"I don't know. It's just so wild. The mayor? Jeez."

Betty sits on the couch next to me, bends over the low table and spins up a joint. She licks the Zig Zag rolling paper and smiles at me again.

"You smoke, don't you?"

I nervously shake my head no. She bounces on the couch.

"Oh, too much fun."

"Huh?"

Betty goes to the stereo and turns up the volume. She sings along, "Time has come today."

She stands in front of me, lights the joint and takes a long inhale. I watch her chest expand. Like a cat she jumps onto my lap and then, opening my mouth with a kiss, exhales her smoke into it. Her lips are big and moist. I ignore the smoke and enjoy the long kiss. She breaks away from me for a moment, takes another hit and does it again.

Whatever the price, I'm willing to pay.

How long has she been in my lap? I'm giggling out of control.

Our noses are touching.

"You like it?"

"Yeah, I like it. I like it a lot."

Her smile is outta sight.

"You like me, too, I can tell."

I have a woody and as I nod realize I'm no longer nervous. I wiggle my ears, we laugh and make out.

When Mike returns, Betty is still under the covers with me. We're laughing at everything.

He sees several unfinished joints on the table and cracks up.

"Betty, I guess you found the stash and my brother. You guys up for a scarf?"

We ravage the lobster. For a moment I take my eyes off the food and gleam at Mike.

"God, everything tastes so good."

"You grooving?"

"Yeah, I'm grooving."

Every day of this past week has been unbelievable fun on the slopes.

Tonight Mike has taken me to the main hotspot in town, the Red Onion. I'm underage but he knows the bartender. Many top international skiers are gathered at the bar. Mike points to one who is surrounded by an army of beautiful women.

"That's Jean Claude Killy. He just competed in the World Cup at Ajax."

"World Cup?"

"Yeah, they travel around the world racing and make a heap of dough."

I'm watching them. Money, chicks, it's mind-blowing. What a great way to live. It's even cooler than being a fighter pilot.

We're back at the cabin. Someone pounds on the door and enters. Mike introduces me to a friend.

"This is Joe. He surfs Maui in the summer and skis here in the winter. He's going to stay here a few days before he heads out."

I shake Joe's hand and am impressed that he has this great routine to surf and ski. He's a tall, healthy blond-haired guy with bright blue eyes. His hand is vibrating and his mouth is set in a permanent teeth-grinding grin.

Mike giggles.

"Joe's trippin.'"

Joe holds out his hand and displays a few small dots of paper.

"Want some acid?"

I ask Mike, "Is it OK?"

"Yeah, go for it."

Mike's cabin is small and box-like, yet every knot in the wood has a story to tell. I think about the small dot of paper I've just swallowed and speak out loud to myself, but my voice comes out warbled. There's too much time between what I think and when I attempt to manufacture a word. I sound like a Martian.

Joe and my brother laugh mischievously. Their fun vibe is groovy, which is comforting since nothing is solid and everything I touch and try to focus on overwhelms me. Mike must be checking out my face because he's telling me to let go of the fear. My hands open from a tight clench and my body melts into the floor. His advice works. Joy explodes through me. There is much more to absorb and so much I have never seen before. In this 'now' everything is connected. There is no 'I.'

An album spins endlessly, like life. The view from the ceiling shows feet stomping on the wood floor. The feet look like they used to belong to my body but there's no attachment. The sound is Creedence Clearwater, definitely the type of music Dad hates but for this moment and this now, it's pure bliss. We love everything. All of Dad's hate flows out of us and good vibes flow in.

Music is a pathway away from the pain of my childhood. Cream sings "I'm So Glad" and "I Feel Free." These songs become a mantra that flows throughout the cabin. It's obvious now how much of a trap 'I'm so sad' or 'I'm so scared' is. A new being is emerging from my old fear-filled body. The avalanche of sound blankets the negative energy. I am glad.

We've been tripping for years or maybe it's been two minutes. This being is timeless.

Mike's VW bug is so dented it's like it's made from crumpled tin foil. We're sliding around in the snow. Driving seems ambitious.

We float into a party and I have to check to see if my legs are moving. There are many beings in this space and an old worry I used to own about sticking out bubbles into my brain. That fear evaporates when we're inside and now I'm absolutely sure that everyone here is just as high as we are. Could the whole world be tripping at this moment?

Being here feels very relaxed but what are we going to do? Sitting still on a couch is an enormous undertaking. For a few moments we gaze at each other and grin until our faces ache. Beautiful girls walk towards Mike. I lose connection with my brother and the view from the ceiling returns. Sound is coming out of Mike's mouth and enveloping the girls. Everyone is laughing at our musical chairs with strangers.

The view drops to the couch as a mane of dark hair tumbles over the seat from behind and slides in next to me. The hair clears and an angelic image beams at me. It's Betty, holding my arm with a face full of love. All the energy outside the two of us is reduced to a hum. I think I could sit still forever.

We're back at Mike's cabin. I still feel high but have returned to my body and have come down from the original intensity of the acid. My hands touch my mouth where Betty kissed me. Did she also kiss me on the cheek? It feels hot. Where did she go? Mike giggles.

"Can't believe her dad just slapped you. Figured you'd at least lose some teeth. Shoulda seen your face when he dragged her out of that party."

My memory flickers.

"Why did he do that?"

"Whatta ya think? The girl's sixteen and she's at a party with a bunch of high flyers. Thought it was cool he hit you instead of her."

"What?"

"Yeah, man. The guy loves his daughter. Makes me feel good to see that."

Mike throws me an ice pack for my face.

"Sleep it off and I'll see you in the morning."

A million thoughts bombard me this morning, and a half million are about Dad. Despite my grooving with so many stoned people last night, only Mike really knows the inside story of my life.

I talk to him while he makes us some breakfast.

"I'm thinking how Dad should take some acid. What did the Navy do to him? Maybe the Navy was like a bad trip."

Mike laughs.

"Oh, that's heavy, man. You better lighten up."

"Alright, Sherlock, what's been going on in your head?"

Mike is wearing this silly Sherlock Holmes hat. Actually, everyone in Aspen is wearing big funny-looking hats.

Mike's eyes open wide.

"I'm getting' all jacked up to go surfing."

OK, he's not thinking about our dad or even Betty's dad.

Joe says, "I'm hittin' it outta here next week. Hope I can bag a few spring swells at Honolua before summer."

Joe is speaking a language that is both familiar and at the same time foreign to me.

"Where?"

Mike fills in.

"Maui, of course, you retard. Let's go surfing next summer."

When I hear 'Maui' and 'let's go,' that's enough for me. Surfing is the icing.

"Yeah, you wouldn't believe it, Bill, the ocean is warm and the chicks are hot."

I think about the five long months until summer break, but counting down to Maui with my brother will make time fly.

I'm back at school and a bit fried from my trip to Aspen. Music soothes my nerves. Lying on my bed in the dorm, the drumbeat of this new song sounds like soldiers going to war but the music and lyrics are tripping me out, especially the part about the 'men on the chessboard' telling you where to go. Are they challenging the 'do as you're told' mentality I've grown up with?

This song isn't the only thing that gets inside my head. Since I've returned from Aspen, many trippy little thoughts that never entered my mind before now make me think about LSD and what happened to my head and my outlook. The old picture of my future is starting to crack.

Just before spring break, a student yells down the hall, "Hey, Bill, it's for you."

I bolt for the pay phone. It's got to be Mike. No one else calls me this late at night.

It is Mike and he sounds stoked.

"Hey, I just got out of the water. The surf was happening."

I can't believe it. Mike the ski bum is back on Maui.

"Aw, man, you're torturing me."

"Well, you'll be here, too, in a few—but in the meantime I got you a ticket to Expo in Montreal for your spring break. I went and it's unreal. It's like seeing the whole world in a big fair. You'll dig it."

I've read that Expo features nations from all over. But I don't really care what it features. I'm just jazzed that Mike wants me to see everything he has.

"You think the parents will say yes?"

"Yeah, I already sold Mom on the educational part, especially since you'll use some of your crappy French. But you and I know the real reason, huh?"

"Yeah. You wouldn't believe how weird it is at home now. Anyway, Mimi has invited me to San Francisco to see what's happening there, so I should be able to escape pretty much the whole summer."

"Shit, man, why go home again?"

What an idea. I don't know how to pull it off, but somehow it's beginning to seem possible.

Meanwhile, he teases me.

"Hey, Montreal is in a foreign country, Billy boy. You're becoming a man of the world."

~

I can't wait to tell Mike about my trip to Montreal and Expo. When I call his number on Maui, though, I get some stony guy who drops the phone to find him. The stoner must have spaced out and after five minutes I hang up. I decide to write him a letter. I see guys writing letters all the time and can't help noticing how excited they are when they get one back. Here goes.

Mike,

It all went down just like you said. Flew to Montreal and moved into the place you set up for me. Like you said, they do speak French and between school and Mama Marcelle I knew enough to get by.

The town was easy to navigate. Took the subway to Expo every day. Saw the exhibits from the different countries and they were cool, but it was the nights that were a blast.

Noticed a poster that advertised some soul groups from Detroit playing at the Place de Nations. Four bands set up at a time. When one stopped, another started. They took me back to the Howard and the other rock concerts you've turned me on to. What can I say—it's all about the pounding beat.

But the biggest thrill was the girls. All the French girls my age strut around in miniskirts. I'd never seen one before and man they sure know how to wear them. Anyway I was scoping out a group of these girls and one of them shot me a look. A blond version of Betty came over and asked me where I was from.

I lied en Français, "Du Hawaii."

She mimed a surf stance and I grew excited and pointed to myself.

"Oui, c'est moi, je fais le surf."

I pointed to the Hawaiian exhibit. Her friends hovered around me. All of them knew about Hawaii. One girl licked her lips.

"I love to eat mangoes."

Another shimmied her body when she told me, "I love to roll around in the warm sand."

Another did a little hula and it didn't matter that

she didn't know what she was doing.

"How is it they move their hips?"

I just smiled. She knew how to move. The Hawaii thing worked well and I got more attention than I ever have. Wish you could've seen me.

Another cooed, "Oh, teach me how to surf."

I got behind her and moved her body into a surf stance. I remember thinking, how am I going to be able to go back to an all-boys dorm?

The first one grabbed me by the hand.

"I am Jacqueline. I saw you first."

Just like Mom's name, huh? I let her lead me away and we danced all night.

I stumbled with my French trying to say, "Je voudrais aller..."

She put her hand over my mouth and giggled at my horrible accent. Then she kissed me. Just a kiss, but she sure knew how. Wow.

Thanks so much.

Bill

~

Summer vacation is here. These last few days of visiting with Mimi in San Francisco have been a groove. I went to an Iron Butterfly concert at the Fillmore and saw the new hippie world that the newspapers have been writing about.

I laugh at myself when I remember being called a four-eyes. Here in San Francisco many guys around the Haight are wearing glasses like I used to, only their glasses are strangely shaped and colored. I wonder if they even need them. But their glasses aren't scaring the chicks away; this is a new way to be cool. Everything is upside down. Mike always made fun of swabbies, but now hippies are wearing pants like those worn by Navy sailors, flared at the bottom. But these bellbottoms have bright wild colors, like the clothes Mike tells me I'll see on Maui.

I enjoyed the hippie style in San Francisco, but it's still a city. Some of the kids, without colored glasses, have a look I recognize from when my brother ran away from home. They seem delirious, tired and hungry. All the kids who aren't getting along with their parents must be fleeing to San Francisco. There's a part of this scene that freaks me out.

Maui. Yep, that's where I want to go. This big city isn't for me. I stare at my 12-21 standby card. I'll fly across the Pacific tomorrow and land on the island where Dad grew up.

Young kids like I've seen on the streets around the city wait for flights here in the San Francisco Airport. Even though I've heard them talking about peace and love, right now they are screaming horrible names at uniformed soldiers returning from Vietnam and appear set on causing a scene.

The girls are the loudest and their scorn is harsh. I'm guessing these soldiers might want to spend some time with a babe when they get back to the U.S., like I do when I leave school, but these girls are holding hands with long-haired guys who probably wash their hair every day with Breck shampoo. I bet these hippies don't know what it's like to have a military buzz cut and look like Uncle Fester. The soldiers keep their cool, but I squirm while I watch.

As I board my flight, I'm wigging out with my anticipation to get to Maui. I can't believe I'll be in the water in a few hours. It's been forever since I left the cold ocean off Coronado. But this time I'm flying right to the best surf in the world—Hawaii. Mike has made my surf dream resurface. I'm not even seventeen yet and so much has already happened to me this year; Aspen and Montreal, and now he's bringing me to Maui. What a great brother.

I grab the June 1967 *Newsweek* from the magazine rack for some distraction. If I don't read something, I'll jump out of my skin.

A stewardess tells us to fasten our seatbelts as the jet starts its engines.

I glance down at the magazine as my weight is pushed against the back of my seat during takeoff. The cover story is about the air battles in the six-day war that just happened in the Middle East.

Could I still become a fighter pilot like Dad? Maybe I'll be able to get an appointment to the Naval Academy when I finish high school and, after that, flight school to fly jets.

What's it like to be a fighter pilot in a conflict that lasts only six days?

I think those Israeli pilots must be heroes in their country to win so fast.

U.S. fighter pilots in air battles over Hanoi and Haiphong have shot down over twenty MIGs this last month. But another article reminds me that the U.S. involvement in Vietnam has already lasted more than three years.

I can get excited about dogfights in the air between opposing jets, but this same article has an aerial picture of fighter jets dropping jellied gasoline, called napalm, on villages with thatched roofs. It's difficult for me to imagine an enemy that lives in a house with a thatched hut.

According to this article, Russian surface-to-air missiles are shooting down many of our planes despite all Dad's efforts with the AWACS program. When their planes are hit, our pilots have to punch out and drop into enemy territory. The report states that pilots who are captured are tortured in North Vietnamese prisons.

The pictures in *Newsweek* also show the empty stare on the faces of soldiers on the ground. Some of them are just a year or two older than I am. I've always separated ground combat from air-to-air, but I'm beginning to see how they are really two sides of one coin. Even though I've lived in the military world all my life, the full reality of this war is grabbing me. I thought flying would be exciting and glorious. Now I wonder if I have the stomach for it.

If I have questions, I'm reading that I'm not alone. Another article shows Martin Luther King and the baby doctor Benjamin Spock leading over 400,000 people in a protest. More young guys are burning their draft cards. The ones who are or will be fighting the war must have their own unanswered questions, just like I do.

But when I think about it, even my arch-conservative father, who had been a combat fighter pilot, voiced his frustrations to me whenever I was home.

"If we're going to be in there, let's be in there all the way. This half-assed pussy-footing around is no way to wage a war."

He'd helped win WWII, so maybe he had a point. According to him, the lack of commitment in Vietnam had resulted in many of our pilots being shot down and ending up as POWs. He told me we should be bombing North Vietnamese ships and missile sites. Then they won't be able to bring the war south.

I stare in horror at this magazine. Burning villagers alive in thatched huts in South Vietnam isn't the way to win. If the government isn't committed, then how can it expect us kids to be? Do I still want to fly jets? If I do, it will be no sooner than three years away—which may as well be forever.

I put the magazine away and dream about my time in Aspen and seeing Jean Claude Killy with the crowd of women surrounding him at the bar. Racing down steep ski slopes around the world sure is a different path than joining the military.

In several hours I'll be swimming in the turquoise waters of the warm Pacific Ocean. Wow, Maui. My biggest wish growing up was to have a permanent home. Moving every other year didn't keep me from yearning for an anchor. At some point I began to fantasize that Maui was my real home because it was where my father was born and raised. This is strange for me, to be going 'home' to a place I've only known from my brother's tales of living there with our grandmother. I wish this jet could fly faster.

Chapter Eight

Lahaina
1967

A huge banyan tree full of birds is growing out of a hole in the middle of the Kahului airport terminal roof. It's difficult to hear a man tell me what kind of birds are making this overwhelming noise—sounds like a million mynah birds having a cocktail party.

A long-haired guy introduces himself as Mike's pal. His car is an old rusted Studebaker with surfboards lashed to the roof. He drops me off at a large house on Front Street on the west side of the island in what he tells me is the rowdy old whaling town of Lahaina.

I suck in a sweet scent as I pull my bag from the car and glance above to see a giant plumeria tree raining down flowers that spin like helicopters to a soft landing. There's a strong smell of pot when I knock on the door of this old plantation-style house.

"You must be Mike's bro from the mainland," a guy says when he opens the door, "'cause no one around here knocks."

A group of sunburnt guys are sitting around the kitchen table, smoking a joint. One points toward the ocean without looking.

"His room is in the back."

The pot smell doesn't bother me a bit. In fact, I love it. No pot for me since Aspen and I'm looking forward to smoking it. Where the hell is my brother?

Someone in another room of the house plays Jimi Hendrix's new song, "Are You Experienced?" I know Jimi means psychedelic experiences on LSD. I've only dropped acid that once and still can't get a handle on what happened. Maybe I'll try it again while I'm here.

Mike's door is open and I see two futons on opposite sides of the room and no other furniture. I drop my bag and look around. Two surfboards lean against the back wall towards the ocean. My heart races but I don't want to expect too much. Still, I'm already seeing myself on the pintail with the balsa wood stringer.

"Just the basics, huh?"

Mike's stripped down to his surf shorts and has just untwisted himself from some kind of pretzel position.

"Got to keep it open for yoga and my mind. Good to see you, Bill."

He's restrained, not what I expected.

"Hey, man, that trip you sent me on to see Expo was outta sight. The French girls, mini skirts. I went out of my mind. What can I say?"

"Well, your letter running it down was cool. That was thanks enough. Knew you'd dig it."

I hear a high-pitched scream from another room.

Mike laughs.

"That's just Paul. He sniffs glue. They call this house the Animal Farm."

Mike sees me eyeballing the pintail. He hands it to me.

"I think this is the first thing you'll need here."

"Wow, Mike, I don't know what to say."

With presents like this, I'm OK with him being low-key.

"Let's go catch a few, Mike."

He waves me off.

"You go. I'll join you later. Want to finish this book."

Mike introduces me to a fat lady who runs the house and rents out the rooms. Mike's housemates are all a few years older than I am and very fit. One of them spots my board.

"Hey, brother, that stick looks unreal. It'll rip. We're just about to go out. Wanna join us to see where the channel is?"

I nod, wave goodbye to Mike and follow their footsteps in the sand.

The house is right in front of a surf break called Shark Pit and I paddle out behind two guys through a narrow, coral-lined channel. At the takeoff spot we sit up to begin our wait. I'm barely able to focus on catching waves, though, due to the overwhelming view of the steep green slopes of the mountains looming up behind Lahaina. The scenery here is breathtaking; it's a long way from Washington, D.C.

Warm. The ocean here is much warmer than what I was used to in Coronado. But the waves are more powerful, too. Sharp. The bottom is shallow and sharp and my first wipeouts shred my feet.

Mike is reading his book about Mahatma Gandhi when I hobble in and show him my battle wounds from the coral. He scrubs my cuts with a toothbrush and applies his special Chinese herbal mixture that he claims will kill the infection from the reef. All I know is that it hurts like hell. After my protests to his torture, he tells me he knows surfers whose infected cuts on their feet have turned into gnarly craters. I get the picture and vow not to touch the bottom in the future.

After Mike has patched me up, he surprises me when he puts on some sharp threads for work. He's working as a food and beverage manager at the Royal Lahaina in the new tourist area of Kaanapali. Was it the yoga, books or subdued attitude? He hadn't looked like a guy with a job when I first walked in the door. But that's my brother. He's always surprising me.

When he leaves, I try to get into his book about Gandhi but fall asleep quickly after my first day in paradise.

I've been hanging out with Mike the last few weeks and every morning I join him for yoga, which is brand new to me. After yoga we go out to Kaanapali for a swim in clear blue water and a run on the long white sand beach. If the waves are up, I'm surfing. I'm getting stronger and can see how the yoga I'm doing with Mike is helping me in the water. Surfing is all I can think about.

Mike spends much more time reading his books than chasing waves. Even when he does get out in the lineup, I don't think he's all there. While we're sitting on our boards waiting for sets, his eyes are unfocused in a spaced-out trance. He often gets caught inside by big sets because he's slow to react.

As much as I wish Mike would get more into surfing with me, I know I can't push him. It's good enough to be here and I set out on my own to discover Maui. Because of the central location of our house I can walk or ride a bike to all the breaks in Lahaina. The other guys in our house take me under their wing and show me the best lineups around town.

Today, I'm waiting for waves by the entrance of Lahaina Harbor, gaping at what other surfers tell me is actor Peter Fonda's sailboat, The Tatoosh. The boat cruises into the harbor with foxy naked girls dancing on the deck. This place is wilder than Aspen.

After surfing, I always feel lean and hungry. It's a light feeling that's perfect for living here in Lahaina. I strut down the street in my surf shorts and flip-flops. This board under my arm is the bitchinest. Hah, my old word back—the East Coast must be losing its hold on me.

Most guys I've seen around the country this year have long hair if they're not in boarding school or the military. The girls dig it so I've stopped cutting mine. It's gotten pretty long now and the sun and ocean are bleaching it blond. I blend in here and look like the other surfers who are skinny and tan. My lats are even filling out. I wish Duke could see me now.

The strong fragrance of Maui pot greets me as I enter the door to the Animal Farm. In the kitchen I get offered a joint.

"Hey, brother, want a hit?"

I nod and sit down to listen in on their rap session but as stoned as I get, I know I only have one brother. Their conversation drifts to the fact that they should be right here on Maui, surfing and smoking pot, forever. I'm stoned and can't find any reason to argue with them. No words come to me and my mind drifts to the bag of chocolate chip cookies on the table. I stick my hand inside the bag but only feel a few broken pieces. Mike enters the room and sees me pouring the remaining crumbs out of the bag, straight into my mouth. He picks up the bag, checks out the ingredients list and scowls.

"Stoned munchies."

I feel his judgment and cringe.

A joint is passed to Mike, who waves it off.

He points to a glass of milk in front of me.

"Mucous."

I follow when he leaves abruptly, shaking his head and rolling his eyes.

"Did I do anything wrong?"

"No. You're doing what you need to do."

"What's wrong with a glass of milk?"

"Nothing. It just carries consequences. You've been pounding milk since you were a kid and your nose has been clogged with mucous all your life. Because of that, you're a mouth breather. Because of that, Dad used to slap you for looking like a retard."

"Why didn't he tell me about milk?"

"He didn't know shit about blue flame food. He never put milk and mucous together. They all think milk is king. For many people it doesn't clog up their noses, but it still ain't good. For kids like you, it's a disaster. Dad thought you were bucking him when you had your mouth open."

"But man, milk and cookies tastes so good when you're stoned."

"Well, you might want to tone that down as well."

"You're not smoking now?"

"Bill, I'm working on my dharma and being blotto doesn't help."

"What's dharma?"

Mike shakes his head.

"You're not ready."

When I eat with Mike, it's all vegetarian. I love the avocado and sprout sandwiches and smoothies from Charley's Juice stand, but mostly we cook at home.

The main kitchen in this house is what Dad would call a pigsty so Mike keeps a blender and a rice cooker in his room. He's into eating a macrobiotic diet so I'm learning to eat tofu, miso and tons of brown rice. It's OK but pretty salty for me.

Mike had told me about mangoes when we were younger and now I'm finding out just how delicious they are. I team up with some of our roommates and raid trees where the owners are letting the fruit fall. We pick around a hundred pounds at a time and freeze what's left after we scarf fresh ones until our stomachs are like drums. Mike was right on years ago when he told me mangoes were paradise.

I try to tempt Mike by showing him a perfect ripe one, cut in half and ready to eat.

"Mangoes are too yin, Bill. You're going to have to learn to control your stoned urges to binge on sweets. Maybe lay off the pot a tad."

Wow, now it's Mike who's the monk, but I can dig it.

He's reading a lot. Books by Carlos Castaneda and Edgar Cayce are piled beside his futon. It looks like he's almost finished with his book about Ghandi. I pick up one titled *Raw Juices, What's Missing in Your Body* by Dr. Norman Walker.

"You've changed your ways since Aspen," I say, "and lost around ten pounds. At this rate I'm headed there myself."

"Yeah," Mikey says, stretching as he sets the Gandhi book aside. "I couldn't keep that up. I've discovered some new ways of living, Bill."

"Like what?"

"Remember that time you fasted once a week to remember your school pal's father who was a POW?"

"Yeah, but we only did that for a few weeks."

"But that was cool. It was about devotion. You wanted to develop a spiritual connection with that pilot."

"Spiritual connection? I guess, but Dad was also getting on me about always stuffing my face and I thought, screw it, I won't eat for a day. My pal liked the idea and we just did it. It was no big deal."

"Well, for me the right thing to do is to unify the mind, body and spirit. Did you know Gandhi fasted thirty days?"

"Yeah, well, he wasn't surfing every day, was he?"

"Believe me, Bill, his issues were much larger than whether or not the surf was up."

"I guess I'd better read his book. A one-day fast was easy, but I was ready to chow down the next day. Thirty? That's incredible."

At age twenty-one my brother has changed radically into a serious adult, leaving not only his Aspen lifestyle behind but our way of life as Navy brats. Right now he's getting dressed to go to work. That really is serious.

We have no TV in our room and the other stoners keep changing the channel on the living room set, which drives me nuts. My only other entertainment is to try to make sense of *Moby Dick*. But without my Papa Bace to interpret the odd language, I know I won't read too far before it puts me to sleep. I don't feel like sleeping yet so I drift down to the harbor to see what's happening there.

"Wow."

It's sunset. Many young people around Lahaina are on the grass in front of the library by the harbor smoking joints and watching for the green flash. My stoned eyes have stared at the sun so long I'm not sure what colors I'm seeing but, like many of the people around me, I keep saying "Wow."

A girl with a mane of golden curls leans her head into her boyfriend. It's obvious that she isn't wearing a bra under her loose shirt.

The sun has been gone for over an hour now, but the sky is still psychedelic purple and orange. I'm hanging around with a few other under-age kids just outside the Maui Bell Bar, hoping I might magically meet a girl like that sunset surfer babe I just saw.

These other kids my age are so obvious when they stare. My head is grooving to the music from inside the bar and I'm pretending I don't even see the girls when they stroll by me. My brother tipped me off—that's how you catch babes.

One of Mike's pals slips me inside so I can see the band. The rock group Space Patrol pounds out a Canned Heat-sounding blues tune. I've seen some of the band members out in the ocean during the day. They're some of the best surfers around here and the girls are checking them out.

Foxy chicks are coming and going. I wish I were a musician or even old enough to talk to them. In this moment, Lahaina feels full of love, especially since I'm stoned.

But then, back outside, a big angry-looking brown man shoves a skinny white guy.

"Looking at me? Like beef?"

"No, man, I'm a vegetarian."

"Wiseass haole. Goin' broke your ass."

The local smacks him hard a few times before the kid runs away, terrified.

I've already learned that beef means to fight. It's good to learn these pidgin words so I can stay out of trouble. There's an edge here. It's not all peace and love. I'll have to watch my step so I don't get my ass kicked.

Some of the locals call long-haired white kids hippies. When I hear the word 'hippie,' I picture what I saw in San Francisco—loner kids with pale skin and hunched shoulders. Here in Lahaina, most of the surfers are very healthy and strut around with tan broad shoulders. But if long sun-bleached hair, low pay or no job, surf-everyday-living means you're a hippie, then many do qualify and, when I think about it, I do, too. It's strange to be called something I thought was so low only a few months ago.

Another word the locals use is *haole*, which I have found out means 'person without breath' in Hawaiian, or 'foreigner' in our way of translating. For most of the locals around here, 'haoles' are any white people from the mainland. They often put 'fucking' before the word to show how much hate they feel. When they get pissed off enough, some locals 'moke out' and beat people up or trash cars. I saw a few destroyed cars on the road when I first arrived, and now I know why.

'Haole' feels like the word 'nigger' that I heard driving through the South with Dad. I wish I could put that redneck cop we saw in Meridian here in front of the pool hall I always avoid on Front Street, to see how he would handle it. I try to dig what it might be like to be black in Mississippi, and I just shudder.

Here, I can see how the locals resent hippies if they don't work and are on welfare, mooching off everyone else. But most of the surfers I know aren't mooching. They work as waiters or busboys at night. Mike tells me tourism is going to take off on this island and it will start right here in Lahaina and Kaanapali.

Outside the legal ways of earning a living, some guys I've met grow the pot they call 'Maui Wowie.' When I smoke it, I'm saying 'wow' all the time as I forget the locals being pissed off and just feel the magic.

Summer is almost over, but I'm not thinking about that now. Mike and I are watching the movie "Endless Summer" in a theater full of pot smoke. Has every surfer who's dropped out from the world of bad vibes come to Maui?

The movie begins and two surfers travel the world searching for the perfect wave. Part of that search takes place in Hawaii at a few of the well-known spots like Banzai Pipeline on the island of Oahu. The crowd hoots and it feels great to be a part of this surfing tribe.

I'm looking at Mike, who's smiling and nodding his head. But with my brother, you can't always tell what that means.

I want to talk about the movie this morning, but Mike's holding out his open palm with a serene look on his face.

"Are those tabs of LSD?"

Mike nods like a philosopher.

"That stuff was intense when I took it with you in Aspen. Even when I got back to school I was thinking about what happened for weeks. Hearing certain songs lit up a lot of weird images from the past. Man, it was heavy. You taking it all the time now?"

"Whenever the call of self-discovery rings, I'm ready."

"Should I do it again?"

"You have to answer that question yourself."

"I've read some scary stuff about it."

"What stuff? The stuff I read was that Paul said all the Beatles have done acid."

I laugh.

"Good enough for me."

I put out my hand and Mike gives me the tab.

"Don't worry. No weird additives. The guy I scored it from was part of the experiments at UCLA. He got the pure shit."

"Experiments?"

"Yep. Like fuckin' lab rats."

We've come on to the acid and are out in the ocean off Lahaina. Mike and I are surfing waves that feel like flowing silk. My perception of time slows down and there are hours to jump to my feet when normally this part of catching a wave takes place in split seconds. There's a sense of being connected with the pulse of the ocean and we never wipe out. The warm Pacific embraces us while we wait for sets and soak in the sensations of colors. I scoop up two hands full of amoeba soup and pour it over my face.

"Life."

Mike reaches over and grabs some of the droplets that drip from my chin.

"Rivers of life."

He opens his hand and we see that it is empty. He's grinning.

"Water, time. No possession. They just flow."

Past and present are blending for me. Four years ago, Duke Grey was searching for his car keys and had just thrown Mike his 1962 bomb shelter handbook.

"We all gotta go sometime," Mikey had said when we were talking about the bomb.

I knew he was copying what I'd heard from the other surfers and decided if he was going to talk like them, I would, too.

"Correctamundo."

"So you're a surfer now?"

"Yeah, Mikey. I'm going to surf forever. I'll never be afraid of the end of the world."

We get out of the water and feel like the ocean has washed us clear of the overwhelming part of our hallucinations—until we get back to the house.

Entering the Animal Farm, Mike gives me a look.

"Let's split. Too much stoned theater. We need to go somewhere safe, without this scattered energy."

Driving doesn't seem safe, but the road is empty. It's a good thing because we're using both lanes. I can't read the road signs; only disjointed letters dance past. We're in the song "Magical Mystery Tour."

The car stops, way off the beaten track. I hope we can find our way home. There's nothing out here but red dirt and lava. Everything's magnetic. We gravitate from the car to the ocean. A blow-hole spits water up like a geyser from a lava tube connected to the surging power of the waves. Salt water rains over us and creates rainbows of hope. The serenity of this harsh landscape helps us shake off the rough edges of our childhood.

Mike tells me, "All that stuff that happened in the past, you gotta let go of it. You can't be pissed off at Dad. He's the result of his own exposure to a reality he couldn't handle. Leave the judgment behind, otherwise it'll keep you from being in the here and now."

An airplane flies overhead.

"We're about to take a special path in life and need to get our minds ready for that."

I nod and feel like I've already made the leap.

Mike starts talking about Jack and Bobby, the Kennedy brothers, and what a great bond they had. Kennedy? I'm scratching my head. I'd forgotten how much Mike was into JFK, but now I remember how upset he'd been when the president was shot. The assassination happened four years ago and I've put it out of my mind. Mike hasn't.

I don't know much about Bobby but it's not important. I like the feeling that we are brothers like those Kennedys and the fact that Mike is planning our future together.

The sun is dropping and somehow he finds our car.

We're driving, but where should we go? We decide we've come down enough from the peak intensity of the trip that we can handle returning to the house. Our plan is to dash into our room and close the door.

But we enter the house and there aren't a million clashing vibes anymore. A thick fog of pot smoke hangs in the air. Our roomates are huddled in front of the TV, watching news about Vietnam. The words and pictures immobilize Mike and me and we get sucked into watching. Looking around the room, I can see that I'm the only one who hasn't yet reached draft age. Everyone else is avoiding the military in some way; we are all one huddled mass of potential soldiers.

They're making comments. Though they're usually laid back about most things they talk about, the war—and being part of it—is personal, and right now they have well-defined opinions. Mike and I have watched the news many times with Dad, but we never felt brave enough back then to comment the way these surfers are doing now.

My acid-tainted perception of this broadcast and the type of warfare it shows clashes with my childhood vision of heroism and glory. Now, I only see psychedelic devastation. My path won't need to be decided for another year, but these guys in this room have made their decisions.

A reporter interviews a middle-aged man in the U.S. who's been kicked out of the priesthood for counseling kids against the draft. Someone points to the TV.

"Right on, that priest says this war is wrong. Even God is on our side."

I agree with these guys about making their own choices, but in the last few hours I've seen molecules move. I doubt God is concerned about anything humans are pursuing, much less picking sides. These stoners are talking like they know it all while they're zonked out of their gourds on pot. They often use the word 'righteous' in their rap sessions, but now they're self-righteous about their path and very critical of guys who are soldiers in Vietnam. I'm thinking about what Mike has just told me about judgment.

Shit, those guys who got drafted are just like what we could be. Our friend Duke was a surfer and now it looks like he could be shipped out. Yesterday Mom told us over the phone that he was at Camp Pendleton. We didn't think he'd really join the Marines, but he played it just the way his father told him to. The way I figure it, he got sucked down the drain.

But what can you do? Avoiding the draft is breaking the law, after all. I can see how a guy can make the decision to resist the draft for himself—but to be down on guys who don't resist just sounds hypocritical. These guys say 'unreal' about everything that is cool. But there's an unreality to their talking like this while we sit here safe and sound.

My feelings are sensitive on this acid trip. Even though I'm trying to shake off memories of my childhood, I know my military upbringing is a big part of who I am. I'm very confused.

Back in our room Mike and I watch the sunset. I could have spent hours trying to grok the big picture of my past, but right now my biggest concern is returning to the East Coast.

"Mike, I love it here. Man, summer is ripping by too fast."

"I can dig it. D.C. could be a million miles away from here."

"Shit."

"Bummer, huh?"

I nod.

"Bill, this is just a moment in time. Everything changes. Lahaina in this time and space is not the Maui Dad grew up on. I saw a brief vision of that Maui when I was in sixth grade here. It was so different than this, and now you've experienced what is more than just a little friction under the veneer of stoned surfers who roam West Maui. That friction won't go away. I don't know where I'm supposed to be, but it isn't here."

If Mike leaves, then my lifeline to Hawaii will vanish. The acid amplifies my fear.

I know Mike can feel my vibe but he's smiling.

"It doesn't mean this isn't good for you. I think it is. You're coming out of your shell and becoming a happy kid. I've told Mom you should finish up high school here. There's a good private school called Hawaii Prep over on the Big Island. If you went to public school, you would constantly be fighting. I think Mom's going for it. Dad has even begun to think about retiring on Maui. In a few weeks you'll be flying south to the Big Island."

As much as I had sunk in my emotions, I'm now soaring with this last revelation. Tears of joy roll down my face. The anxiety of returning to school on the East Coast has been keeping me up at night. I'm all set now, and it's all because of Mike.

"But what about you?"

"Remember that stock I bought? Mary Carter Paints. Just sold it for a killing. I'm flush and I'm hittin' the road, Bill."

I have to chuckle.

"You're always hitting it."

"This time I'm going a little farther than usual."

"Where?"

"I'll let you know when I get there."

He gives me a wild-eyed look.

"Edge City, man."

I'm scrunching my face with misunderstanding. Sometimes I wish he would just spit it out straight.

"Mike, it's not so bad here on Maui."

"Yeah, but it won't work for me. This has just been a first step."

"What'll you do?"

"Bill, things are starting to shake up all over and some people are getting involved politically trying to make changes for the better within the structure that exists. Others are taking off to more remote places in the country and the world. I'm with them. I'm disillusioned with the political process and see no hope in that path. Shit, I need to work on myself before I can tell anyone else what to do. I like the concept of gardening, eating right and setting an example by living in a non-violent way. My path will lead me to a power spot that works for me."

Mike has spoken to me before about power spots as described in his Carlos Castaneda books. It makes me feel good that I'm not the only one in our family thinking about a place to call home, or power spot.

"My idea of getting back to the land is the South Pacific. Mimi told me about her travels and I know I need to see the world for myself. I'm not going to spend my life jetting back and forth from Aspen to Lahaina like a hedonistic yo-yo—so I've bought a ticket to Tahiti, Fiji, New Zealand, Australia and who knows where after that."

"Wow, Mike. Far out."

"Yeah, very far out."

I grab *Moby Dick* off my bed and quickly turn to the first chapter.

"You know, I've been tripping out on this book since I've been here. Here it is, Ishmael in the first chapter, 'As for me, I am tormented with an everlasting itch for things remote. I love to sail forbidden seas, and land on barbarous coasts.'"

"So you think I'm Ishmael?"

"Nah. I just like that sentence. Your trip sounds more like *The Endless Summer*."

"Yeah, well, you never know."

"Doesn't sound like I'll be seeing you for a while."

"Soon enough, Bill. In the meantime, you'll have a great place to evolve here in Hawaii."

It's been a week since our acid trip and I'm wondering if what seemed to happen or what Mike said will really come true. My life has been filled

Mike Boyum, Lahaina, 1967

with plenty of expectations that have turned out to be false hopes. I've been subdued until today.

Mom just called and confirmed that Mike's been communicating with her about all this. Sure enough, Dad is going to retire on Maui, so having me finish high school in Hawaii makes sense in a logistical way, apart from my indescribable love of this place. I'm jumping out of my skin with joy.

I give Mike a huge hug as he boards a plane to the South Pacific, astonished by how light he's packed.

"Hey, Bill," he says, "keep writing those letters."

"I'll be in school. It'll be boring. You want to hear about my algebra?"

Mike gives my arm a push. "No, asshole, but something might happen you could tell me about. You never know."

Chapter Nine

Jet Stream
1967-1968

I've been at my new school on the Big Island of Hawaii for two months, but it's still a thrill every time they call out my name for having mail. The only letters I get are from Mike and it's been frustrating that he has no return address because, as he writes, "I'm island hopping..." One letter is from Tahiti and the next from Fiji. The pictures he sends of each place are breathtaking. Even though I've heard people talk about these places, seeing a picture makes each new paradise more real. Mike appears skinnier in each picture he sends.

Here's one from New Zealand—he says he'll be there a while. He's met a girl. They got together in Australia and are now at her home in Christchurch. The great thing is, he left me an address.

Mike's skin has an orange tint to it, apparently from the amount of carrot juice he consumes. But he has a great glow and seems to be on the right path, so I buy a juicer, along with a fifty-pound bag of organic carrots, and attempt to duplicate his diet in my room.

Many guys in this all-boys school have write-away girlfriends and tease me when I'm enthusiastically writing a letter to my brother. Sure, I wish I had a girlfriend, but I miss Mike. Where do I begin?

Hey Mike,

The vibe is so great here and our dress code is
shorts, t-shirts and flip-flops except on Sunday
chapel when we wear a coat, tie and hard shoes.
I'm really stoked to still be in Hawaii and constantly
remember that you were the one who set me up.
I only wish you were still nearby.

My roommate thinks I've been living here all my life.
I wish I had so I don't correct him. I don't feel like
explaining our life and this does feel like home now.

Things are pretty cool these days. Before you left, your outlook seemed so gloomy about living in the U.S., but there are many things happening this year that seem hopeful, even on the mainland. It looks to me like people are trying to change things for the better.

Next year is the election and my 18th birthday. The war looks like the biggest issue. For sure the draft is— for guys my age. All my friends talk about is the draft.

The hippies aren't the only ones protesting. The TV reports say that Gene McCarthy and Bobby Kennedy also want us to pull out of Vietnam. You know I never knew much about Bobby before, but lately I've been reading up. He's in the news all the time. But McCarthy is the one running for president—not Kennedy, even though many people want him to run. If he steps into the ring, he'll be a hopeful vision. I'm hoping he will. If either of these men becomes president, then my decision will already be made about Vietnam. I bet you would want Bobby to be president. Maybe you left too soon.

Bill

It's taken two months to hear back from him.

Bill,

Hey, you dummy. You think you know it all just because you devour Newsweek? We get all the news magazines here, plus I hear about things you'll never read in those American mags. I know what's happening and know all those peace candidates don't have a prayer. Kennedy is the only guy who can take Nixon and, like you said, he ain't running.

Mom gave me Duke's address in Vietnam. He's in some shitass base called Khe Sanh. I wrote him and told him to keep his head low.

Hey, got you set up with my pals to stay with them in Aspen during your Christmas vacation. Maybe you could go to college somewhere in Colorado? Catch you on the rebound.

Mike

I'm back from my ski trip to Aspen. It's time to report.

Mike,

It's so cool you set me up to go skiing again. Had a blast. College in Colorado? Sounds great. Pretty sure the Naval Academy is off my list. Colorado kind of looks like where you are in New Zealand. Hope the girls are as pretty as the one you're with.

Man, it's a new year. Hope this one is as good as '67. Can't believe the year started and ended in Aspen with Montreal, San Francisco and Lahaina in between. All those adventures were because of you. What can I say? You even put the idea in Mom's head for me to go to school here. Right now I'm taking in a spectacular view of snow on top of two 13,000 peaks. This place is far out. I love it, even when we have this cold driving rain. It's like winter on the mainland but I know the warm beach is only 3,000 feet of elevation below me.

Up here I can get warm by the fire in the common room. Right now I'm watching the news about the battle of Khe Sanh and the Tet Offensive. They say public support for the war is dropping fast. A large transport plane is doing a touch-and-go at the tiny airstrip of Khe Sanh while hooking and dragging out a shipment of supplies from the rear hatch. Then the behemoth plane lifts off immediately as mortar rounds explode around it. I'm thinking about Duke, the meanest hot-dogger in Coronado. The report is comparing this battle to Dien Bien Phu, where the French were wiped out to a man. That's so heavy. It seems that something big is happening every week over there. I think about Duke and feel like I'm

cheering for the main character in a movie, only
that's not what he is. He's your best pal.

Bill

Here's a postcard of a beautiful sailboat keeled over in a strong wind.
The caption reads, Wonderful Auckland.

Bill,

On the move again. Didn't work out with the girl. I'll
post you when I land... somewhere.

Another postcard from Mike shows a smiling Asian woman with rotten
teeth balancing a large basket on top of her head.

I'm sleeping under a gazebo right on the beach of this
quiet fishing village of Kuta Beach, Bali. The white
sand is empty and stretches for as far as I can see.
Coconut juice every day and body surfing in the crystal-clear water of the Indian Ocean.

Vietnam ain't no joke. Keep up the good work in school.

Write me at Poste Restante, Bali.

Cheers,

Mike

Bali? Even the name sounds like paradise to me. The way Mike
writes about empty beaches, it seems like it is. Is it Bali Hai from
the "South Pacific" musical?

Hey, Mike,

Man, you just go from one beautiful spot to another.
I had to look Bali up in the atlas. Indonesia? Wow.
No one has even heard of it here.

So radical that King got shot. Can you believe that
shit? But Bobby is running now and LBJ isn't. I

think things might turn out OK. I know I can get behind Kennedy. A few days ago I saw Bobby give a moving speech on TV about King. I was thinking about the word 'charisma' that Mimi taught me after she saw JFK speak when she was at San Diego State. I have a better idea what the word means now and Bobby has it. From what I read, I'm not the only one who thinks so. I know JFK meant something to you and I'm beginning to feel the same way about Bobby.

Pretty sure my SATs will be good enough to get into college. This last year has been solid honor roll for me. Can you believe it? English lit is my favorite. You know how "Moby Dick" has been my favorite story. Turns out it's an American classic. All the stories from Papa Bace's old library are classics. I even re-read "Treasure Island". Remember that one?

I also read Robert Louis Stevenson's "The Strange Case of Dr. Jekyll and Mr. Hyde." A wild guy made up of opposing emotions and desires—some good and some evil. What a tale. It's the story of our life, don't you think? There's the ugly and violent Mr. Hyde and his weird link to the respectable Dr. Jekyll. Jekyll created a drug that separated his good and evil natures—purifying the doctor himself but with the frightening side effects of periods spent as the monstrous Hyde. Don't you think it's just like the whistling, finger-snapping, swing-dancing Maui boy who is Dad versus his clench-jawed Captain Bligh? The last time I was home I called something trippy while I was talking to Mom. Dad overheard me and yelled at me that I didn't have the right to corrupt the English language at my pleasure while I lived under his roof. Don't mean to get so heavy but man, just a crummy word and he flips out. What are you doing now?

Bill

I just spent the time after my last class reading the letter I got from Mikey. Now I'm dashing to my dorm common room for our headmaster's lecture. A cold wind is driving horizontal rain across the campus, and it's going to feel really cozy sitting around the fireplace. I'm the last one in. Our headmaster is giving us his Horatio Alger speech that's intended to inspire us. He must have been in the theater when he was young. Right now he's acting out each motivational explosion.

"Wipe the muck out of your eyes!"

His hands swipe away make-believe muck from what look like the eyes of a madman.

"Pull yourself up by your bootstraps!"

He almost falls over grabbing those imaginary bootstraps.

"Hitch your wagon to a star."

The boys up front wish he would hitch his lips to a bottle of mouthwash.

The headmaster's act is always the same and I'm tuning out... the warmth of the fire pulls me back to Mikey's letter.

Bill,

What kind of drugs are they feeding you there? That's some weird shit. Maybe true, but weird. Forget about Dad. You're out of the house now. Think happy thoughts.

I'm grooving and traveling. I've started a rock-and-roll group that we call The Prophesy. Cool, huh? Prophets have a special place in Islamic culture and I'm now on the Islamic island of Java. Rock-and-roll is even taking this part of the world by storm. In Bali I got high with a wild bunch of out-of-work musicians from all over the world and figured it was Indonesia's turn. Flew to Singapore and invested in musical equipment. Our rock group rented a huge house in a beautiful high-elevation town in West Java called Bandung. We've been touring throughout all the Indonesian Islands, putting on rock concerts that are wildly successful. Dig this—my new nom de guerre:

Jet Streeeeeaaammm

Wow, I remember the last time he wrote, he was living a self-described monk-like existence on pristine Kuta Beach. That's Mike for you, hard to pin down. Prophets, Java, rock-and-roll... The fireplace is so warm and my eyelids fall shut.

"Mr. Boyum! Wake up!"

~

Bobby Kennedy was shot today.

Everyone is walking around school in comatose-like shock. Summer vacation is still a few days off, but we are already disconnecting from school. Dinner is eggplant Parmesan, which I normally scarf, but tonight it just looks like a sour-smelling pile of goop. All my senses have shut down.

I study the two summits of Mauna Kea and Mauna Loa, which are covered in a volcanic haze, a sign of at least a minor eruption.

One of the underclassmen with affection for Hawaiian mythology says, "The volcano goddess Pele must be angry."

Hey, Jet,

I feel like crap. Guess you know what happened. Shit, Mike, all the hope leading up to Bobby's assassination made me want to prove you wrong. Now I'm not so sure. Just before you left, I remember your words about how futile political change was. Was that a lucky guess? The name of your rock group—Prophesy—wow, it seems perfect now. So far your predictions have been right on. Unfortunately.

I'm going back to Maui for the summer. Now that Dad's retired they've bought a house in Kula. Finally we have a real home on Maui. Hope I have as much fun as I did last summer with you. Too bad you won't be there. Can't wait to see you again.

Bill

I receive a postcard from Mike. The caption reads, 'Have a smokin' good time.' There's a picture of a tribal man with a large turban smoking something from a long pipe. It puzzles me that the stamp is from Karachi, Pakistan.

On the back Mike writes:

Mail is slow and I'm moving fast. Post me at my

Bandung address.

Jet

I don't understand but am glad he's written.

Hey, Jet,

Karachi? It's nowhere near Java or Bali. Hope this gets to you. I'm in Kula for the summer at the new house. Dad looks like he's pretty excited to be back

on Maui. I hope he can mellow out in retirement and show me some of the good vibes we shared crossing the country together four years ago. Maybe we can both put the rough times behind us.

Today I went with them to buy tomatoes at the Omura's farm and hot Gregullo's bread from the Portuguese baker by the Morihara store in Kula. Mom makes jam from the strawberry guavas in our yard and Dad and I dive into yanking weeds. It's like 'Green Acres' on TV.

I got my driver's license a week ago and when I finish my chores Dad lets me use the car to go down to the beach. I think without the stress of Dad's work everything is going to be copacetic.

Bill

No word from Mike but I know he's out there, somewhere. I don't need to wait before I write again. There's too much on my mind.

Hey, Jet,

Dad's childhood friend, Wilson Cannon, is now president of the Bank of Hawaii. He offered him a job. But Dad isn't a banker and he knows it. I don't think there is much he knows how to do in the work world. But only a month back on Maui he got re-commissioned as a Commodore for the fleet to carry out maneuvers around Kahoolawe. I thought he was here to retire???

At the beach I was talking story with some Hawaiian surfers who were going on about how the Hawaiians have been looked down on for years and now it's time to assert their pride and culture. The rallying cry of their cause is the bombing of the same island that Dad's in charge of blowing up. The bombs are destroying ancient archeological sites and Hawaiian heritage with it. They want the Navy outta there.

Sounded cool to me and I want to be friends with these guys, but I felt horrible since Dad is the bomber. The Navy has used his local boy status as a public relations maneuver—as if he would be sensitive to local issues. But we all know he isn't a local boy anymore. He's still a Navy guy, and sensitivity???

I'm sure not pounding my chest about what Dad does for a living. He just told me I need to get a job. Trying to find a place to stay in Lahaina.

Bill

Summer vacation is almost over.

Hey, Jet,

Summer has been a bummer. Didn't find a place to rent in Lahaina. Didn't get to take chicks for catamaran rides like I'd imagined. Only job I could find was picking pineapples. Not cool, no girls, no fun.

I was the only haole in a work gang of eleven hitched to a conveyor belt swung across the row of fruit, walking with my head down, picking as fast as I could. A Portagee Luna followed behind me, barking in heavy pidgin. "You one dumbass haole. Dis one no ripe. You stink, buggah." It was a full-on downer and got worse.

Last night at the end of the shift I got in a fight with a short Japanese kid who was kicking dents in Dad's car. Knew I would get it from Dad so I jumped on the kid and we got into it. The rest of the gang circled around and began kicking me hard everywhere—ribs, face and especially teeth. Every kick and punch they shouted, "fuckin' haole." One tooth was knocked clean out—those work boots have steel toes in them. The rest of my teeth were floating like jelly in my mouth. They beat the shit out of me.

I was stoked about being branded a 'Maui boy,' but the fact is that for me the term only applies at my mostly haole school. Here on Maui outside the protection of school or family it doesn't matter what

I'm called—I'm white. I talked to Dad after I got beat up. He told me, "I never had any trouble like that growing up here. What did you do to provoke them?"

Pissed me off. When he first got back here, I thought he had changed, but he's still the same Dad we always knew. I don't know why he got along OK growing up and I can't get along—but I know I'm not the only one. Can't wait to go back to school and escape his bummers.

Bill

Mike hasn't written back and I'm growing impatient to get news from him. Dad answers the phone and then slams it back onto the cradle.

"Can you believe the nerve? A collect call from a wrong number in a foreign country."

When he leaves the living room, I grab the moment.

"A phone call, Mom? That's what pisses him off?"

"Oh, someone is always calling about voting for their candidate and it peeves your father to no end."

That night, I sleep out in the living room where the phone is. It rings and I answer it quickly so it doesn't wake Dad up.

The overseas operator speaks in a strange accent.

"You have a collect call from a Mr. Jet, do you accept the charges?"

"Uh, yes."

"Hey, Mike. How come you never write?"

"Hey, maann, don't bring me down."

It's Mike and he's obviously stoned. But it's still great just to hear his voice. He tells me about some of the interesting islands he's been to on his band's concert tour.

"You wouldn't believe Ambon, Bill. It's right out of a Conrad novel. It has a conical volcano surrounded by jungle. And spices."

"Spices?"

"Yeah, man, all kinds."

He chuckles.

His good humor is contagious and we're laughing on the phone until I ask if he got my letter about Bobby Kennedy.

"I just got all your letters. Been on the road. But yeah, that stuff is depressing. Bill, Indonesia is the fifth most-populated country in the world, but nobody gets killed with guns unless there is some kind of war. They have absolute gun control. Sad shit about Bobby."

Even though the subject is sad, it's just good to hear from him. But now Mike is mumbling some stuff I can't decipher and I wonder what's going on. Is this what he meant by Edge City?

The connection is lost.

Finally, a letter from Mike:

> Bill,
>
> Sorry I was so loaded when we talked. I know there are serious things on your mind and life with Dad is still what it is. Think of it this way, that chapter of your life is almost over. But watch out. The next thing you know you'll have politicians lining up to rope you into the war. Bobby's assassination was only the beginning. This shit won't stop. You should figure out what's happening for you. You need to decide who you are, what side you're on and what you will fight for. You think the government is watching out for you? Like I've always told you, I don't think there's much hope in the U.S. The good news is I'm getting things together over here and it's fan-tastic. You'll see soon enough.
>
> Jet

I don't wait to write back.

Hey, Jet,

You sure got that right. Man, things are heating up. I was stoked to get back to school early to train in a three-week pre-season football camp. During camp our regimen after practice was simple—eat, sleep and read comic books. The coach said no TV, which didn't matter to anyone, even me the news hound.

Now that classes have started I just got to watch the tube for the first time. It's been sooo heavy. Mike, you wouldn't believe what's happened in Chicago. Barbed-wire barriers, heads being bashed, tear gas exploding, demonstrators throwing rocks and police charging into them. All the good guys got bumped off this year. Man, what's happening? Well, next year I'll be in college and have my deferment. I think it's going to be Nixon in November.

Bill

The national election returns are on TV. I'm using my pen like an ice pick and have had to restart this letter a few times.

Hey, Jet,

Fuckin' Nixon, just like I thought. Humphrey was so close. Only half a million vote difference. Maybe if all the pissed-off college kids had voted, it might have been different. But you know what? I don't care about politics and thinking I can change things. You were right on about all this crap, even before King, Bobby and that whole deal in Chicago. I'm so god damn numb. Mom just told me Duke got killed at Khe Sanh. Sorry to give you such bad news. Where are you? Please write.

Bill

As I mail the letter, so many questions keep running through my mind. This is my last year of high school. Then what? On one hand there is the safe path of going to college. Without a deferment, I'd be going into the military. On the other hand is my brother's adventurous life on exotic islands. Wasn't his last letter asking me to join him? But he hasn't written in a while. Is plugging into his life an unrealistic fantasy? If I join him, how would we carve our way in the world?

Chapter Ten

The Gun
1968-1969

Christmas vacation. Mom just picked me up at the Kahului airport. What she's telling me is making me squirm as we drive up the slope of Haleakala.

"I don't know what's wrong. Your Dad just seems so distant."

"Yeah," I say, "I noticed the same thing during Father's Day weekend. When I told him I thought Navy would win the Army-Navy game, he just said, 'Oh.' And when you guys left, he shook my hand as if I were a politician, and we all know how he feels about those guys. How long has he been this way?"

"Since he finished with the Navy exercises off Kahoolawe. He gets so mad at me when I do the littlest thing that isn't his standard operating

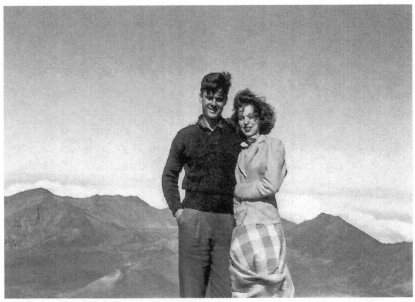

Mom and Dad, Haleakala Summit, August 1945

procedure. Sometimes he looks like he wants to hit me. When I start crying, he drops into this awful silence."

"You know he loves you, Mom. Didn't you tell me you were his cheesecake shot on his ship locker door?"

"Did I show you that picture?"

"No."

"Well, everytime he was on leave during the war we would go to Sandy Beach. Oh, it was so wonderful, Billy. He could bodysurf all day long. It always revitalized him."

Mom glances at me with tears in her eyes.

"You know, he was so nice then, Billy."

"Sure, Mom, you've always told me that."

"I just don't know what to do."

"It'll be all right. Let me talk to him."

Maybe those words will make her happy for a moment, but I know it's probably ridiculous to hope I could ever change Dad's mood.

We pull into our driveway and it does feel great to be home. I enter the house and shake Dad's hand energetically. I'm going to at least try to make this a cheery Christmas.

"Hey, Dad, you finally picked a winner."

I know he voted for Tricky Dick for the second time, even though Humphrey is from Minnesota, the Boyum family landing point into America from Norway.

"It's not a lottery, Bill."

I glance at Mom, wondering what to say next. Maybe my news will make him smile.

"I've been accepted at CSU."

"Oh? Who's paying for it?"

Jeez, there he goes into that same old inquisition mode.

Mom pipes in, "We are—I mean, I am. Of course."

I stare at Dad, baffled. Doesn't he want me to go to college? Why is the money thing such a big deal?

He's glaring at Mom.

"So you didn't feel the need to talk about this with me?"

Mom turns on the water works.

Dad stares back at me. I can hear Mom crying, but feel defiant enough not to look away from him the way I've always done before. This moment lingers for a few seconds and I expect him to yell at me, but instead he storms off to their bedroom.

Last summer it became obvious Mom and Dad's retirement wasn't going to be like 'Green Acres,' but this is worse than I ever imagined. And my initial attempts at connecting are just making things more tense.

"Mom, what's going on? Don't you two talk to each other?"

Each of her sentences is punctuated with a sob.

"I'm afraid to talk to him. He just explodes. So I do everything behind his back. You know, it's my money, Billy. My parents gave it to me."

"Talk a little softer, Mom." I point in the direction of their bedroom and whisper, "I thought he would eventually loosen up."

Mom calms down a bit without Dad around, but is still crying.

"All he knows is how to be a Naval Officer."

I hug her but she looks away vacantly.

"Billy, I keep thinking about the last year of the war, when he was flying into combat from his aircraft carrier."

I interrupt, "He told me once about flying back to the Wasp by the

Jacqueline M. Boyum (Jackie), Sandy Beach, Oahu, 1942

stars, but that's it."

"I thought he told you all about it."

She waves her hand in the air to show it's no big deal.

"Which battles was Dad in?"

"Every little pile of sand they captured, he was there."

I realize it's going to be impossible to get detailed information from her and let her continue on to make her original point.

"During the last year of the war, he'd been fighting for over a year and was finally given shore leave in San Diego. When his leave was over, he went back to the Pacific on the Intrepid. It was anchored off Kahului when they came here to practice touch-and-goes with their newer planes before they went off to fight the Japanese again."

"Mom, where were you back then?"

"Oh, I was here, too, though I wasn't allowed much time with him. Then right before he was supposed to ship out again for the western Pacific, they dropped the atomic bomb and the war ended."

"You were here with Dad when the war ended?"

I'm stunned and try to imagine it.

She smiles at me with teary bright eyes.

"Yes. We drove up to the top of Haleakala and gazed down at the whole island. It was such a happy moment."

Mom slips into the past.

"Back then I didn't know he would make the Navy a career. He was home where he had grown up, and I thought we might live on Maui. You know, many other pilots retired after the war. They'd had enough, but your father was different. He wanted to fly jets."

"Well, you're here now."

"Yes, but it's different. It's different here now, and he's different."

She wipes tears off her face with the back of her hand.

"Let me show you a picture of us on top of the volcano."

"Mom, don't bug him."

She waves me off.

"It's just a picture. He'll be OK." She cracks open the door to their bedroom and checks for Dad. I follow her and see he isn't there. He must have gone out back through their room's sliding glass door. We enter and she starts rummaging through her closet to find the picture.

My eyes dart around the bedroom to examine their current life. There is little to focus on. It appears Dad has finally had his way about clutter and his coins are still stacked neatly on top of his dresser. That's why my eyes land on the open cherry wood case on their dresser. I haven't seen it for eight years. A memory floods of placing the WWI pearl-handled .45 carefully back in that same case, closing and locking its lid, and returning the key to where it had been hidden in my grandparents' house. That moment seems so far away. I walk over, slide my fingers over the smooth felt that lines the box and think of my grandfather.

Mom emerges from the closet, excited to have found a memento of happier times.

"Here it is."

I leave the case and join her to check out the picture of her and Dad on top of the ten thousand-foot summit of Haleakala. Dad has his arm around her, dashing in a thick-collared sweater. He's twenty-six and his dark hair is long enough to part. I laugh at myself for presuming he'd always worn his hair in a flat top. Without his signature haircut I can barely recognize him, but his smile is unmistakable. Here is the real Smilin' Jack. Mom looks cold but very much in love as she hugs Dad tightly.

"Mom, you look so fantastic and Dad looks... happy."

"He was happy. Happy the war was over. He'd had many Japanese friends here on Maui when he was growing up. The war was difficult for him."

I try to imagine Dad battling with his emotions and just shake my head. There's no sense arguing with Mom about that right now. Her tears are drying up and I don't want to upset her.

My focus shifts back to the gun case.

"So who inherited Papa Bace's .45? I just noticed the case."

Mom's eyes shift to where I've pointed at the dresser and freeze at sight of the open case.

She screams, "Oh my God, Jack!"

My mind digests the enormity of the open case. Somehow when I first saw it, I couldn't allow for the possibility that the gun had gone along with it. There are many little boxes and cases my parents own for memorabilia that don't contain their original contents.

Mom's frantic.

"Where is he, Billy?"

I race to each empty room in the house. My heart pounds out ticks on a clock that has an unacceptable alarm.

"Billy, you have to go find him, quick!"

He isn't in the house and I'm panicking—but at the same time angry.

"That gun, that fucking gun. Why did you keep it?"

I accentuate the word 'you' because it could have easily gone to her brother or sister.

Holy crap. I never told anyone about my brother's suicide attempt. Mikey swore me to that secret. A wave of guilt breaks over me.

"We thought it would be good to have for protection."

The stupidity of it pisses me off.

"You can't hit anything with that gun unless you're ten feet away. It's only good for..."

Mom is already melting and I don't need to finish the sentence to state the obvious. This is no time to lay blame.

A strong pulse throbs in my temples and sound begins to muffle. I go catatonic for a moment and attempt to connect with a sensory perception that I've only experienced on LSD. This feels like a trip—everything that's happened since I first walked in the door has blown my mind. The intensity of the natural elements draws my vision out the window to a view of the crater behind the house. It's sunset and all the clouds on the mountain have cleared. Cinder above the treeline glows brilliant rust red.

It's obvious now that he must have left the house through their bedroom door. My eyes follow to our immediate backyard, which Dad and I had worked to clear the summer before. The tall cane grass beyond our property moves slightly against the windless sunset.

I point to the movement and turn towards Mom.

"Let me try this alone."

I charge out the back door but then enter the cane gently, remembering the enormous hole the .45 put in the tree Mikey hit at Sans Souci in 1960.

"Dad?" I whisper.

There's some moaning just ahead. I part the cane and stand above him. He's in a fetal position. My eyes land on the pearl-handled gun. That god-damn gun. Dad presses and turns the barrel into his temple as though it's a key that won't fit.

I wonder for a brief moment if he thinks he can anticipate the explosion by pressing it so hard. Why had General 'Black Jack' Pershing given the gun to Papa Bace in WWI? It's weird having these disjointed thoughts. I shove them from my mind; I need to focus immediately. Is the man I've feared the most throughout my life on the edge of suicide?

Dad finally lifts his eyes from the gun towards me. Tears roll down his face.

But he surprises me by suddenly turning defiant.

"When you came in the door, you were staring at me like you are now, just like your brother stared at me when he was your age. You wanted to hit me, didn't you?"

Jesus, there is a huge gap in his perception of what he thinks I'm thinking and what I'm actually thinking. I'd forgotten about that show-down between my brother and him about four years ago. This is a dangerous situation and I'm flying by the seat of my pants.

I drop to my knees next to him and cry, "I didn't want to hit you. I love you, Dad."

It seems like the only place to begin. I can't remember any time I've said 'I love you' to my father growing up and if I did, it was probably out of fear. I don't remember him saying it, either. But instead of comforting him, my words release what I can only imagine is a lifetime of grief. Red slashes of setting sunlight slice through the cane grass to reveal the anguish on Dad's face. My own face must reflect extreme panic because he turns away from me, curling onto his side, his face in the dirt, moaning. Standing over him, I see his khaki dungarees and torn t-shirt. His bare feet remind me of all the starched uniforms and spit-polished shoes I've seen him wear throughout his life. I love this grubby look and remember my grandfather, Papa Bace, another naval officer with a casual side. But right now these tattered clothes are a symbol of Dad's breakdown.

I lay my hand lightly on his shoulder and curl up beside him.

His emotions erupt with choking sounds for what seems like an eternity. His sweat stinks. I smelled it last summer when I was working with him, but this time it smells sour.

As the sky darkens his sounds subside.

I spot a star and squeeze his shoulder.

"Dad?"

His head lifts from the ground but he's searching for a focal point, like a drunk. The gun wanders dangerously in his free hand.

"Can you put that gun down for a second and talk to me?"

He turns towards me, but his eyes are still unfocused. He hasn't loosened his grip.

My dad. There are parts of him that I admire to such an incredible degree. Mom has just revealed a little more about his past to me, the depth of which I hadn't known. What an unacceptable time to lose him. There is so much more I need to learn. Maybe we could turn our lousy connection around?

Where can I start? Football and politics have already been exposed as points of zero interest. He has never expressed his feelings to me. Why should I expect him to start now? What does he love more than any-thing? Mom, of course, but right now that is obviously a sore spot.

I twitch when I feel some unknown bug wiggle against my skin. We both saw gigantic centipedes crawling around in this cane prison last summer, silver-colored ones that had a ton more wallop in their sting than the common brown ones. I've been bitten by them before and it hurts like hell. We would never curl up in this dirt without the greater threat of the .45 hanging over us.

The sharp edges of the cane grass cut into my skin as I try to get comfortable. I'm grasping for something to say as I huddle with Dad and his sweat. Will the darkness again bring the comfort I've seen this former night fighter pilot enjoy? The sunset has been replaced by an intense full moon. I go with what I have.

"Look at that moon. I can't believe they have a moon mission planned for next summer."

Changing the subject from this grimy field to the heavens might be the right move.

Dad mumbles, "Test pilots."

Even though I can tell he's not ready to talk, my tension relaxes a notch. He belongs to a close fraternity of aviator pioneers… but I want him to belong to me.

His head drops back to the ground and his arm is outstretched. Moonlight is reflecting off the gun.

There were sunsets and early evenings when I was a kid where my designated job was to barbecue the steak for our dinner. Dad would always check up on me to make sure I wasn't overcooking the meat.

"See the skin between your thumb and forefinger?" he'd say. "If you push on the meat and it feels like the texture of the skin when the thumb and finger are together, it's still too rare. If it feels like the skin when the thumb and finger are wide apart, it's overdone. So right in the middle is where we want it."

Those were special moments; it felt good to have him teach me, even when he was repeating the same drill every time. I wished he could have trusted me to remember but he always worried I'd forget. He'd take a moment to smile up at the stars as if he were saying hello to a friend. One night Dad was especially relaxed and I was hoping he would stay and talk with me longer. But he told me he forgot his beer and went back inside the house.

Now Dad's forearm is exposed and when I touch it, it feels like overdone steak. His grip on the gun must still be strong.

He's not moaning anymore, but he didn't bite on my moon mission hook. Maybe it's better to just lie here in silence.

My mind drifts to another night of fear from when Dad and I crossed the country in 1964. We were driving in Mississippi near the Naval Base named after Admiral McCain and Dad was telling me about the night the Admiral allowed him to land on the Wasp with enemy traffic in the area. "I only had twenty gallons left in my tank," he'd said, "fumes for a two thousand-horsepower engine."

Again I try to imagine what landing in the ocean at night would have been like if Dad had run out of gas.

"Twenty gallons."

I didn't mean for my inner thoughts to become vocal.

A few minutes later Dad stirs.

"Twenty gallons?"

At this point, any words from Dad are a sign of life.

"You only had twenty gallons in your tank, Dad, almost fumes. Admiral McCain saved your life."

He rolls slowly onto one knee, still clutching the gun.

"You remember that?"

"Of course I do. I remember that and all the great times we had on our trip across the country."

He brings his other knee to join the first and I can see his teeth again in the moonlight.

"Yes. I also remember."

He drops the gun and grabs my forearm. There's force in his grip for only a moment before he lets go.

I carefully slide the gun away.

It's getting late, with cold mountain air descending on us from Haleakala's summit. I shiver from many things.

"I'm going to take this inside the house, Dad. Why don't you take some time? Stay out here as long as you want."

I get up to leave.

"Bill, one more thing. I love you, too."

When I enter the house I find Mom drinking. She breathes a sigh of relief when she notices the gun in my hand and slurs her words.

"Is he all right?"

"Yes, Mom. He's fine. Why don't you go to bed? He'll be in when he's ready."

In the morning while drinking his coffee Dad tells me, "I want to show you something."

This is a good sign.

We drive along Holumua Road above Hookipa Surfing Park. The road leads up to where Dad went to Maui High. The school is out for Christmas break so we have the grounds to ourselves. Dad's prepared for the chilly December air, stepping out of the car wearing his leather flight jacket which still has his insignia sewn on. I sit with him on the front steps of the school and try to imagine this stern man as a high school student like me. We admire a line of towering royal palms that grace the entrance.

"Those palms were planted when I was in school here. I have many fond memories of this place, especially the debates."

"You debated?"

"Yes."

That doesn't surprise me. He's always had a way with words.

"Did you have any nicknames?"

"My classmates used to call me The Admiral after I got accepted at Annapolis." He frowns. "If I were an Admiral today, I'd still be in Foggy Bottom, listening to moron politicians."

"You liked the Navy better when you began flying, didn't you?"

"Yes, I did."

"How did you get the flying bug, Dad?"

"I don't know exactly, Bill, but a PBY seaplane landed here on Maui to refuel on its way to Canton, China for a mail run in 1936. We thought that was extraordinary and dedicated our senior yearbook to that Pan Am Clipper."

"So that was the first plane you ever saw?"

"No. My mother had gone to California when I was nine to grab my brother Sevath by the ear and bring him back to Maui. He was twenty-five and she was adamant that he needed to wake up to his responsibilities, stop doing foolish things and get to work."

"What was he doing in California?"

I think I detect a glint in his eyes.

"Flying airplanes. Sevath caught flight fever in the wake of Lindberg's success that year with his Atlantic crossing. We all thought that was pretty special. Sevath's argument was that Lucky Lindy was from Minnesota so it followed that flying was part of his Scandinavian heritage. That logic fell on deaf ears."

I almost crack a smile about flying being called foolish.

"But Sevath brought a WWI Curtiss Jennie back to Maui. He started barnstorming at the old Puunene airstrip."

I can't contain my enthusiasm.

"Did you get to see it?"

"Yes, in fact, without our parents' knowledge, he took me up for a ride."

He smiles for the first time since we've been talking.

"Sevath was taking people on short flights around the island to make a little money. He was a pretty good pilot."

"When you were in high school, did you think you might become a pilot?"

"No. My inspiration to go to Annapolis came from ships. Ships brought everything to Maui in those days. If your vision took you to a broader horizon then, it was a ship that took you there. Sevath and I rode

John Hoag Boyum (Jack), Maui High School, 1933

horses up to the top of Haleakala in 1935 and were able to view across the channel to the Big Island. We witnessed seven lines of lava flowing down from the top of Mauna Loa. It was stunning and made me wonder what other horizons were waiting for me."

I can only imagine that he saw ship captains as the astronauts of that era. Last night, when we were huddled in the cane grass on the brink of I-hate-to-think-what, I gazed up at the silhouette of the mountain above us. It was glowing in the moonlight. I can easily imagine now the magic of the lava flows Dad saw on that night with his brother in 1935.

He pauses and exhales deeply.

"Educational opportunities were limited for high school graduates on Maui. I had no idea that war was only six years away."

Is this the sore spot about my college expenses? He went to a free school, where a candidate was actually paid to begin his service. I'd better stick to the conversation about ships and flight.

"Did you see airplanes at the Academy?"

"No. Aviation at that time was a string of disasters. In the spring of 1937 we heard about the Hindenburg blowing up in nearby New Jersey. The Navy's opinion was that aviation was an unproven asset, at least for Naval operations."

"What happened after you graduated?"

"I graduated in June 1940 and by the fall we were listening intently to war broadcasts from London. The war in Europe had just begun and we

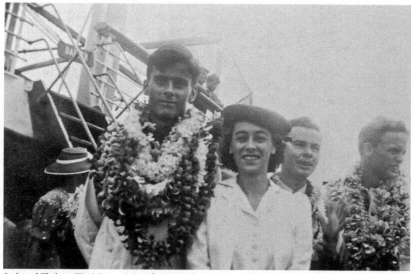

Jack and Thelma (Tita) Boyum, Frank Foss, Wilson Cannon, USS Lurline, 1936

wondered if it would spill over in our direction. We didn't know what the Japanese were up to. British fighter planes were on front stage and some reporters wrote that if the Nazis weren't stopped in England, they would be at our doorstep next. That got our attention."

Wow, my first thought is that Dad might have fantasized in the same way I had when I read about air combat in the Battle of Britain. The difference is that the battle was happening in real time when he heard those broadcasts, rather than in past history.

"Your attention?"

"For war, yes, but flying came later. My first sea duty was on the heavy cruiser Northampton, which was assigned to the battle group with the carrier Enterprise. In late November 1941 the Enterprise was sent to Wake Island to deliver planes. Our task force was scheduled to return to Pearl Harbor on December 6th."

"I think I've heard this part of the story, where you met Mom for the second time."

"Yes. Admiral Halsey knew about increasing tensions with Japan and already considered his fleet on war status, but junior officers like me were just looking forward to the start of another great weekend... girls at the beach and those wonderful falls behind Manoa. It all started going to hell on the return trip from Wake. The weather was rough and we got tossed around. That turned out to be the same storm that hid the Japanese fleet. Then, to further slow us down, some sea garbage fouled our props. Our battle group was 152 miles west when the Japanese assault began on December 7th, too far away for me to locate them from my post in the radar room. Some of our spotter planes saw the fleet after the attack, but by then the Japanese were already pulling away. In any case, we were no match for their fleet and there was no effort to pursue. We pulled into Pearl on the 8th. We found complete devastation where all the heavy cruisers had been berthed. They all were sunk and the majority of their crews lost. It was evident to us that the Japanese had revealed the true power of a carrier task force."

Holy mackerel, these are some heavy details I've never heard before.

"And what happened to you next?"

"In late May we were about to be deployed again. I proposed to your mother the night she graduated from Punahou. In early June, we were still part of the same task force group attached to the Enterprise, off Midway. Remember you saw the Battle of Midway on 'Navy Log' when you were a kid?"

162 / JOURNALS FROM THE EDGE

Despite the fact that I didn't think he ever paid non-violent attention to me growing up, Dad had been watching me watch 'Navy Log' without my knowledge. This brings up a whole different line of questions for me. But for now I'll stick to the war. He's talking to me, which is much better than last night. The war seems to be working.

"Yes, sir, and you were there?"

"I was. It was a spectacular display of naval aviation. We didn't know then that it was the turning point of the war. For what turned out to be a major victory, things went to hell in the beginning. Many of our pilots were lost in the initial engagements. It was incredible, Bill, there were so many planes in the air. My station in the radar room gave me a detailed account of all the air groups in action. We had to be on alert for a Japanese counter-attack. They came, but they concentrated their fire on our carriers. The Northampton was spared any major damage. But the writing was clearly on the wall—it was going to be a carrier war."

"And those carriers needed pilots, didn't they, Dad?"

"Yes. There was a big call-up for flight school. This was the point of no return for me. I was going to be a pilot, no question about it. The British had given us their secret technology called radar and I'd been involved with our first use of it on the Northampton. This is where I received my background for the night fighting program that I later entered. After Midway, I went back to the States to learn how to fly."

"What happened to the Northampton?"

His voice chokes up.

"I was fortunate a second time; the Northampton was sunk a few months later off Guadalcanal. It was in a large surface fleet battle and took two torpedo hits."

Maybe I'd better be careful; there are so many painful pitfalls for Dad. "That's when you learned to fly?"

His voice elevates, "Yes. At Pensacola. I got my wings in the spring of 1943. During all of 1944 and '45 I flew combat operations on the Wasp as squadron leader of the Night Fighters. The Night Fighters reported directly to Admiral McCain. You know his grandson was shot down over North Vietnam two years ago. He's a prisoner of war."

Resurfacing the memory of Admiral McCain worked to free Dad's grip on the gun last night, but his last words about the Admiral's grandson sound gloomy. Even though I'm reveling in his war history, it's time to talk about something else.

I stand and he follows my lead.

"Dad, did you grow up near here?"

NIGHT FIGHTER SQUADRON VFN-77C ON THE WASP FLIGHT DECK, 1944
Back Row: Charles A. Soderlund, James Bruce,Jr., Daniel Rengier, Daniel B. Kelly, Irving L. Straus.
Front Row: John L. Carter. John H. Bovum. John D. Zeilinger. Lawrence W. Brown.

"Yes. I used to walk to school."

We pick our way down a washed-out dirt road until we arrive at a ruin of an old sugar mill. A banyan tree envelops the walls and makes it difficult to recognize the mill until he points it out to me.

"This is where my father first worked when he came here in 1906. A few years later he built and ran the lime plant over at Baldwin Beach Park. It was just a beach at that time, no park. The plant crushed coral and produced lime for sugar production."

He points to the east from where we stand.

"Our house was up in that area, near those palms and mango trees. It was a plantation village called Hamakuapoko. Everyone did his work and got along."

He cracks a slight grin as he says, "If they didn't, they would answer to Sheriff Joe Mitchell. He was a big Hawaiian who carried a blacksnake bullwhip."

"So what happened to Hamakuapoko?"

"After the war there were labor strikes, the Democrats took over and the plantation system began to break down. All the homes in H-poko were torn down and plowed under into cane fields."

I think back to the story he told me on Papa Bace's pier in 1964 of how he would take off from his carrier, not knowing if it would be in the same spot when he returned. His situation now seems similar to me. He has come back to find his old home buried under a sea of sugar cane.

"Are you happy to be back on Maui, Dad?"

We pull away some branches and vines blocking our entrance into the old mill ruins.

"I struggle with your mom, Bill. Her thyroid condition hasn't improved and she's remarkably stubborn about taking her medication. Her problem is also exacerbated by alcohol. Since I retired I'm drinking more, and she is, too."

That's a deeper answer than I've bargained for, and I wonder where he's going with this.

I step inside the old mill and grab a hanging Banyan tree root.

He sits down at the entrance.

"In my career I've grown accustomed to order and efficiency. When I would come home it was sometimes aggravating for me, yet I could always count on that order when I returned to work. You probably know my job became frustrating at the end of my career and now this retirement has proven even more so. I'm not used to dealing with your mother's emotional instability on a daily basis, and yet that's what my life has come to."

I yank hard on the root.

Guilty feelings surge through me as I realize I was part of the aggravation when he got home every evening when I was a kid. But Mom? Mom is the problem? You met this young, beautiful athletic girl not even out of high school. She falls in love with you and does your every bidding to become a great Navy wife with all the entertaining it entails. It isn't her fault that this included a lot of social drinking, which turned out to aggravate her thyroid condition.

No, it's you, Dad. From what Mom told me last night, you and Mom gazed down on Maui from the top of Haleakala when the war ended in 1945. You decided to continue flying and make the Navy your lifetime career, with all its consequences. The latest consequence was your complete freak-out last night. You're an emotional basket case as a result of failing to adapt to civilian life. You can't blame this on Mom.

But I keep all this to myself.

What I tell him is, "I'm sorry, Dad," as if I understand why he's upset.

Even in his broken emotional state, he still wields so much psychological power over me.

"Well, I'm sorry, too."

We get back to the car.

"You drive, Bill."

Getting in the driver's seat gives me the same feeling I had when we drove across the country in 1964.

Holumua Road descends toward the ocean through a canopy of iron-wood trees that have been warped into an arch from the constant trade winds. I pull over to take in the view. The wind roars so loudly here that for a moment I'm back in our house in Coronado with Mom, startled by the sound of yet another jet taking off. Time is erased by the wind.

"Did you say something, Dad?"

"No."

He points to the ocean.

"There she blows."

The way he says it sounds like Ahab in *Moby Dick*. I shudder at the memory of Ahab's obsession and the spooky parallels his character has to Dad's. When I see a whale explode from the ocean surface like a Polaris missile, my dark thoughts fade.

"Wow," I say. "I hear they're going to make the ocean off Maui into a whale sanctuary. No more whaling."

Dad lays his hand on my arm.

"I've got a little bit of a headache, Bill. Do you mind if we go home now?"

Today I'm having a tough time keeping it together and drive out to a secluded end of the island. The serenity doesn't work. I need my brother and have brought pen and paper to sort out my confusion.

Hey, Mike,

I'm at the blowhole. The same place where we went to figure things out after we dropped acid two summers ago. But I didn't take any drugs today. Didn't need to. I need to be straight to clear these thoughts that have messed up my head. Christmas at home has been a really bad trip. I don't know where to begin, but as usual it has to do with Dad. Something pretty radical happened that I should probably wait to tell you about in person. I've been changing these last two years since I've been here in Hawaii, but this deal over Christmas really shook me to the core. Before this happened, even though I've always been on your side, in the back of my mind I always believed Dad had a strong mind—and that made his outlook more convincing. I know that sounds weird but that's what I thought all those years he was being so rough on us. So while I thought you were right on, somehow I always thought of Dad as just being right. But now I see he isn't strong at all. I think there's something really wrong with him. And now I'm re-evaluating everything. I love Dad in a certain way but wow, I'm just not going to follow in his footsteps. Sorry to be so heavy but that's the way it is. I know you already figured this stuff out and that's why you're over there. I can dig it more than ever.

Bill

No letters come from Mike but writing him still helps me get a grip.

Hey, Mike,

I'm back at school. Senior year is wrapping up and everyone is set for college next year. Most of us seniors have just been cruising. On weekends my pals and I explore the empty lava-strewn coasts stretching from Puako to Anahumalu Bay and Kona. We also check out the deep valleys on the north side of the island and we always come back to school covered in mud.

One of my pals asked me what I'm going to do after I finish college. Can you believe that? Right now I'm just thinking about this summer and what I can do for work. My pal's dad is a roofing contractor and he thinks that'll probably be what he ends up doing. I told him I got nothing like that. I wish I could just surf but that's not realistic, is it? Remember that tune 'Get a Job?' That's going to be my theme song.

Bill

It's spring and I'm jubilant to receive a letter from Mike.

Hey, dummy, you don't need a jooooob, I'm sending you a ticket. No sweat. We don't have to worry about dough. I'm even sending tickets for Mom and Dad. One big happy family here on Bali. Can you dig it? It'll be a gas. You'll come out first so we can catch up— and surf! Perfect surf as far as you can see. And get this, there're no other surfers here. Get in touch with Dick Brewer on the North Shore. He's making us seven boards for you to bring down here.

Mike

Mike isn't forgetting about me just because he's on the other side of the world. But what does he mean? Is the rock-and-roll business that profitable? I'll find out soon enough. Hell, he's on to something great like he always seems to be, and my previous bummer summer is still strong in my mind. I need to get out of Hawaii.

On graduation day Mom, Dad and Mimi show up and give me leis for the ceremony. I say goodbye to all my pals and a silent farewell to the Big Island, which has given me so much grounding. It has also cemented a feeling that I belong somewhere and that I do have a home.

But right now my heart is pounding at the thought of going to Bali.

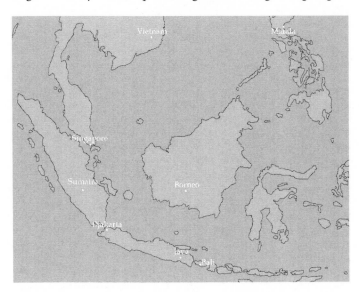

Chapter Eleven

Bali High
1969

I'm settled in my seat on the Pan Am Clipper and recall what Dad told me about the Clipper that landed off Maui in 1936. This aircraft is no longer the seaplane that had stopped back then to refuel on its way to the Orient. Dad's high school yearbook celebrated that seaplane as Maui's transition into the modern world. Thirty-three years later, I'm flying in great comfort in a huge jumbo jet with hardly any people onboard.

With her job at TWA, Mimi has managed to get all seven Dick Brewer surfboards on the plane for free. I'm going surfing.

I've been so excited about this trip and told everyone where I'm going—but no one knows where Bali is. They say the same thing I first thought, "Bali? Like Bali Hai in 'South Pacific?'"

I told them, "Next to Java." And still I got blank faces. I quit trying to explain something I don't really know myself. This flight feels like a trip to the moon, just like what they have planned later this summer.

We stop in Fiji on the way and I check out the islands I can see from the plane window—they look like a jeweled necklace stretching across the turquoise sea. What an adventure this is going to be.

Mike has arranged for me to stay overnight in the Indonesian capital of Djakarta at the home of his friend Joe Galloway until the following day, when I'll complete the last leg of my trip to Bali.

Having moved around for the last eighteen years does little to dull my enthusiasm. I try to tell myself this is just going to be one more place I've seen in the world.

My flight lands at Halim airport in Djakarta. The airport seems small and dingy for a capital city. Right away I can tell this isn't just another country, like Canada. The air is hot and humid like the southern U.S. But instead of tobacco, the exotic smell of clove cigarettes permeates the air. The airport is very hectic, with an overwhelming crowd of people and their accompanying din. All this has a disorienting effect on my already jet-lagged body.

Baggage boys in orange jumpsuits walk around with their arms draped over each other in an innocent child-like way and giggle as they stare at me with eyes like dark pools. I think about "The Wizard of Oz." They're munchkin-size in height but very slender. I don't see any fat people.

My own look is Levi jeans, a sweat-soaked Gant shirt and Bass Weejuns—a prep school kid very far from the prep school world.

No one speaks English even though they nod their heads as if they understand what I'm saying. Their glazed eyes tell me they don't. I keep repeating my mantra of directions to Joe Galloway's address.

I see some bicycles with small carriages on the front and point at one. A wiry man with legs like steel cables answers my silent question.

"Betcha?"

I nod. These vehicles appear cool and airy—perfect for me. I ignore all the taxi drivers who tug on my shirt as I jump into this small bicycle-powered cab.

It's a mistake. My betcha driver peddles our vehicle so much faster than I think possible, but not fast enough. The merging of speeding cars and these slow throwbacks to another age make for a constant succession of near misses. When I manage to suppress my fear long enough to look around, I see ornate statues and memorials dominating each intersection. They give an impression of wealth, a weird contrast in this city with its acres of tin-roof slums. We pass over a bridge and I see people below using a smelly canal both as a latrine and a laundry.

My focus shifts to the shirtless back of my driver. His sun-leathered skin is stretched tight over his ribs. He says something to me in his own language and I shake my head while I repeat Joe's address. I'm thinking of my new favorite movie, "Cool Hand Luke." Like Luke, I'm experiencing a failure to communicate. Unfortunately, I also know how that movie ends.

I might be able to handle this skinny guy, but what if he takes me to some poor part of the city and a hundred of his pals descend on me like rats? How could I be so out to lunch?

Somehow my mantra works because suddenly we're in an upscale neighborhood. I arrive at Joe's soaking wet from heat and fright. My feelings for my driver change instantly and I feel guilty for not trusting him. His face beams as if I have just changed his life when I give him a five-dollar bill.

Joe Galloway is friendly, with a slight Texas accent. The only thing Mike has told me about him is that he was the head of UPI, so I ask him about his job.

"Now I get to do stories like your brother's rock concert fiasco."

"What?"

Mike hadn't let me in on this. What am I walking into?

Joe grins at my lack of information.

"He didn't tell you about that? Mike and his musicians posted a no-show at a concert ticketed for around 50,000 fans. The crowd did show, the band didn't, a riot ensued and the fans ran amok. That's the word in this country that describes chaos. Amok. I did an interview with him before he got blacklisted. Turned out to be a very interesting guy."

I panic.

"Blacklisted? So he's not on Bali?"

"Oh, he's back. He's a very resourceful guy who knows how to land on his feet. Don't worry."

I settle down and glance at a map of Southeast Asia on the wall. Push-pins dot several action areas in Vietnam.

"You've been there?"

"Quite a bit. I have a friend who's a photojournalist for *Time* magazine. I'd like you to meet Sean. He's just arrived from Vietnam for a little R&R. I'm trying to talk him into flying to Bali to spend some time with you and your brother. He just went to the market and should be back soon."

After a well-needed shower, I rejoin Joe just as a tall guy with mov-ie-star looks walks into the house with the swagger of a fighter pilot.

Joe introduces me to Sean and I listen to their passionate but easygo-ing conversation about developments in Vietnam. Both men are jour-nalists, a profession I hold in very high regard. Vietnam has become such a huge issue; listening to firsthand info from these two experienced men is an inspiration for a news and history buff like myself.

The conversation turns to my brother and his wild times with his rock group.

I mention surfing and Joe lifts his eyebrows at Sean and points to me.

"These guys know how to have fun."

Sean gives me a conspiratorial grin.

"You know, I'm jazzed on surfing. Grew up in Palm Beach with my mother. The surf deal always flipped my switch, but I never got to do it much."

Something about him makes me like Sean right away. I tell him he should come with me to Bali.

Sean and I arrive on Bali, which is much less busy than Djakarta. But like Djakarta, it's a world of contrasts. The airport is adorned with Hindu art and the entrance of the road to Kuta has a large white marble statue of a Hindu god charging into battle on a chariot. Our chariot is a vehicle called a bemo. It has a noisy three-stroke engine that sucks exhaust back to where we sit in a passenger bed consisting of two opposing bench seats with a half round of sheet metal over it. The combination of pot-holes and a lack of shocks creates the impression that the bemo has square wheels.

We drive by several road crews where women labor with enormous piles of crushed coral in baskets balanced on their heads. A few men sit comfortably in the shade, directing the women while cigarettes dangle from their lips.

We're eager to escape our gas chamber and jump out at 'bemo corner' at the head of Jalan Pantai (Beach Road). Sean points to a hanging wire with a light bulb at the end in one of the small warongs that surround the intersection.

"Just like in many little villages I saw in Vietnam."

Past the shops, the road is dirt and there is no more electricity or commercial operations. We walk the remaining mile through the sleepy fishing village of Kuta, toward what Joe told us is Mike's home near the ocean. The only sounds on this road are crickets and soft voices speaking in an unfamiliar cadence. Large trees drape over the road and the smell and haze from burning coconut husks hang in the windless air.

Mike startles me when we walk in. He's skinny and doesn't look fit. I give him a bear hug and Sean introduces himself.

Mike beams when he meets Sean.

"Joe's told me all about you. Stoked you're here."

I keep staring at Mike and he notices.

"I've lost a little, huh?"

All my expectations of seeing my brother are rattled and I don't reply.

"Here, try this, it's durian."

My finger pokes at a football-size nut pod with woody spikes around the outside shell. Mike pries it open along fracture lines and withdraws the creamy yellow fruit. He sucks the custard off the seed.

I try a small piece while Mike fills me in.

"Only tigers and humans eat this. It's full of protein."

"Protein? Looks like you could use some."

Mike checks out his ribcage.

"That bad?"

I nod, grin and start devouring more durian.

"Don't OD on that stuff, Bill. It'll give you bad dreams."

"Man, you turn me on to this and it's like our grandmother's eight-layer cake. One bite?"

"You guys want a smoothie? Bill looks like he wants to eat me."

Sean says, "Sure."

Mike leans out a side window, pushes a giant banana leaf aside and half whispers towards the fruit stand that neighbors his house.

"Genik, *minta tiga smoothie* (three smoothies, please)."

Moments later we hear the whir of a blender.

Mike tells us, "I bought Genik that blender and a generator. It's the only one on this road."

Soon Genik, a beautiful Balinese woman, walks in with our smoothies and smiles at Mike.

"*Adik* (brother)?"

Mike nods and then Genik turns toward Sean. She barely gets the smoothie into his hands before she blushes and runs away.

Mike giggles.

"I've never seen a Balinese woman react that way with a Western guy," Mike says. "But then, you are Sean Flynn."

I feel like I'm missing out on part of the equation.

"What don't I know about Sean?"

Sean sighs.

"It's one of those things I don't bother telling strangers, but now that you're going to be watching me in the waves maybe this is the right time for you to know: I'm the son of Captain Blood."

Mike chuckles and says, "Well, we're the sons of Captain Bligh." Then he turns to me. "But yeah, Bill," he adds nonchalantly. "Sean is Errol Flynn's son."

Wow, it seems incredible enough to have met a photojournalist for *Time* magazine—but now this.

Mike is talking to Sean again. "We were big fans of your father's films."

Sean says, "From what I've heard, your stories would rival just about anyone's."

I'm interested to learn more about Sean, but can't wait to see the Indian Ocean.

"Hey," I say, "let's check out the surf."

We walk down to a white sand beach and see that it stretches for miles in either direction. It's empty except for a few naked girls.

Mike sees me lift my eyebrows.

"Euro chicks. They backpack through Asia and end up here."

"That's it? No surfers?"

Clean waves peel offshore as if carved by a machine lathe.

"None."

Mike points towards a consistent section.

"That'll be a great place for Sean to start."

I size up my emaciated brother.

"Yeah, but where are you going to start?"

I place my leg in front of his and push Mike down in the sand. Then I jump on him and playfully but energetically rough him up, pushing his face into the sand.

"You don't look like you could handle baby waves at Waikiki," I tease. "What the hell have you been doing to yourself?"

Sean's shaking his head. "You guys play rough."

"This is just pay-back," I say, letting Mike up so he can gasp for air.

"That's how it's going to feel when you go over the falls," I needle him.

Mike takes our tussle in stride as he slowly rights himself.

"You're right. I deserved that, especially from you." He looks up at our companion. "Truth is, Sean, I brought him down here to get my sorry ass back in shape. You look fit, though," he adds, standing now.

"I've just spent a good amount of time out in the jungle with Special Forces, hucking a big pack full of camera gear," Sean says. "Don't know if it'll help for surfing, but I'm ready to try."

I'm staring at Mike again, certain he needs way more help than Sean. It worries me that he's so thin. Plus my jet lag is getting to me and I need a workout.

"Let's get started."

We take off for a jog down this never-ending beach. I could live here. It really is paradise.

The beach calls each of us for a different reason. Mike needs to get in shape, Sean's unwinding and I'm pinching myself every time I see the waves.

Our days begin with an hour of intense yoga followed by a beach run-swim-run. It makes me happy to see Mike resurrect his fanaticism for getting fit. Swimming in the clear water revitalizes the three of us. After a few weeks of this regimen, we're swimming like Johnny Weissmuller.

The surf comes up and I break out my quiver of Dick Brewer surfboards. Sean's picking it up fast, I'm in hog heaven and Mike is still working on his take-off timing. We're all buzzed from being in the ocean.

When we get back to the house Made, our main houseboy, hands me a chilled young coconut with a straw. Mike has different people to do our laundry, cook and shop. I wonder if we're living like our grandparents did when they were stationed in Haiti. In restful moments I read Melville and get stoned. Human activity around Mike's house stops by five-thirty in the afternoon. This is the most peaceful place I've ever experienced.

One afternoon when Sean is out sightseeing with his camera, Mike and I lounge in a roomy area that looks out to the sea.

My brother grins at me.

"Man, for a guy who thought high school would be boring, you sure had a ton of shit to write."

I give him a push. "And you sure didn't. I never heard from you after I wrote about Duke."

Mike lets his gaze move outside. "That did set me back. So bummed. Wrote to him in Khe Sanh a few times and invited him to come here. Got one short letter. He wanted to check this place out."

"Man, he would have flipped for Bali."

Mike nods. "At least you're here. You're saving my life, you know."

I glance at him, still bothered by how sickly he looks. "I had no idea what you'd been doing. Writing you felt like a one-way street."

"I've been in a tailspin, Bill."

"Yeah," I say, "Joe told me about the no-show."

"And that was just the end of a long stretch of crazy theater. Things just spun out."

I knew there must be more to the story than that, but for now I let it pass.

"I think I know what you mean."

"Hey," he says, changing the subject, "that letter about Dad seemed heavy. What happened?"

My hands cover my face and I try to get everything straight in my head before I start talking. Then I take a deep breath and think about what Mike has just told me about being spun out. How much should I say?

"You know Dad is going to be fifty next week... amazing how he cheated death a few times in the war. All those battles he fought. But now he's got one more."

"Finding happiness is a battle for everyone, isn't it?"

I shrug. "Guess so. It just seemed sad to me. Now that he's finally gone back to Maui, I don't think he feels like it's really his home anymore. Plus the Navy dropped him into retirement completely unprepared. Maybe he can make a new start. You'll see what I mean soon enough when he gets here."

"Yeah, we'll see. So that was it? You call that intense? Man, you haven't seen nothin' yet."

"Well, that was just…"

I don't finish and am grateful to see Sean stroll in the door. I'm not sure if I even want to finish and decide maybe I've covered it enough without the heavy details. We're having a great time. Why ruin it with a bummer?

Workouts, surfing and fat joints of Thai grass give us tremendous appetites. The three of us are powering through a huge dinner out on an expansive lawn by the ocean, watching another beautiful sunset. The only irritation is an ever-present pack of dogs that keep coming around our table.

I ignore the dogs and ask Sean, "How did you come to this part of the world from Florida?"

"My mother was an actress, Lili Damita. So even though I didn't see my dad much growing up, acting came my way. I quit college and went to Spain to star in a remake of—can you guess?"

We are pretty stoned so he fills in, "'Captain Blood.' Yeah, 'Figlio del Capitano Blood.'"

He shakes his head, amused by his own story.

"I was twenty-one then."

"Was that the only movie?"

"No. Do you remember 'Zorro' when you guys were kids?"

"Yeah, sure."

"Well, I did 'The Sign of Zorro,' caps, masks and all. There were a few other B movies for me in France. I had money, Porsches and chicks. Couldn't be happier, right?"

Mike interjects, "Yeah, I know that one. Just went through a year of heroin, rock-and-roll and groupies."

I snap out of my haze.

"You were a junkie? No wonder you were so screwed up, Mike. Jeez."

I think about Mike's clean living in Lahaina, as well as his description of his life when he first arrived here. I can't imagine how he fell off that path.

I jab him in the shoulder.

Mike points his thumb at me.

"He'll have his tests someday."

Sean says, "That's it, isn't it? It's those tests that make us who we are. I burned out with the movie thing and wanted to taste some real life. You know, my father had connections all over the world and wherever I went it invited uncomfortable comparisons to him. I felt empty and wanted to do something I could really test myself with. The same year Joe was dodging bullets at the battle of Ia Drang..."

I interrupt, "Joe was at Ia Drang? Wow."

I'm shaking my head in amazement.

"Yep, he was there. Anyway, that same year I went to Africa to start a career in journalism. That gig didn't pay well so I went to Singapore to do another movie and make some dough. The action was heating up in Vietnam so I popped over and got signed on as a UPI photographer. You know all that background with movie camera work really gave me an eye for what I thought was a good shot. Got lost in the jungles and mountains with Special Forces for some long stretches. It was pretty wild."

He pauses and reflects.

"But I'm jazzed to be here now and learning how to surf. Shit, this place is..."

Mike interrupts, "Let's start calling it home. Bill and I were just talking about this. We've moved around quite a bit growing up, and this feels like the place to make our power spot."

Sean nods in agreement.

The dogs wait until our conversation turns so consuming that it distracts our attention from the food on the table. At that point they rush in, grab some ahi and race away before we can react. We begin to pile coral rocks next to us to keep them at a safer distance.

It's so hot and humid in Mike's house that we remain on the beach into the evening. There is a slight cooling breeze out here, where we can soak up the stars and talk into the night about Vietnam, Indonesia, surf and girls. We don't drink alcohol but puff away on powerful Thai pot.

It's a different world here. I'm not even thinking about TV or anything else I ever did in the evenings at home, wherever that was.

Things go quiet during marijuana minutes when we lose focus on the conversation. In these moments of short-term memory loss, we watch the lanterns on the small fishing boats just offshore bob up and down. When they disappear behind a swell approaching the shore, we can forecast rising surf.

Tonight Mike tells me we're going to a barong dance but won't say anymore than that.

"Barong dance?"

"Just watch and figure it out for yourself."

Since I've been here he's told me a few times that he's tired of my asking so many questions about this place and what Indonesian words mean.

We smoke a joint and go to join the few Westerners hanging around the boundary of the action.

The arena for the dance is the dirt street that runs through the village. It's common to see people in the cool evenings use the street as a community center.

I can tell the barong isn't meant to be a tourist event like the hula dances I've seen at Hawaiian luaus. Almost all of people gathered here are village people dressed in ceremonial batiks called sarongs, which are wrapped around their waists the way I wrap a towel around myself after a shower.

Wow, what a sound. Across from us are simply dressed musicians playing an instrument kind of like a xylophone. It's the most enchanting sound I've ever heard. The musicians sit in the dirt, smoking clove cigarettes as they play. They appear as stoned as we are. A light haze floats like magic in the air on this windless night, and I feel like I've gone back in time.

A moment of doubt enters my mind that maybe we shouldn't be eavesdropping on what is a serious ceremony for these villagers. But I relax as young smiling children kneel in the musician's laps, soaking up the ritual performance along with us. I laugh to myself when I think about fidgeting in church when I was their age.

A different note from the *gambang kayu* (xylophone) and a change of tempo startle me. A colorful dragon with bare feet enters the arena, followed by dancers in ornate costumes with gold trim. The dancers' faces are made up to look very intense and alert, as if they're on a hunt—or maybe being hunted. Their hand movements are very intricate, even more than in any hula I ever saw on Maui.

We hear a terrifying growl and dust rises from the street. A hideous

Medusa-like witch stomps into the arena and begins a fire-and-brim-
stone speech in a language I haven't even heard the locals speak. Maybe
they're speaking in tongues like Pentecostal church devotees. The children across from me look scared. I am, too. But in the next moment the
witch is making a different sound, like a belly laugh. Is she laughing at us?

My attention turns to the right. A man wearing the only white hat
among all the colored hats everyone else is wearing is splashing blood on
the faces of another group of dancers. A few people turn their heads to
look behind us and I'm sucked into doing so myself. A headless chicken
body is still twitching on a chopping block. I'm stoned but I know these
guys are way farther out than I am. I'm guessing this white-hat guy is a
priest of some sort.

The dancers must be entering a trance-like state after being baptized
in a chicken blood bath. Their trance appears way more extreme than a
marijuana high, more like an acid trip.

But these trippers have gold daggers at their sides when they enter the
arena, and they dance around the witch in aggressive postures. Oh shit,
now they've pulled out those daggers and are pointing them at her.

This is getting wild. They're stabbing into the air towards the witch
but without making contact. She booms out more fire and brimstone
and the dancers fall back. The crowd also falls back and now I realize
there is no difference between the crowd and the dancers. I'm not a
spectator anymore, either. This whole event is breathing in and out as
one body.

The dancers begin moaning with sounds of frustration. Oh, man,
now they're sticking the blade points into their own cheekbones and
chests. The blades bend dangerously. There, one of the daggers breaks
without penetrating the skin of the dancer. And now another. It's all
getting very freaky. Their actions and the results are defying reality as I
know it.

There's no time to space out on this unbelievable sight. Everyone is
running. I turn and run with them. There's a Western tourist on the
other side of the street from me who's walking with a cane. The crowd
knocks him over and he disappears from my view.

God, this is like a crash at an air show.

We return to Mike's house. I start to talk. Mike puts up his hand and
emits a rushing exhale. Without any discussion of what just happened, I
crash into a restless sleep of weird dreams.

Mike and I are driving to Denpasar, the main city on the island, to extend our visas. I'm thumbing through the book on orchids that Mike had me bring from Hawaii.

Suddenly he says, "So lay it on me. What did you think of that theater last night?"

I shake my head. "When we went to bed I couldn't stop dreaming about it. It seemed like there were two opposing characters, but neither one came out on top. Were they like good and evil? Then there was that disturbing suicide deal they couldn't pull off."

As soon as I say it, I stare at Mike for a moment and wonder if he's thinking about his past—because I suddenly am. I don't want to get into that and try to move on before he goes there.

"But those breaking daggers," I add, "man, that was wild."

"Your dreams are from too much durian, Bill. But good and evil? Those are Western concepts."

We pass a rice field and Mike points at a huge VW bug-sized volcanic rock in the middle of one paddy.

"Well," I say, "what were they?"

"Just forces, opposing forces, like that lava rock in that field. See that volcano way over there? It's called Agung."

I see the cone shape on the far side of the island and nod.

"In 1963 that baby threw that rock all the way over here. This island has many natural forces at work, and these people just want harmony so they can pull off their next rice crop. They do it by acknowledging the existence of both sides of nature so those forces don't feel neglected or spiteful and hopefully return to some sort of equilibrium. They put on those dances after disasters like flood, drought, drowning, disease or a volcanic explosion."

Mike shakes his head in wonder.

"But sometimes things go haywire, like last night."

"So are things balanced now?"

Mike shrugs.

"Who knows?"

We arrive at the immigration office and wait for three hours to get in to see the Chief. I'm staring at a gold Rolex watch on Mike's wrist that I've never seen him wear.

Mike tells me, "These guys were forced to sit and sweat it out in Dutch offices for years. Now they're in charge and this is pay-back."

"But this shouldn't be a problem, right?"

"Shit, I don't know, Bill. This is my first time in this office since I was blacklisted. Some of my oil pals in Singapore snuck me back into Indonesia through Balikpapan this last time. Those guys don't even use their passports in this country."

"Balikpapan?"

"Yeah. It's a big oil town in Borneo."

Balikpapan? I can't even fathom or pronounce the places Mike has seen the last two years. He's pretty adept at getting around these uncomfortable corners of the world and smoothing them out, even if he did stray off of what I think his path should be. My job now is to keep him pointed in the right direction. We're brothers, after all.

But here in this immigration office I'm worried our stay here could end soon. I remember the rock concert fiasco Joe told me about and wonder if we'll be successful after this long wait. My experience is that long waits aren't good. I think Mike will have to pull a rabbit out of his ass to extend our visas.

We're finally led into the immigration office and Mike taps my arm that cradles the orchid book. I take my cue and present the book to the Chief. He smiles and sets the book aside without opening it for even a short glance. I'm disappointed but he points for us to sit. Is this a good sign?

Mike begins a long speech in Indonesian and there are toothy grins on both sides. After several minutes I follow their lead and rise from my chair. Mike flashes his best smile and locks the Chief into a long handshake. He maintains this cheerful eye contact while I dare only a quick glance to see him slide the Rolex off his hand and onto the wrist of the Chief. What a move. The Chief directs us out and his secretary stamps our passport extensions.

Now we're driving back to Kuta and I'm trying to figure out how things work.

"Mike, are all these guys corrupt?"

"Corrupt, Bill? Corrupt is a matter of perspective. An official like him doesn't make that much money. But his position gives him the opportunity to receive a private tax of sorts. Do you have a say in where all that tax money goes in the U.S.? A bribe just serves to prioritize a situation. No matter where you are in the world, grease makes things happen. That was only minor grease, pal. A baksheesh, as they say in Karachi."

I mime my brother's move with the handshake.

"I can dig it. That was a pretty smooth move, Mike."

"Subtle, that's the key. Some people complain about it, but maybe they're just too cheap to do it or lack the cool to pull it off. It's gotta be cool or you can get yourself into trouble. But yeah, it's a way of life here, just part of the cost of living."

I'm thinking Mike has it wired.

"Well," he adds, "whatever you have to do, it's worth it."

"Fucking A it's worth it. We're here with a few euro backpackers and hardly anyone else. This is like hitting the surfer jackpot, isn't it?"

Mike flicks me in the chest with the back of his hand. He has a huge grin on his face. It's great to see him so proud of himself.

We're surfing every day. I think Mike has forgotten the Lahaina days when he told me there was more to life than surfing. Our daily routine is now totally dedicated to riding waves. When we aren't in the water, we're eating healthy or training hard.

"Hey, Bill, today let's shine the food."

The reminder of my one-day fasts for the POW pilot brings back a fond memory of my time in boarding school.

"Sure, man. But I remember the last time I did this, you asked if I was a monk."

"Well, now I can dig it. That's what we are. Surf monks."

"Cool."

We're exploring more surf breaks around the coast of Bali when Sean spots a little pocket beach that has huge palms and exotic plants. It looks like it's been landscaped for a Cleopatra movie set. He calls it the Cecil B. DeMille cove.

I overhear Sean tell Mike, "Yeah, let's buy that piece out on the cove. I'm ready to live here for the rest of my life. I just have to go back to Vietnam for one more piece for *Time*. It's going to be big and I've made commitments to a friend to be there with him for the assignment."

Mike and I are enthusiastic about future plans with Sean and establishing a base here on Bali, but I'm concerned about his immediate future.

"Don't you worry about going back into the line of fire?"

Sean nods. "Yeah, you have to keep on your toes and I've had my share of close calls. But it's intriguing at the same time. One thing I have going for me is that the VC know they have an opportunity to use correspondents to promote their cause. The war is reading well for them in the U.S. media. So generally they have a hands-off policy towards news guys. I have some pals who were captured and ended up with intimate interviews with the VC and NVA regulars. Their reports exposed how spartan these guys lived and showed the world their dedication. Then they were released. Sure, it's scary, but even if you get captured it isn't the end of the world."

Mom and Dad arrive and Mike puts them up in a private bungalow on the beach. I'm wondering how Mike and Dad will get along in this world Mike has created.

We all go to the beach and take in some bodysurfing. Dad looks happy. When we talk, it seems like Mike and Dad have put away their past mental swords and miraculously they get along, just like he and I did after the gun incident on Maui.

Dad works up an appetite after a long swim and bodysurfing in the crystal-blue waves off Kuta. Mike sets up a huge spread for us at a restaurant on the beach. Dad tells us he loves this regimen with fruit in the morning and one main meal with huge platters of ahi and veggies.

Mom and Dad are also pleased to meet Sean. When Sean leaves for a moment, Mom asks us, "Wasn't his father a spy?"

Dad puts a finger to his lips, which occurs to me is a much kinder way to tell her to keep her mouth shut than he used to use on us.

But when Sean returns Mom can't control herself.

"Isn't it interesting that your father was in Spain with Hemingway during the Spanish Civil war and now you're a reporter in Vietnam?" she says.

Mike and I are cringing because we know how Sean dreads those comparisons with his father. But he's gracious with her.

"Maybe we both needed to test our wills in conflict and record the sacrifice men and women make."

I'm amazed to notice Dad nod approvingly.

"The code the Naval Academy drilled into midshipmen was sacrifice, duty, honor and country," he says.

I notice Dad's eyes lock on Mike for an instant before he diverts his attention back to Sean. But Mike doesn't notice. He's ordering more food from our waiter.

Sean asks Dad, "You served in WWII?"

"Yes. When the war broke out I was on the heavy cruiser Northampton."

"Your sons told me you were a pilot."

"Yes, later on. A carrier pilot."

"I met some carrier pilots from the Oriskany. Great guys."

Sean mentioning the Oriskany turns Dad into his best Smilin' Jack persona and his answers to Sean's questions become much more detailed. Mom tries to have a separate conversation with Mike and me. We know that bugs Dad and soon take Mom back to their bungalow.

Sean catches Mike and me in private two hours later.

"I thought you said your father was a prick? He's great. Man, he was in every engagement across the Pacific, from Guam to Leyte Gulf. I could talk with him for hours."

Mike shrugs.

"What can I say? It's like he's a different person."

"I think I understand. It's lucky you guys had a father around at all, no matter what happened. My parents were divorced soon after I was born."

I realize Sean doesn't know what happened to my brother and me and it would be impossible for him to gauge that fall-out. We really haven't figured it out ourselves. Our father, who is only a few years younger than Errol Flynn, has impressed Sean as a real-life warrior.

Mike rubs his face.

"Makes me wonder if what we thought happened growing up was real."

Wait a minute, it was real and I'm not ready to forgive or forget. I know it's still real from the judgmental look Dad started to lay on Mike at dinner. He's been behaving himself since he's been here, fooling everyone, and I know why.

Until now I've thought I would keep the image of Dad pressing the .45 into his temple to myself. Why bring up that downer when we're having such a good time? But after hearing what Mike and Sean just said, I'm changing my mind. I'm not going to forget the past just because Dad doesn't intimidate me anymore. And then there's the guilt I still feel about keeping Mike's attempted suicide a secret. Maybe that gun ended up in Mom's inheritance because I kept that secret. I'm thinking secrets are bullshit.

The barong dance with all its suicidal implications has invaded my dreams too many times. Maybe Mike and Dad wouldn't have really pulled the trigger and were just going to the edge like those barong dancers. Me? I was there, having to witness and carry the weight for both of them. I don't want to carry it anymore.

I blurt it all out to Sean and Mike: the blow-up about the college tuition costs when I came home; the story of Dad's war experiences from

Mom; his contemplating life from the top of Haleakala and making the Navy a lifetime career; my putting the gun case away and not telling anyone about it in 1961; then me discovering the empty case seven years later and then searching for Dad and talking him down from the brink.

"He's gutted. That's why he's so polite. But I'll tell you what, he hasn't forgotten about your discharge from the Navy."

I tell Mike all this in front of Sean and don't mind him hearing it now. We both respect Sean and I don't want him to think I'm some whining kid complaining for nothing about his upbringing. He needs to hear the real nitty-gritty.

Sean and Mike sit silently for several minutes after my bombshell.

Finally Sean says, "I've seen soldiers in Vietnam that were just hollowed out, exhausted, mentally ruined. Some so bad they killed themselves. It's like some kind of shell shock. Have you ever considered that your Dad came out of WWII with battle fatigue?"

Chills go down my spine. I've heard that word a few times before, and now I flash to when I told Mikey what I'd learned about shell shock from our grandfather.

"Papa Bace told you war stories?" he'd said.

"Yeah, when we were crabbing. He knew tons of stuff about war and fixing soldiers."

"Yep, Papa Bace knew everything."

"Nope. He told me there were some things he couldn't figure out."

"Like what?"

"Something invisible that soldiers get. But I'm glad no one we know has it."

But someone we know does have it: Dad.

"No," I say. "I hadn't considered that. I guess it makes sense—the stress of night flying, the intense thunder of warfare, the loss of good friends and any of the hundreds of unknown events that he experienced and will never tell us."

Sean nods.

"For him, coming home to family life was maybe too much of a gear shift to handle."

Mike has tears rolling down his face.

"Don't feel bad about that gun," he says. "If he hadn't had it, he would've found another one."

Maybe, I think, but that was the gun that was accessible to him.

These last few days it seems like my revelation about Dad has put a damper on Mike's spirits and disrupted our routine.

"Listen, Bill," he says, "Sean has to go back to Vietnam and I have a business opportunity. Maybe it would be good for you to head back to Maui with Mom and Dad. We'll definitely do this again after you finish school next spring."

I feel a little guilty about dropping such a downer on our good times. Did I make a mistake dumping all that stuff about Dad? I feel like I've pried enough already and don't ask about Mike's 'business opportunity.' Maybe that's just an excuse, anyway. He might need some time alone to figure things out.

"Yeah, no sweat."

My brother pops me in the shoulder.

"Can't believe you're going to be a college guy now."

We say our goodbyes to Sean, who promises to return to Bali next June or July, maybe for good. We privately think he's nuts to go back to Vietnam. But Sean seems bigger than life to us and we're reluctant to express our negative feelings to him. He's so confident. From what he's told us, it's like the seas have always parted for him as he walks through life. We say nothing more to change his mind.

His parting words are, "My father told me this: If you really like to do something, do it twice."

That sounds like he's bound and determined to return to this land of surf. I know I'll be back.

Mom, Dad and I are leaving in two more days. Mom reports to Mike and me in private.

"Your Dad is having some headaches and uncomfortable dreams. Maybe it's this new diet and all the exercise, but it's shaking him up."

I know Mike can't blame Dad's dreams on durian. He won't touch the stuff.

Mike tells Mom and me, "Don't worry. It's well known among travelers that Bali is a place of dreams."

I add, "Maybe it's the warm humid air; I've had a few of my own."

Mom asks, "Do you wake up screaming?"

Chapter Twelve

Swept Away
1969-1970

I'm in Fort Collins, reading the end of Mike's latest letter in the student plaza.

...Don't let up on the letters. They keep me solid.

Mike

I look up from his hen-scratched pages. Girls. There are so many beautiful girls at this place. After years of all-boys schools, I'm going crazy looking at girls.

I'm writing him back. If he liked my letters about chicks from Montreal, he'll love this.

> Hey, Mike,
>
> Classes have started but it's not as hard as I thought it would be and there's plenty of time to write. Last night I had to ditch my date. Couldn't stand her New Jersey accent and found another girl in the elevator. This one was pissed off at her boyfriend and went up to my room with me. I put on Marvin Gaye's 'Too Busy Thinking About My Baby' and that did the trick. The great thing about this situation was she had to get back to her room after she'd had her 'revenge' with me and I avoided the morning thing, which I wonder if I'll ever learn how to manage.
>
> Bill

There's been no response from Mike in a few weeks. Maybe he's bored with my exploits with girls, so I've just written him another, more serious letter about seeing a TV report that Art Linkletter's daughter had jumped off a building after taking LSD.

> ...Was it the acid that made her do it, or was she just plain old unhappy enough with her life that she chose to end it? I thought blaming it on the acid was a convenient solution for those who didn't want to bring up some painful questions, like what could they have done to prevent it? Or how should they explain it to others? I was there with Dad when he broke down. If I hadn't been, maybe I'd be passing off his death as an accident and not a suicide attempt. We've all seen Art Linkletter on TV and he looks like a jovial guy but as we know from Dad, smiles can hide shit.

Before I sign it I remember Mike and his time with the gun. I rip the letter up and toss it.

I've written Mike four letters and have none in return until today, when I receive a postcard from Penang, Malaysia.

> Bill,
>
> Blew thru Kuta where I found my stash of reports of your wicked ways. They're a gas. Glad to see you've got your eyes open. Vietnam ain't no joke. Keep your grades up. Wrote Sean but haven't heard back. On the road again but all set for your return next summer.
>
> Cool, Jet.

Hey, Jet,

It's May and everyone has been stoked to be warm again. But we all feel cold today. We heard that four students were gunned down by National Guard troops at Kent State. The scene has gotten so political. I even let myself get sucked into going to an anti-war rally. Everyone was amped-up. But it was a happening. Met a girl there. Can you believe

it? Another one named Jackie. She's smart and cute.
I've really got the hots for her, but she's always
pulling me into late-night rap sessions with other
students about the war. I try to add some reality
about how the guys in Dad's generation react to
change, but I'm not good talking in groups and get
interrupted by other guys' arguments. I think
they're trying to one-up me while they're eyeballing
my babe.

I'm with you, Mike—not these guys. I'm not
changing the system. Canned Heat plays my favorite
song. I love their new hit 'Goin' up the Country'
about water tasting like wine and jumping in it to
stay drunk all the time. And about leaving the USA
because of all the fussing and fighting. I've decided
it's my song. I want to be drunk with surfing in
Indonesia. That's my idea of a romantic cause. I'm
not going to be a political activist.

Bill

Jackie is shaking me from a dead sleep in the middle of the night. She's
holding the telephone.

"Come on, wake up. It's Kabul, Afghanistan calling, do you accept a
collect call?"

"What?"

I try to clear the cobwebs from my head. It's got to be Mike. He's the
only person I know who could be in as strange a place as Afghanistan.
Still oblivious to time zone differences, he's once again calling me when
I'm sleeping.

"Bill."

Just the way he says my name focuses my attention.

"Sean is missing in Cambodia."

Two bombshells. First, Mike is in Kabul, why? Second is Sean. Before
I can respond, the line goes dead.

I can't sleep the rest of the night and when Jackie wakes up she begins
quizzing me.

"Who's calling you from Afghanistan in the middle of the night?"

"My brother."

"Is that what's bothering you?"

All of it's bothering me. The student rumor is that the FBI has a blank check to operate. I'm concerned about the alleged political wiretaps that I've heard J. Edgar Hoover has implemented. From the rap sessions I've gone to with Jackie, they must have this whole campus bugged. And now I've received an overseas call from Bananastan, as my sister Mimi likes to call any central Asian country. They could be knocking at my door at any moment. What's Mike doing?

Buffalo Springfield guitarist Stephen Stills has written about paranoia. I look into Jackie's worried eyes.

"I can't tell you right now."

"I thought we said no secrets."

I shake my head.

"Sorry."

It's been two weeks since I last heard from Jackie. I'm torn up about her, but I'm also torn up about what I'm reading in *Time* magazine concerning Sean. Just like Mike told me, he's missing in Cambodia. A reporter had spoken to Dana Stone, Sean's cameraman friend, just before they were last seen.

Dana Stone had joked with the reporter.

"Sean wants us to get captured for a report from the other side."

I feel a chill as I remember our conversation with him about this exact scenario.

I've been feeling especially lonely during these last weeks of school and am anxious to get back to Indonesia. Anyway, this isn't the time to get permanently involved with a girl. My future is going to be with Mike. That's what I keep telling myself as I search out my favorite escape. I haven't smoked much dope this year. At this college, alcohol is the accepted way to loosen up. But right now, feeling this blue, a beer just won't cut it. I have some privacy and I'm sneaking a hit from a joint I got from the black guys down the hall. They know I don't get along with most of these mid-western students in our dorm and dig it that I'm as good at finding girls as they are.

Being stoned is the road away from the do-as-you're-told mentality of Dad's generation. I had hoped the pot would help me find my way through the inner dialogue I'm having about all this crap that's coming up for me, but it's not working today. It's adding to my confusion. I don't know who's doing the talking.

I finally figure it out. Whether it's the student raps I've been in on or the hamsters in my head, it's all this talking that's the problem. I push the talk away and the dope allows me to slip back to Bali, where I'll be in just a week. Paradise.

~

I arrive at Mike's house in Kuta Beach and drop my bags. Colorado to Bali? It blows my mind how far away and different the two places are on the map and that I travel to each place with such ease. But Bali no longer seems like a far-away place. I like to think it's going to be home. Every sense in my body opens up when I'm here.

Mike's looking fantastic now. He hasn't stopped working out since I left. I have a million questions about Sean but instead of answering me, he's searching my bags.

"Where's the medium-grain brown rice?"

"In the surfboard bags just like you told me. The Bali customs guys couldn't believe I was importing rice."

Mike's agitated.

"Did they open the rice bags?"

"No. Why?"

"Just like to know how it is. They haven't been searching much, but this election has everyone uptight."

"Searching for what?"

"You already gonna start asking a lot of questions, Bill?"

"Yeah. You called me from Kabul. You said Sean had been captured. It cost me a girlfriend and I want to know what's up."

He rolls his eyes.

"There'll be many more girls, Bill."

"This one was special."

"Yeah, sure."

Why have I come? I'm pissed and haven't even unpacked. There's a familiar aroma in Mike's house.

"You're smuggling hashish?"

He points at me.

"Hey, you're learning to figure things out all by yourself."

His sarcasm is annoying but he's giving me that subtle grin I know so well. Does he think this is funny?

"I'm a rug merchant, only with a D."

"Yeah. D for dumbshit."

The smirk fades from his face but I'm not finished.

"How can you act so cocky about this stuff, Mike? You want to go to jail?"

He yells, "You know anyone who's gone to jail?"

I yell back, "As a matter of fact, yeah. Some Brotherhood guys on Maui this last December."

We're glaring at each other and I'm wondering if we're going to end up wrestling like we did last summer when I first arrived. A few moments pass. His eyes lose their tension and his voice lowers.

"I did hear about that. My connect in Kabul told me. Bill, they were arrogant shits. Those guys were living flamboyant lifestyles in plain sight. When you live outside U.S. laws, you have to live outside the U.S. Anyway, we have lots of time. No need to work everything out right now. I'll explain later."

"What about Sean?"

"Nothing. No news. If he were going to be released, they would've done it already. I do know the Cambodians aren't like the Vietnamese. Everything he might have assumed could have been wrong."

I'm trying to take this all in. Every time I try to corner Mike with my emotional feedback, he slips away by changing his attitude. Is that how he handles challenges in the Third World?

We decide to drop our initial attempts to figure it all out. I know if I press when the time isn't right we'll probably end up punching each other. Wrestling Mike to the ground won't be as easy a victory as it was last year when he was still weak from drug use. He's fit now and as hard-headed as ever. I'm sure he feels the same way about me.

Mike and I set out to repeat all the surf routines of the previous summer, but Sean's upbeat energy is missing. A welcome addition to our gang is Mike's pal Joe Barness. He's a tall lean square-shouldered guy with longer hair than mine and a beard. Barness could be the mellowest guy I've ever met.

"Where did you meet my brother?"

He cracks a wry grin.

"Oh, we've been around."

He's mellow but outside of surfing it's obvious he isn't going to offer any personal details. I don't care. Joe is a great goofy-footer and a fun guy to have in the line-up. He likes to eat everything we like, especially durian. When you get right down to it, surfing and eating are the only things that matter.

Traveling the roads around Bali is jarring and to avoid that Mike has brought an Avon rubber boat from Singapore. Now we can zip straight out to the airport reef from the beach in front of his home. Mike has had a hard time surfing the more challenging reef at Uluwatu and has let Joe and me avoid the long hike by blazing out there in the boat. The two of us have even been spending the night, anchored outside the line-up at Uluwatu so we can surf well after the sun sets and at the very first light of day. The water surface during those sunset and sunrise moments is like velvet. Checking out the stars at night from inside the Avon feels like being in a space capsule and only total exhaustion and hashish allow us to sleep. Our food is a jug of juice with mangosteens and rambutans mixed with it. The stars are psychedelic. Joe takes it in just like I do without trying to put the experience into words. He's the perfect surf partner.

Last year when we walked down the beach road of Kuta, the locals would call out to us about finding a wife or gaining weight. This year that same walk is eerily quiet. Mike tells me the CIA has helped General Suharto, the new leader of this country, arrange an 'election' to start a democracy in order to qualify for military aid from the U.S. government. It will be this country's first election. If he wins, Suharto will have to morph from being a general to being a democratically elected leader.

Mike has learned all this info on his trips to other surrounding countries in Asia. Here in Indonesia any article in a news magazine concerning this country is blacked out.

In the streets of Kuta Mike points at soldiers goose-stepping through town in full battle gear.

"Guess they'll know who to vote for."

Made, our gentle forty-year-old houseman, is the head of the local National Party. They're not as radical as the socialists or communists, but Suharto's Golkar Party doesn't want competition from anyone.

It's the night before the election and Golkar thugs have stationed themselves outside our house, waiting for Made to leave to go home.

We peek out the window and see them with their machetes.

Mike says, "Check out the KKK. Made won't stand a chance if he walks home. We'll keep him here overnight."

This morning everything appears calm and I don't see any thugs outside our place waiting to hack up Made.

Mike walks in with a *Bali Post* newspaper.

"Who won?"

"Who do you think? Suharto and Golkar by ninety-eight percent."

"So what now?"

"Don't sweat it. Things will cool down. That Mississippi-style vibe we witnessed will disappear. Suharto's foreign aid from the U.S. depends on favorable feedback from Western visitors. We're golden."

Mike's right. No one has been hassling us. As visitors from the U.S., we can lead a carefree life on Bali with little interference. Our surf monk existence rolls on.

A few more surfers have started to show up, but it's still very uncrowded at Kuta reef. The point break of Uluwatu is always empty and there are only monkeys on the cliffs to watch us play in the waves.

The surfers here come from all over the world. Most of them end up at Mike's pad to find out where to go for waves. One of them is Bob Laverty. He's from California and looks very fit—like some wild Viking with long bleached-out hair and a blond beard. We've hit it off with him and he often joins us for dinner. Mike has trained Made to shop for the very best food, so we eat like kings.

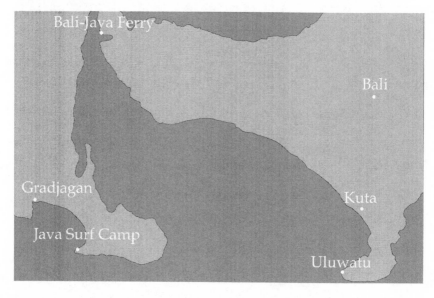

Bob Laverty is back from a short trip to Djakarta. He tells us that he checked out a long peeling left-hander from the window of his plane. After seeing this, he traveled on his own to a small fishing village that would be the starting point for the last leg of his journey. The village had a narrow dirt road like Kuta, but when he walked down that road to catch a glimpse of the ocean, he stepped on some half-buried smoldering coconut husks and burned his feet. He had to abort his exploration and never got a ground-level look at the mystery wave.

Mike spins a joint and passes it to Bob, who shows him the palm of his hand and politely says, "No, thanks."

He's looking over some British Admiralty charts my brother has just brought from Singapore.

He points at a specific spot on the chart.

"Unreal."

I peek over his shoulder. Bob's enthusiasm is contagious.

I'm stoned and blurt out, "Where are the roads?"

He chuckles.

"These maps are for ships."

As stoned as I am, the word ships makes me feel anxious. Mike is smuggling hashish and these charts aren't meant to search for surf. We both glance at my brother.

Bob's bright blue eyes recapture my attention and he changes the unsaid subject.

"But we can use them for finding surf spots. See how the map shows reef depths?"

I watch Bob match up the reefs at Uluwatu with the southeastern tip of Java. Our small cadre of pals already know what a fantastic point break Uluwatu is. The map shows the reefs of the two spots are roughly the same depth, as are their alignment to the southeast trade winds.

"We gotta check this out," he half whispers.

It's obvious that Bob wants to keep this find a secret.

Mike points at Bob's burned feet and shakes his head.

"First, you need some decent medical attention. We'll go next year."

I take a hit.

"Why, though?" I say. "It's not even crowded where we go now. Why bother?"

"How long do you think it's going to be like this?" Bob asks. "This is the golden time for Bali, but it won't last forever."

Mike steps in for a hit and his voice squeaks while he holds his inhale.

"Edge City, man."

The smoke explodes from his lungs.

Bob nods and flashes a wide grin.

There's that word Mike used three years ago in Lahaina before he took off for this part of the world. Edge City? It seems to me we're getting closer all the time.

The surf is flat this morning and our routine shifts to swimming. Mike and I always hold off on getting stoned until after our swim in order to keep our carburetors clean.

After the swim I feel fantastic. Every muscle in my body is loose and strong.

"Let's do a dope fast today."

Mike nods.

"I can dig it."

Back at the house we're scarfing a large plate of rambutan and mangosteen when Rahim, one of Mike's pals, pops in the door. He has a noticeable southern California accent.

"You guys ready to burn one?"

"No, we're passing today."

He lights up a hash joint and puffs away.

"Just heard Johnny got popped in Penang. Fucking goons are radical. They got the death penalty for dope."

This news terrifies me. We've surfed with Johnny and he's a great guy. Now he's locked up in a Malaysian jail facing the death penalty? Maybe I should take a hit. Rahim looks relaxed but after a second I decide against it. Mike and I are quiet, thinking about Johnny.

Rahim is a talker and doesn't look like he digs our silence.

"Hey, I'll catch you on the rebound."

Rahim leaves and Mike says to the void he's left, "Yeah, thanks for the downer."

"Hey, Mike. Rahim? He's obviously from the U.S. What's with that stupid A-rab name?"

"Yeah. He's from L.A. Like that alias could fool anyone."

"So he's hiding from the law, right?"

Mike tilts his head and shrugs, but doesn't say anything.

He sees me shaking my head.

I ask, "And what about Johnny?"

"Listen, Bill, they won't hang Johnny. The worst he'll get is the raps of the cane."

"What the fuck is that?"

"They have their executioner knock the flesh off your tail bone with this cane whip. Then for every day you're sentenced, they knock that wound open again. You can't sit or lie down comfortably for a long time."

"Great."

Mike ignores my sarcasm. Since I've been back here we've had a constant stream of distractions from people, getting stoned and being just too downright tired to talk about anything of substance. But right now we're alone, not stoned and I feel energized from our swim.

"How did this all happen?"

I don't need to say more than that. He knows what I mean.

"Bill, you know I had all that dough from my stock sales. Man, that gamble really paid off. Anyway I made it last pretty good until I hooked up with those musicians. They could spend money faster than a chick and soon enough we needed more. There were a few guys here on Bali who'd been to Afghanistan to smuggle hash. I made friends with them and figured why not? Before I knew it, I was off supplementing the band's war chest with hash money."

"All this happened before I got here last summer? Why didn't you tell me?"

"Shit, Sean was here and Mom and Dad were coming. Guess I just didn't want the cat out of the bag. Wasn't sure where you were at."

"Secrets, huh? I know." I shake my head. "Man, it's such a big jump."

"It is big, but the payoff is huge."

I still can't grasp the totality of it. Smoking dope is one thing, but the idea of smuggling scares the shit out of me, especially with the consequences we've just been talking about for Johnny in Malaysia.

"Don't you feel like—I don't know…?"

"A criminal? Yeah sure, like all the criminals throughout time. You like history. Remember the Kennedys? The Kennedys' father, Joe, started his family fortune with shady stock sales and importing booze. His son became president. You know, I met this old Chinese man in Penang last year. He told me the first bucket of gold is always dirty. The buckets you get after that are for cleaning up the first one."

I can dig what he's saying, but maybe the Kennedys are a bad example. I'm thinking about what kind of karma came their way because of that dirty gold.

"OK, but why you? Can't you do something else to make money?"

"Like what, Bill? Remember when I got discharged from the Navy?

That was a section eight, pal. In the straight world back in the U.S., I'd be digging ditches."

I knew Dad was bummed about Mike's discharge but hadn't realized how it would affect his job options.

"You see what we have here? There aren't very many places like this in the world. This is what I want. From the way you're digging this, I think it's what you want, too. I need you to scout that new surf spot on Java with Laverty next year. We can surf here the rest of our lives if we play our cards right. If I went back to the U.S. and dropped into any kind of work there, this would all slip away. You're here or you're not here."

He's right about wanting to be here—the idea of not being here rattles me. We had traveled throughout the U.S. growing up and I have a vague idea of what options exist there for carving out a life in the straight world. When I think about it, most of those jobs would be like encasing yourself in cement.

I don't need a fancy car or house; I just need the freedom to be here and ride waves. If I could make money surfing that would be even better, but who would pay someone to surf? We shouldn't need much dough. Living is cheap here on Bali.

But I'm still struggling with the concept of smuggling. Despite his rap, Mike can see I remain baffled by how he's come to this solution.

"Look. This kind of smuggling is a new frontier. It's not the type of business you prepare for by growing up in small-town America, helping out at your father's business on the weekends."

I remember how one of my classmates told me about his father's roofing business.

"You got that right," I say. "We lived in a different world, didn't we?"

"That's for sure, Bill. No profession was being passed on to us, unless we chose a military career. That whole deal is so screwed up."

I had almost chosen that path, but whatever happened to Mike when he was in the Navy sure looked like a bummer. Now it feels really good when he includes me when he's describing the life he wants to put together. I nod and let him roll.

"But on some level, something was passed on to us, wasn't it?"

Mike seems to be shooting from the hip as he speaks. I wish I could put words together the way he does.

"It's more a projection of spirit, isn't it? Our Dad flew jets, for chrissake. That was his buzz. He was checking out what was possible in his era. That's what we picked up."

Mike is giving me his best conspiratorial grin and I remember something he told me when we were kids: "When you fly jets, you don't have to live like the rest of the jerks in the world."

We didn't fly those jets, but the glamour of Dad's world was there for us.

"Man, I can dig it but smuggling, breaking the law, it's just so..."

"Laws? Bill, we're on Bali. Laws are different in different places. Don't sweat it. We won't be doin' jack in Malaysia. I already scoped it out in Penang. Besides, you've seen laws at work recently. How are they working for everyone?"

If he's referring to the politics throughout the world in the last five years, that world does seem to be falling apart.

"Our law out here is the extreme law of nature. We're livin' on the edge, man. That's the world we live in. Look, Dad got high in his own way. For us it's surfing. I'll do anything I have to do to make it happen."

His words have a very seductive appeal and when I examine my attraction for this place, I start to see it his way. It would be hypocritical for me to enjoy this place and not acknowledge how he's pulling it off. I don't feel as judgmental as when I first arrived and don't want to knock heads with my brother anymore.

"Yeah, Mike, remember all that cheap booze Mom brought over from Mexico? When I think about it, I suppose there was a lot more than booze coming back from your trips to Baja with Duke."

I smile with the memory, but Mike looks sad at the mention of Duke's name.

"Too bad about Duke. He musta' listened to his dad. Why the fuckin' Marines? He should be out here with us right now. Can't believe all the shit I went through to get out of the Navy. But I'm here now and he isn't. We owe it to him to do it right."

"I wonder what his number was?"

"What?"

"You've heard about the draft lottery?"

"Yeah, read about it in *Time.*"

"Well, they had the first lottery this last December. It was for all you fuckers born before 1950. I did see what your number was."

I have a little grin on my face and wait.

He hits me in the shoulder.

"OK, dipshit, what was it?"

"365. The best number in the universe."

Mike's jaw drops.

"Shit. You mean all that hassle, screwing up my ankle with that anchor chain, damn. And I had that golden number coming my way."

"My birthday had a high number this year but it wasn't my year. Hope I get as lucky next year."

Mike hugs me.

"We'll work it out no matter what. You're not going to be a grunt. I'm going to need your help. Get college done and we'll go from there."

His last sentence makes me feel a part of something big. I love my brother and once again he's swept me off my feet. Does it mean I'll eventually join him doing this stuff? I'm scared and excited at the same time.

Mike tells me, "Man, I've hung out in some shitholes—Karachi, Goa, Delhi, Rawalpindi and all over Afghanistan. I've been stuck waiting around for people and product in some crappy scum-infested places. But you know what? I can do this. I can make it happen. Remember that movie 'Giant' with James Dean? I've struck oil. Hash oil. And when I get back here with you, it's all worth it."

It's reassuring hearing this from Mike. I feel like I've taken a huge step just listening to him.

Our upbringing did create initiative and independence, even though that path for Mike has taken a criminal turn. Navy brats know how to move. I flash back to Coronado, Baja Mexico, huarache sandals, tire wells, hollowed-out surfboards and Duke with his new hearse. The mystery of Baja is solved for me and now Mike and I are living a surfer's dream, just like Duke predicted. We've found our own path to search for perfect waves; it's 'Endless Summer' but with a twist.

Mike and I scarf some Thai durian, growl and start an exercise routine on his chin-up bar out in the yard.

Surfing gives me a huge appetite and today we get more than just food at the restaurant. I go back to Mike's house after a lunch with Joe Barness and Bob Laverty.

"Hey, Mike," Laverty says, "I can't believe what I've seen. All a guy has to do is hang out around here to get connected. Just watched someone get offered big cake for sailing a boat back with a load. Same guy offered me ten grand to carry some cash across a border to make things happen."

Laverty chuckles. "But when I just wanted to shoot some casual shots, that same guy told me, 'no pictures.'"

Mike says to me, "It's smuggling 101, right?"

Made emerges from our manure-smelling courtyard with a blender full of magic mushrooms.

"Who's up for a smoothie?" says Mike.

Tonight I'm in a mescaline fog, re-running my new reality. The conversations at the juice bar today inevitably turned to stories of drug scams from all over the world. I dig these tales of surfers taking big risks, sailing across the ocean with their loads of hashish. It reminds me of Sinbad. Like him, surfers are a spartan breed. I remember the tales of the Arabian Nights when I hear about Morocco, where there are both waves and hash. Morocco is one of the places The Brotherhood of Eternal Love operates, and there is even a rumor that one of the surfers in 'Endless Summer' is part of the Brotherhood.

The Brotherhood are smugglers who fled from Laguna Beach. I've seen them surfing on Maui. They're older than I am and all we do is nod at each other but I know who they are. When they pull up to the beach in a Mercedes, I'm pretty sure that Benz has almost been around the planet. Parking a luxury car in the salt spray does look flamboyant to me, especially when they talk like they're supposed to be on some kind of spiritual path. Some of these guys are notorious for handing out orange sunshine LSD. They're a loose connection of surfers 'working' for a common goal. Loose is the key word. From the stories I've heard, it's disorganized crime by a bunch of stoners.

Wow, I wonder if I'll be able to remember all these stories. Right now all I can think about is how to end this inner dialogue and go to sleep.

Mike is hanging upside down from our chin-up bar and I'm sanding out some nicks on my surfboard fin.

A skinny guy wearing only swim trunks and a military haircut steps into our yard.

"Hey, man, looks like I found the right place."

We know every Western person in Kuta but have never seen this guy. I blow the fiberglass dust off my fin and examine the surface. Mike swings upright. "You looking for someone?"

"If you're the one they call Mike."

"Who's asking?"

"Just me. I'm Butch. The locals in this village told me you guys were the ones to see about finding good waves."

"You're a surfer?"

I can tell Mike is suspicious. None of the surfers we know look like this guy. There's a moment of silence as Butch and Mike lock eyes.

"Yeah, I am. But I've looked at cops the way you're looking at me, and you couldn't be further from the truth."

Mike slides his hand across his temples in reference to Butch's short haircut.

"Oh, this? Marines."

"You still in?"

"No, I'm out. Thank God I'm out."

Mike Boyum hanging out

"Well, we're out, too. Yeah, I'm Mike. Have a seat."

"Just got back from the States getting my discharge."

"You were in 'Nam?"

Butch nods and fires up a joint.

"Shit, man, you don't know how great it is to be here. Man, being in the U.S. was like weird."

I can guess what he means but I'm not going to ask him since he has such a pained expression on his face. Mike must see it, too and changes the subject.

"How did you hear about this place?"

"In 'Nam, man. In 'Nam. It was wild. Had a buddy in recon. Ever heard of the Nimbus satellite?"

I try to dig up the word Nimbus from the past. That's it. Dad had talked about cumulus nimbus clouds in one of his weather lectures. Satellites?

"Mike, remember Sputnik? Remember how pissed off Dad was when the Russians were the first into space? Scared Mimi's dog so bad it peed in the house."

Butch grins and passes me his joint.

"Well," he says, "things have come a long way since then. Now we can see pictures of the Earth from outer space."

That's the thing I know I missed out on when I bailed on a military future. Here's a former Marine who knows something about goddamn satellites.

"Anyway," Butch continues, "my buddy shows me these sat weather maps of the Indian Ocean. Shit, from the tip of South Africa there was one low pressure stacked up against another, aimed at Indonesia. Always figured these islands must be loaded with surf."

Mike appears overwhelmed.

"You found this place from space?"

Butch grins.

"Yeah, I guess so. How did you find it?"

Mike shakes his head.

"Just blundered in here. Blind luck."

Butch replies, "It's better to be lucky than smart."

We all know what he means by that.

Butch sees us looking at a good-size dent on his neck and touches it.

Mike asks him, "What happened?"

"Yeah, not so lucky, huh? I was green. First week in. You know, they put me on this three-man team to carry this heavy-ass mortar. Took fucking minutes to set up the god-damn thing. When you're walking along..."

Butch takes a long hit and his eyes open wide.

"Can't tell you how much fucking walking we did."

His eyes roll around.

"Anyway the tree line suddenly lights up and you got your face in the dirt and all I got is part of this heavy-ass piece of shit and no rifle. Now those Charlies have got their shit together. They don't wait around while you set up your heavy shit to pound them. They hit a couple of your guys and disappear without a trace in less than a minute. So the mortars were useless, total bullshit, until I cut off all that heavy crap and took off all the aiming bullshit. Then you could set up fast and shoot from the hip. I practiced. I got good. That first time I got creased 'cause I wasn't shooting back. After I modified the piece of shit, I was. One way I found to stay alive in 'Nam was to shoot back. Don't aim, just fucking shoot back. The ones that hid in the dirt always got it. You want to kill them first."

I see that Mike's mouth is as open as mine.

I ask Butch, "So nothing else happened to you?"

Butch shrugs. "A shrink told me my neurotransmission pathways are fried."

Mike and I twist our faces.

"What?"

"Big word, huh? They got plenty of big words. Asked the doc if that was why no one wanted to be around me when I got home and he just nodded."

Mike's eyes are like saucers.

"No judgments here, pal. We've fried our share of neurons."

Butch is silent for a moment and finally gives Mike a warm handshake.

"You know what, fuck those doctors. I know what fucking works. Some fucking hippies offered me that crappy Mex pot to mellow me out. Wait till they try what I brought back. A little Laotian present from the Ho Chi Minh trail. Golden Voice ganja. That'll kick their ass. But hey, it ain't smack."

We all laugh because it's currently kicking our asses.

Mike asks, "How'd you do it?"

"Just personal possessions. They don't check much for us. A little payback, for using us like bait."

Mike drops his head.

"At least you're here. We lost a pal at Khe Sanh."

"A Marine, huh? I wasn't in that neck of the woods."

No one speaks for a few moments until Butch's face lights up.

"Hey, let's go surfing."

We like Butch. We feel that military bond with him yet he's out here like us, in Edge City, where a ruined guy can mellow out.

We're surfing at Uluwatu and the waves are jacking up in size. Huge sets crack and explode on the reef. I catch a few but notice that Butch is sitting motionless, facing out towards the sea with a stare like Superman's, X-ray style. Maybe he can see all that life under the water that we don't want to think about.

But my concern gets the best of me so I paddle up to him.

"Hey, Butch, if you ain't the hunter, you could be the hunted."

He snaps his head up from his thousand-yard-stare.

One of the basic laws of surfing is that if you're not catching waves, you'll eventually get caught inside—but it's obvious I've hit a nerve.

"You OK?"

"I'm fine."

"OK, but this ain't no time to space out."

I think surfing or any single-focused activity is fine on hashish or grass. But Butch's detachment looks different from any normal drug high. The waves are big enough that it's serious business. I flash—is this what Sean Flynn was describing when he told us about those Special Forces guys wigging out?

Colorado is a place that used to feel like nirvana. But I've been to the other side of the world and come back again. It's like being from another planet... and maybe a bit like Butch in the big waves.

It's the fall of my sophomore year. School's bleak, even with the steady stream of girls. I love the moist warm air in Indonesia—by comparison, this cold dry stuff in Colorado feels harsh.

The student dramas have lost their edge and my mind is far away. I'm occupied with thoughts about my brother and his plans for our future. He has his finger on the pulse of the Third World and I'm hooked on the lifestyle he's shown me.

My future is shaping up like the clean wall of a perfect wave. That future includes freedom, surf, travel and probably some illegal activities. The questions I had are fading away in the wake of current events. The war in Vietnam is still raging and the world is falling apart. It could mean my life if I don't make the right decision. There's a strong current pulling me away from the mayhem of war and into a life with my brother.

That future contrasts with my present situation, enrolled as a college student with only a deferment keeping me from the draft. The draft represents total loss of freedom and I'd be stuck, maybe somewhere dangerous. Using smack? Losing my mind like Butch? Maybe that's the path if I were in 'Nam. I'd better write Mike.

Mike,

My Vietnam problem is in my face. Instead of waiting until December to pick bingo balls, like they did last year, the Selective Service decided to do it in July, when I was still on Bali. My number was waiting for me when I got back to school.

I guess I used up my good luck a year ago. My number this year is 74 and they'll be drafting at least up to 100 if not higher. Dropping out of school to trip out with you isn't an option.

School is boring and I'm especially frustrated by the lack of choice I have about what subjects are available to me. So I'm just taking easy shit, like Home Ec, which is loaded with chicks. The teacher knows why I'm there—girls and a credit.

Bill

I've been surfing perfect waves at Honolua Bay every day since vacation began, but even the surf isn't washing away my problems.

Mike,

I'm back on Maui for Christmas. Man did I fuck up this last quarter at school. You know I couldn't even see out of my freaking window it was so frosted up. The snow was knee deep and I had this babe in my bed. Man what a tiger. I love tigers in the morning and figured I'd walk to classes later when it warmed up a tad. So I failed that class. No big deal, I thought. But when I got home to Maui, Mom handed

me a letter from the Wailuku draft board informing
me I was a credit short so my status would be
changed to 1-A. Or I could put myself on this new
deal called extended priority which means that for
three months I could be called before number one, if
they call up anyone.

From what I'm reading the opposition to the war is
pressuring call-ups down to zero. The draft board
even told me it's a pretty good bet that the next
three months will be OK. If I make it, then my
number will be placed behind 365. I hate depending
on luck or the government—but Canada sounds too
cold. Never thought I was a gambler before, but I'm
going for the extended priority.

Had a conversation with Dad about the draft. He
told me this is a decision I'll have to live with for
the rest of my life. In one way I knew he was right.
I remember you told me how your discharge gave
you the section eight and maybe Dad was talking
about those consequences, but I was pretty sure he
meant his position would sustain the test of time
about the validity of this bullshit war. Totally
disagree with him about that. This war isn't valid
and I know I will have to live with the consequences
for the rest of my life if I fight in it. My opinion
isn't being formed by war protesters, but by the
actual veterans I've met at school returning from
'Nam. They told me stories about officers being
fragged because they were so gung ho they signed
up for too many combat patrols. All these stories
were unnerving as they totally called bullshit on the
myths of patriotism and commitment to this war.
These guys have been there. Guys like Butch. It was
really cool meeting him in Bali but man, he was out
there. I ran into one vet who told me simply and
with conviction—Don't go.

I'm not going to end up with a dishonorable
discharge and a section eight. If I do get called up
I'll deal with it then.

When I told Dad my decision, he shrugged and said,
"So be it."

Dad says this phrase for other things he confronts in his life around the house these days and it unnerves me. Isn't he going to try to control things around him anymore? Has he given up?

I'm glad I don't have to argue with him about the draft. He's still clinging to the domino theory, but that grip is no longer strong.

Bill

It's February and cold here in Colorado. In the library I spot a *Time* magazine cover with the leader of U.S. forces in Vietnam, General Abrams. The title, "The War: Getting in Deeper To Get Out Faster?" I shudder.

At home during spring break Mom says Dad is having more night-mares. He wakes up screaming at Mom.
"You put the devil in my head!"
Mom can only cry.
I grab my now dog-eared *Moby Dick*. One passage jumps out at me about Ahab's demons.
"Often, when forced from his hammock by exhausting and intolera-bly vivid dreams of the night, which, resuming his own intense thoughts through the day, carried them on amid a clashing of phrensies, and whirled them round and round in his blazing brain, till the very throb-bing of his lifespot became insufferable anguish; and when, as was some-times the case, these spiritual throes in him heaved his being up from its base, and a chasm seemed opening in him, from which forked flames and lightnings shot up, and accursed fiends beckoned him to leap down among them; when this hell in himself yawned beneath him, a wild cry would be heard through the ship; and with glaring eyes Ahab would burst from his state room, as though escaping from a bed that was on fire."
Moby Dick is great input, but I need to spill my guts.

Mike,

You could say Dad has been lucky. He dodged a bullet at Pearl Harbor and then chanced to meet

Mom for the second time. He left the Northampton for flight school before it went on to Guadalcanal and was sunk. He did all those carrier landings at night and never landed in the drink once. Dad survived the war. But the thing with luck is that it runs out like those damn bingo ball numbers. I can't believe our invincible dad has brain cancer. The doctor told us that his case is terminal. Even so, Tripler Army Hospital is giving him cobalt radiation and chemotherapy.

The treatments have turned him into a caricature of himself. He's all puffed up like the Pillsbury doughboy. It freaks me out. And our uptight dad has turned into a giddy space cadet. He's been telling me stories he's never told me about his childhood and tricks he played on his buddies. Enjoyable as his stories are, the erosion of his health is hard to witness. His time left is unclear. There are ups and downs, with hopes and dismay. I wish you were here.

Bill

My letter must have grabbed Mikey because he jumped on the first flight back to Maui and now I'm dumping all my problems on him.

"I'm bumming. All this with Dad, and my classes have already started back in Colorado. If I lose any more credits I'm screwed."

Mike is shaking his head and has that far-off look that means he's not listening to me.

"Remember all that shit he ate? That barbecued steak fat that disappeared off his plate when we weren't looking. What about those fucking pickled pigs' feet? And man, that scrapple he loved. They sweep up the floor of the slaughterhouse and that's the ingredients for that shit."

"So you think that caused this cancer?"

"Fuckin' A."

Mike and I think Dad should check out some alternative therapies. The Tripler doctors have already admitted defeat. But Dad's brother and our mom overrule us. For them, it's too big a leap of faith to embark on wheatgrass therapy.

I can't handle it. After his breakdown, I'd held out hope for Dad to finally change, but now he's going to die. Jesus, he's only fifty-two.

The enormity of his terminal illness and my diminishing options are overwhelming. I've got to get back to school. This crisis has already made me late for the new semester. Everything is so messed up. How will I be able to concentrate on classes?

Mom hands me a letter.

"Oh God, Billy, it's from the Selective Service."

I rip it open and scan the short paragraph. A smile grows on my face. "I'm free!"

The time period for my gamble has passed. There have been no call-ups. My luck has held out; 366 is my new number.

It's great to see Mom smile. She's so happy she doesn't have to worry about me going to war and tells us she's already been through enough of that. I'm thinking she's probably pretty shell-shocked herself. Holding the fort, as Dad always says, is a tough job.

Mom leaves and I'm facing Mike. He's grinning at me.

"Why go back to school now?"

My mouth gapes open. It's a shocking revelation. He's right. School holds nothing for me now that my looming draft problem is resolved. I can almost feel myself dropping into a clean wave on Bali and silently mouth the word 'wow.'

"A ticket to Bali is less than next semester's tuition," I say.

Mike nods. "But before we go surfing, why don't we extend your education?"

"I don't get it."

"I got a load in Kabul. You could come along."

"Afghanistan?"

"Yeah, it'll be a gas. Think about it and if you want to go, make that ticket to Karachi."

I've thought about it the last two days. Why not? I've got no reason to go back to school. Bali has become my new home and helping Mike in Karachi will help keep it that way. Besides, flying east to the cold Rocky Mountains doesn't hold a candle to flying west with my brother. He wants me to come and I'm stoked to be invited.

Mom is devastated by Dad's terminal prognosis and her goodbye hug is limp until tears stream down her face.

"You boys need to watch out for each other."

Mike says, "Yeah, Mom, don't worry. I got it together."

Chapter Thirteen

The Graduate
1971

From my Pan Am window seat there's nothing but blue ocean and clouds. Man, we're flying to Karachi, almost halfway around the world. I glance at Mike sitting next to me. Since the day he returned to Maui he has slowly changed into a wild-looking hippie with a beard. I give a questioning pull on a strand of hair from his chin, and he swipes my hand away.

"Where we're going, beards are in."

"You mean they're grubby?"

"No, they've got their shit tight. You're the grub. But don't worry."

"I'm not worried. I'm a surfer."

Mike snickers.

We arrive and it doesn't take long to realize that being a surfer won't mean crap in Karachi.

Mike's a big spender these days and wants to use our chips on the best digs. We're staying at the InterContinental—the only decent place in town. Mike has been at the gym and when he returns to our room, I'm taking in the view from our window.

"This place isn't safe for us. When you went for your work-out, I cruised around out there on the streets. Felt like that Jack London story where the guy is alone in the woods with wolves surrounding him. Once we leave the doors of this hotel, we're in the woods."

"Oh, quit being so dramatic. It's cool. And besides, we're covered."

He sounds a little edgy.

"What's that mean?"

"It means don't worry. I'll be in charge of our safety."

That bothers me. But he does seem enthusiastic about our trip and his positive attitude is always infectious.

"Pack light. We can leave most of our stuff here at the hotel. We'll be back."

It feels like I've just fallen asleep when Mike shakes me awake. The sun is coming up as we jump into a rugged Jeep parked in front of the hotel. We're not alone. Mike tells me we've been provided with these two men to act as our guides. Both our driver and his front seat partner are big bearded men wearing sidearms. There are also two automatic rifles racked above the front seat. Mike surveys our ride and nods.

"I guess we're good."

Karachi is a huge city of desperately poor people and I'm glad to leave for the open country. My enthusiasm quickly dims, though, when I see that the roads are crowded with military traffic going in the same direction we are.

"What's happening?"

Mike pushes a newspaper across my chest. It says the Pakistanis are gearing up for a war with India over the provinces of Kashmir and Bengal. I'm startled that we have arrived with such bad timing. There's something very disturbing about setting off to smuggle hashish via roads swarming with fierce, grim-faced soldiers hauling heavy artillery and automatic weapons.

"This doesn't look good."

"These two countries go to war all the time. It's no big deal."

I can't believe how self-assured my brother is.

"Is your nose bleeding?"

Mike turns away and wipes his nose.

"Yeah, it's these dusty dry roads."

I doze off but a bump opens my eyes just as Mike is throwing a small vial out the window. I close my eyes again.

Our jeep is freed from the traffic jam when the Pakistani army makes a turn towards Kashmir in the east and we follow the signs to Peshawar.

We enter Peshawar and I tell Mike I'd like to buy some apricots. I've been a vegetarian for a few months now. He stumbles in his communication and our driver stops in front of a bazaar that sells guns. The shop owner proudly points to his own gun as though to ask if we want to buy some hardware. Mike appears interested and inspects a few pieces in detail. I'm watching over his shoulder, interested in the people who work in this shop. The gray-bearded gun merchant has a group of teenage boys working for him who are experts at putting together weapons from all kinds of parts. Their hands move rapidly, mixing and matching. My eyes settle on one of the boys who has only one hand yet is still remarkable in his ability to put a complete gun together. Mike notices my attention.

"Remember when we were kids? Dad told me, 'In some areas of the world, they would chop off your hand for stealing.' Well, guess where we are, pal."

I'm stunned and shake my head with the rough memory.

"Apricots. Please."

Mike waves the owner off; there will be no sale. Guns still make me uneasy and Mike knows it. He hits me playfully in the shoulder and passes me a joint.

We're driving again after failing to find any fruit. Mike tells me, "Peshawar is the last Pakistani city before the Khyber Pass, the eastern entrance into Afghanistan. It also marks the boundary of any national influence from the country of Pakistan. From here and well into Afghanistan, it's Edge City."

I'm guessing that means whoever has the best weapons makes the rules. The hash and this information don't relax me. I'm checking out the stark scenery as we begin to climb into the mountains, imagining all the ambushes that must have occurred throughout history on this same road.

We stop. Apparently this is the border, although there is no sign like the one that declares "Entering Beautiful Mississippi" with a giant magnolia. Our driver is conversing with a group of locals. I'm able to see these Pashto tribesmen up close, and can see their lives have cut rugged crags into their faces that echo the harsh landscape around them. The man next to the window has fierce blue eyes like a hawk's. Is he looking right through me, fully aware of what we're up to? My face must look soft and untested.

Mike can read my mind.

"Hey, he's just counting heads. We're going to buy some hashish. It's no secret. They know. Hashish is an old business in this part of the world."

The man in our window reaches into his vest. Whatever it is, it's hard to pull out. Despite what Mike has just told me, my heart races an instant until he finally produces a stamp for our visas. We enter the Khyber Pass.

I want to show off what I know to Mike.

"This is a historical place for ambushes. I read from Kipling how only one soldier from the invading British Army survived the slaughter."

"Then you should be happy we aren't invading. Our mission is just commerce. Commerce is a highly esteemed activity here. The local population is just trying to carve out a living in this tough world. Can you dig it? Money and baksheesh speak volumes."

'Baksheesh,' the word Mike used after he bribed the immigration official on Bali with a Rolex, is an Arab word. My Asian history class taught me about the Silk Road, the once well-used trade route for the spice caravans. Buddhists were the first on the Silk Road, followed by Moslem Arabs and then Mongols. They each made a huge impact here. This was an important trade route before the age of nautical discovery.

We're bumping along this dusty road and I'm thinking that the educational appeal is as strong for me as our repeating history with profit as motive.

But it still looks like the Wild West. I see weapons on many men, but they're one-shot Enfield rifles from WWI and I doubt some of them fire at all.

We also see backpackers hitching along the road to Kabul. They flash us peace signs.

Mike tells me, "Hippies. They've been here since the mid-'60s, when Mimi was here."

"Peace, love. Cool, hippies."

"It's wild, Bill. They're from all over North America, Europe and Australia. If someone wants to travel to a far corner of the world that's as different as possible from the West, Afghanistan is the place. It also has the treasure of the best hashish on the planet. Anyone who has an interest in cannabis of any form couldn't be in a better place. Hashish is everywhere."

Mike's right. As we approach Kabul, I can smell hashish in the air. Restaurants put it in food, and bricks of it are piled high in almost every bazaar.

"You know, Bill, this place has a king. Mohammad Zahir Shah not only proclaimed hashish legal, but he also promotes its trade. That's the law here. For stoners, this is the kingdom of heaven."

He chuckles.

We eat well in Kabul. The smell of kabobs doesn't turn me on since I've become a devoted vegetarian, but I love the tangerine juice, melons and apricots. Tons of apricots. Despite this arid environment, there is sufficient irrigation for extensive orchards, fields of wheat and, of course, huge fields of poppies and cannabis.

Kabul is a pleasant city, nicer than cities in Indonesia. It's also at a very high elevation, like the Front Range of Colorado. I like it here.

We meet Moussini, our man with the hashish, and arrange its refinement into honey oil, a new high-powered product. He's dressed like most locals around here in a floppy hat, vest and linen trousers. I remember some of the Brotherhood guys on Maui dressed the same way. Moussini speaks English in the strangest way I've ever heard.

"You-show-me-mon-ey-I-give-you-ha-shish."

I keep repeating his line. It sounds so funny to me, especially when I see the huge smile on his face when we fork over his money.

Many travelers are coming by Moussini's to sample his product. From what we gather rapping with people in restaurants, most smugglers have entered this country from the west, through peaceful Iran.

I ask Mike, "Why did we enter through a war zone?"

"Because the Pakistani border doesn't give a shit. They already have tons of hashish, just not as good. Iran? The Shah supports the U.S. by enforcing a tough policy on smuggling. Believe me, you don't wanna find your ass in one of those pits they call prisons. Pakistan is the way to go. We don't have much sway there outside of all the crappy out-of-date weapons

Mike Boyum

we give them. They're just trying to exist as a country. Nope. We're not going to load our stash into panels of luxury cars. Those Brotherhood guys can do that. They can drive their cars to Germany and ship them to North America. They can have that border. I have a better plan."

There's some waiting time in Kabul, so we rent motorcycles to race out to the Bamian Valley in the Hindu Kush Mountains, over a hundred miles to the west.

Mike tells me before we head out, "This road was built by the U.S. and the Ruskies during the mid-'60s. That's why there're less potholes on it than on the Khyber Road."

It's easy riding for us, even if we look like dust ghosts by the end of each day.

The Bamian Valley is as high as the ski town of Telluride. This area was the heart of the Silk Road long before the Moslems invaded and was a center of Buddhism during the fifth century. A few large statues of the Buddha were erected during this period, and the one in front of us is called the Standing Buddha. It's 173 feet tall, carved out of a solid rock cliff. I remember admiring a photo of it in my *Life Atlas* as a kid.

A barrel-chested Afghani with lungs like bellows places a piece of hashish the size of a chunk of coal into a hookah. At an elevation of 8,500 feet he puffs the meteorite of hashish into a fiery glow. When I take my turn my legs crumble beneath me. We smoke the pipe while we stand in rapture of the statue. It has been there for so long and I figure will be there forever, a timeless treasure.

I respect and fear the Afghanis from the little I know of their history. Mike and I attempt to fit in with our long hair and beards, but it's pathetic. We're stoned skinny surfers and they're tough men who put up with us only because of our money. I wonder if the lure of profit is the only thing that keeps them from slitting our throats. I notice them glance at our bodyguards. For now, they're being friendly. Our unwritten contract works.

After arranging for the oil to be transported, we head back to the Khyber Pass. The same terrain we saw entering this country two weeks ago now has an element of timelessness.

We return to Karachi and check back into the InterContinental. After what we've been through, Mike and I are eager for clean sheets and soft beds.

Mike hits the gym to consume his free time and I spend days curled up on my bed with a novel titled *The Flashman Chronicles,* a tale about a dashing British Army officer, Harry Flashman, who romps through Central Asia during the peak years of the British Empire. The story portrays Afghanistan, India and Pakistan as lands of enchantment—ripe territory for Flashman, a charming rogue who often entangles himself in history's turning points and either cheats death with each turn of the page or cavorts with a princess or the wife of a rival.

Harry's adventures and earthly pleasures contrast starkly with my state of mind. Even though I've enjoyed the relaxation for the first few days here, the only excitement since then has come from these pages. Mike and I have just passed through Harry's old stomping grounds, but we hardly romped through them the way Harry did.

I don't need any more rest, but the book slowly slips from my hands and I drift into yet another half sleep.

The days wear on, five, and then ten—but it feels like years to me. Why are we still here? Whenever I question Mike about his plans, he gives me an irritated look. Why is he edgy now, when we're comfortable?

A bang on the door interrupts my reading. It's Mike and he's grinning. He has his hands full with a heavy stainless steel sugar cane juicing machine he's bought at the Sadder Bazaar. Mike always manages to dig up a diamond in the rough wherever we find ourselves. Here in Karachi that diamond is cane juice.

He glances at my novel lying open on the bed.

"*Flashman* is a gas compared to that bummer whale tale you haul around. I've got the whole series."

Right before he plugs in the machine, he adds, "We might be here for a while."

I catch his last add-on but the shiny apparatus stifles my response as it rumbles to life and crushes some fresh stalks of sugar cane with explosive snaps. The juice squeezes out of the machine—effervescent and seafoam green. Mike holds out a glass.

"Drink this quick before it turns brown and tastes funky."

I grumble at his last recommendation.

"We were supposed to be here how long? Ten days? Now what? Yeah, brown and funky, that's it."

But when I walk over and slug down the glass of juice, I grin.

"This is unreal."

Mike flashes me a twinkling eye. I figure that look silently advises what he has told me many times before: Stick with me, little brother, and you'll be farting through silk.

Out loud he says, "Come on, this place isn't so bad. I know I've been a shit. Let's go for a beach run. That'll cheer you up until the girls get here."

I've been resisting getting out of our room. Every time I've ventured into this city, I feel overwhelmed by the poverty. All of Pakistan is poor, but the boundaries of this city accentuate misery to such a degree that escape and hope seem impossible. Mike is right, though; exercise, especially next to the ocean, has always worked for me.

We sprint down Karachi's long Clifton Beach, and the last ten days seem to recede like an empty past. There is nothing like a beach to bring me back to life. The sky is clear and the air cool, but this beach on the Arabian Sea is dismal with rocks and garbage. A camel with a passenger bounces past us, casting a throat-gagging smell. I bump Mike hard, steering him around a pile of camel dung.

Mike stops for push-ups dangerously close to a snake charmer, whose cobra is halfway out of its basket. This beach isn't charming me and my mood still stinks.

I'm getting sick of curry. We've missed turkey and Thanksgiving by being stuck in Karachi, and Christmas is coming. If we were surfing, I wouldn't care about holidays, but here in a city, especially this city, it bothers me. Waiting is a huge part of what we're doing.

Mike strives to make it fun, which isn't easy here. He's also stressing how important it is for neither of us to get sick. Karachi isn't known for great sanitation.

"Hey, our wait is almost up. I have some babes flying in tonight. Dancers. We're going to do some fiberglass work on their Samsonite suitcases and then fill in the false bottoms with our oil."

We take a taxi to the Quaid-e-Azam International Airport and wait for the girls to arrive. Aside from the part they are going to play in this operation, I look forward to some female company.

"So you heard they were cute?"

"Like Katharine Ross, baby."

I love that movie star's eyes and go along with Mike's fun.

"So they like outlaws?"

"Of course, they love outlaws. Who else would they like? They look like fancy chicks from New York City, but they're just like us."

My anticipation is high as we wait to greet the girls at the baggage area. The way I see it, things will begin to move forward to what I hope will be our eventual departure. The girls are in Karachi on business, our business. They want the same thing we want—to make some big money fast. Maybe we can have some fun with them at the same time.

The airport is busy. Many airlines use Karachi as a hub to different destinations around the world, which suits our plans. What doesn't suit us is the continued heavy presence of Pakistani military. India isn't just in between Bali and where we are; it's between West and East Pakistan. The Bengalis in the east are in rebellion and things are tense with India because they're supporting the Bengalis. I'm not taking sides, but our recent experience on our way to the Afghan border still makes me nervous.

The two girls, Samantha and Ann, arrive at Pan Am's baggage claim and are waiting to collect their hard-shelled Samsonites. The girls are conservatively dressed and made up but obviously worn out. I think they are possibly cute and try some small talk.

"Long flight, huh?"

Samantha does a quick inspection with her makeup mirror and doesn't even give me a glance. They also say little on the way to the hotel, and my lustful fantasies dim.

We check them in and Mike has them dump their belongings out on their bed so we can modify their suitcases. I try not to look at items like their lace underwear but I can't help myself. The taller blonde, Ann, notices me.

"So. Are you going to show me the town?"

Girls never fail to blow my mind.

I mumble, "Sure."

She gets my best smile as we leave with their luggage.

We've left the Samsonites with the fiberglasser in town and now Mike is briefing me about Karachi's nightlife. A military dictator is running the country. Apparently he's oppressing Bengali dissidents but leaves the nightlife in Karachi alone.

Mike kids me.

"So Ann?"

I shrug.

"She looks like a schoolteacher. I'm into beach babes."

This isn't what I want to talk about.

"So this means we're out of here soon, huh?"

"I don't know, Bill. There could be a snag."

"Snag?"

He's irritated again.

"Why do I need to answer so many damn questions? I'm getting tired of it. When we're set to go, I'll let you know."

Mike was patient on our trip into Afghanistan but since we've been back in Karachi, he's been weird. Maybe he doesn't know how it will play out and it bothers him? Perhaps he knows enough to worry and doesn't want to worry me. I let it go. I like the happy Mike, even when he bugs me.

On the way back to the hotel he goes into a bathroom and, when he returns, he's happy Mike again. We cross Club Road to buy some fruit. He starts to dance across the street like Wilson Pickett boogalooing to "Mustang Sally" on the streets of Karachi. I know you don't get high like this from hashish.

He starts to howl, "Guess you better slow your Mustang down."

I roll my eyes and point around us to show him where we are.

He stops dancing and turns me around.

"Hey, want to see some Paki belly dancers?"

He knows Paki women have no appeal at all for me.

We dig out a wad of rupees and pay for a melon, a jackfruit and a newspaper. I point to the jackfruit.

"You can have it. I'll take some melon."

Mike bites off a piece of jackfruit.

"Makes your dick hard, Bill."

"Great. I can put it in a door and slam it."

He grimaces.

"You get the front page, asshole."

Mike snags the sports.

"I'm taking Miami over Dallas. The Super Bowl is in New Orleans."

"And bet against Navy's best-ever quarterback?"

"Sure. The Navy has no nostalgia for me."

"Well, that's about a month away. Man, I'd take New Orleans over Karachi any day."

Both are ports at the delta end of major rivers, but the similarities end there.

The front page says war is imminent between India and Pakistan. Karachi is heavily fortified. Nixon backs Pakistan. The Pakis are equipped with superior American weapons. India has crappy Soviet weapons.

I wonder how much damage either side can do as they appear to barely subsist as countries. Military planning takes organization and there are no clear examples of it in either country. I can't even imagine an Indian military of any kind. It's an oxymoron. The India in my mind is full of mystics, yogis, gurus and sitar players.

"Hey, Mike, wasn't Gandhi like some kind of peaceful protestor?"

"Yeah, man."

"Well, Indira Gandhi doesn't seem so peaceful."

"You dummy. There's tons of people in India named Gandhi. It's like Smith."

"Oh. Well, it looks like they're pals with the Ruskies."

"Don't worry."

Mike's right. According to the paper, the war will take place somewhere else, probably in the north around Kashmir in the direction we saw the Paki army marching a few weeks ago.

We call the girls' room. They want to sleep off their flight, so I read more of the *Flashman Chronicles* until I crash.

The paper and I are wrong. India does have a capable air force. I wake up the next morning to the rumble of air raids over Karachi. Sporadic attacks continue all morning and jets roar by our window. All the action appears to be over the port and nothing significant happens over the city. Small wisps of smoke and the constant pop of anti-aircraft fire are the only signs of battle. But we'll pass on our daily beach run and obey the hotel advisory to stay in our rooms.

The girls come by in the late afternoon and want their night out. They are either oblivious or jet lagged because they seem unaware of the commencement of hostilities. We explain the situation but tell them we'll take them to the Nasreen Room inside the hotel—it's famous for having foreign bands. The girls giggle and feign fear. They need our protection. Is this like taking a date to a horror show?

They're pleased that they can wait out a war in a bar. I'm not so sure. This certainly qualifies as a snag. How long will we be stuck in Karachi now? The Indians can't last too long, can they?

The girls leave and say they'll be waiting for us at the Nasreen Room while we clean up. When I come out of the shower, the sun has set and the battle has intensified. Our hotel window reveals a staggering scene over the skies of Karachi. I keep the curtain panels close around my face as I watch to prevent any light from escaping our room. It's early December and though I can't expect Christmas decorations in this city, Karachi is so lit up I can't even spot the stars that might have guided the three wise men. Man, some kind of compass would sure be helpful right about now. Twenty-one years old and I'm facing a crossroads, maybe even crosshairs. The wisdom of investing any faith in my brother's four-year age difference is being challenged.

On the other hand, I'm no longer bored. My attention turns to some huge fires maybe five miles away. Horrendous explosions light up sections of the city. Karachi is being bombed. From our window I can hear, but barely see, the attacking planes roar by, dark specters trailing blue exhausts. Bombs, fighter jets, explosions—I can barely believe what I'm seeing.

The press has been writing about the Pakistan-India conflict for a while and—for a time, at least—it seemed to be simply a war of words. But now it's turned deadly and, worse yet, it's right on top of us. Jesus, no more saber rattling; these ragheads are at war.

I hear Mike sniff loudly in the bathroom. Shit, he's getting a cold, just what we need. He comes out holding a small mirror with lines of white powder on it.

"Want some?"

"Coke? Is that what you've been doing?"

He nods and cranks up the Rolling Stones to top volume. I shake my head as he screams in a wretched falsetto the Jumpin' Jack Flash line about being born in a hurricane. Then he's strumming an air guitar and dancing in front of the mirror, flashing me a toothy smile as he sings about things being a gas, gas, gas!

Mike has been able to draw from the well of our common experience to turn even a rowdy rock-and-roll song into a metaphor of our current situation. It's his way of bringing me back into the fold, even when that bond means ignoring what I now know to be common sense—the need for us to get the hell out of Dodge, pronto.

Mike howls about being schooled with a strap across his back.

Yep, we know that school. Is Mike Jumpin' Jack Flash? I laugh to myself, thinking I'm in Karachi to make sure Flash doesn't burn himself up.

Another loud explosion reverberates nearby. I run over, turn off the room lights and return to my observation window. Lights four blocks away suddenly dim, courtesy of the Indian Air Force.

I shake my head in fearful appreciation of our predicament and twist towards Mike again.

"We're so screwed. These guys are dropping in on their runs right over our hotel. We've got to be next."

Mike turns down the stereo and turns on the lights. He mocks me in the impish manner that always pisses me off.

"What gots to be, gots to be."

Words don't come to me. Why isn't he scared—like me? I know he's holding something back to keep me on my heels. He's too cool. Is he keeping me on edge and out of the planning loop? Does he even know what the plan is? I know he's playing me, but how?

Our situation is grim and for me it's totally real. You wouldn't know it by observing Mike, though, who is calmly putting his hair in place with a fine-toothed comb, like Kookie from "77 Sunset Strip."

Mike begins to flick the lights on and off while contorting his face into a fearful but ultimately comedic mask. Despite my fears, I laugh.

He wasn't this cocky two years ago when I found him strung out on Bali. Now he looks like a million bucks. Heavenly Bali has been good for both of us. Being here in Karachi has not. I'm witnessing bombings from our window and thinking we're descending into hell. Perhaps we've already arrived.

Mike postures in the wall mirror and flexes his pecs, stretching his shirt tight across his chest. I remember the Vic Tanney muscle shakes he used to drink when he hoped to be like one of the UDT candidates who scored the babes when we lived in Coronado. Right now scoring with a chick doesn't seem that important to me. I haven't anticipated an air war and know this situation isn't going to make splitting this dump happen any faster.

I'm scared and feel pathetic. But I'm not going to let Mike know it.

"Hey, Muscles," I say, "is this nightclub underground?"

I remember London civilians took refuge in underground bomb shelters during the Blitz in WWII. Dad once told me Edward R. Murrow had signed off his reports from London with, "Good night and good luck." But as long as I'm resurrecting the dead, I figure Kipling should be here; he's the most adept at describing slaughter in Central Asia. My mind is wandering all over the map.

Mike is in a typically sarcastic mood.

"Underground? Yeah. Sure. You ready?"

He can barely conceal his disdain for my loose-fitting aloha shirt and standard Levis. His trousers and shirt display every contour of his body. A last-second hit on a hashish pin joint inflates him like a balloon.

"Let's go," he squeaks, without exhaling.

It's been a long day and the safest choice would be to stay put. But hanging out alone isn't an option. I need more distraction than Harry Flashman and my inner dialogue can deliver. I'm ready to roll with Mike.

The Nasreen Room is not underground. It's well above ground, giving us a fantastic view of the city and, of course, a close-up view of the continuing explosions.

I check out the room. Wow, what a scene. The usual foreign band is absent this evening. Pakistanis in goofy cowboy outfits dribble out a wretched version of "Tracks of My Tears." If Smokey Robinson were here, he would crawl under the table. The room, decorated as a country-western bar, is shabby and has seen better days. Merle Haggard's picture has a spider-web crack in the glass inside a frame that hangs cockeyed.

I barely recognize our girls even though they are the only Western girls in the joint. Their hair is down, over their shoulders, and their skirts are up, way up. They've lost the librarian look they had yesterday at the airport. I'm changing my mind about them but can't help notice the two well-groomed Western men sitting with them.

One of the men hands the waiter a thick wad of rupees when their bottle of wine arrives. Competition for the babes? Yep, that's the way I see it. One wide-shouldered guy looks like a swimmer or maybe a surfer, and the other is obviously a weightlifter. Both appear to be about ten or more years older than Mike, and their expensive clothing would be right up Mike's alley.

As we approach the table I spot gold Rolexes and gold chains and get a whiff of cologne. The weightlifter shoves his chair back and stands.

In a cheerful British accent he shouts, "Hey, Mike," as he mimes an isometric pectoral flex to my brother.

Mike has a huge grin on his face and nods appreciatively, as if he's reuniting with a long-lost pal.

"Ian." Mike stretches the name slowly in a raspy, stoned voice.

He initiates a complicated handshake I think should be reserved for a couple of Black Panthers, and Ian enthusiastically participates with his well-rehearsed part.

I note the two guys' pale complexions. They aren't surfers.

Mike grabs my arm and shakes it playfully.

"This is my baby brother, Bill."

I rip my arm loose. I've always despised that introduction and I'm especially pissed off here where I have my sights set on Ann, who is looking very hot.

Ian extends his hand, and I offer only the standard Navy-issue handshake that I learned from my father—a strong squeeze and quick release. But when I attempt to let go, Ian holds tight with two hands. My hand feels like it's encased in concrete as he intensely locks his eyes on mine.

I'm never comfortable with that kind of immediate intimacy and always prefer to check people out from a distance. But now I'm caught, and I sense that he's checking me out in his unsubtle way. I know it will be easy for him to determine I'm out of my element. I'm not wearing any watch, jewelry or expensive cologne, and my well-tanned face does little to hide my anxiety. My eyes dart back and forth between Ian and my brother.

"Relax," Ian whispers in a sympathetic tone as he finally releases my hand and rests one of his on my shoulder. He stares at me with a weird gleam. Then suddenly he's louder.

"We meet Mike at the gym every time he rolls into town."

Ian grimaces for a moment.

"Though it's hardly ever this town."

Then he flashes a quick smile.

"It's usually Singapore, Hong Kong or Kuala Lumpur." He turns to Mike, "Remember that time in KL?" and then back to me. "Anyway, your brother is a madman!"

Ian has a noticeable lisp and spins around.

"How about this place?"

I realize he's gay and laugh inside for initially thinking these two were competition for the girls. But if they aren't chasing chicks, what are they doing here in Karachi? My interest in Ann will have to go on the back burner until I figure out what's up with these guys.

Ian slides his hand over the tattered mechanical bull.

"It's so giddy-up."

He leers at Mike and me.

"So American."

I'm irritated. Does he have us pegged as mainstream American just because Mike has shown him the Huey Newton handshake? What a joke! I couldn't care less how this joint is decked out. My opinion is that Karachi is the pits, period.

I grunt, "Yeah, great view."

Ian tells me, "Did you know American oil and tool outfitters steadily traveled through here in the mid-'60s? They were competing with the Soviets to develop Afghanistan's infrastructure. Afghanistan is loaded with natural gas, but the Americans eventually gave up and pulled out,

46 / Journals from the Edge

leaving behind this seedy bar, a watering hole for anyone advancing or retreating from Central Asia."

I don't care about this history or Ian's lecture. All that's important to me is the choice of friends Mike has made. Maybe he has good reason to cultivate Ian's friendship, but I can't help remembering some real losers he's connected with in the past.

I ask, "Are you in oil?"

Ian smirks and tilts his head, as if my question is ridiculous.

Who the hell are they? Tourists? Yeah, right. I've seen zero tourists in this city. Who would want to come here to see the sights? Peace Corps guys? No way. No hope. And not CIA, either—we spotted some spooks on Bali wearing their safari suits and Ray Ban aviator specs. Narcs?

Perhaps my question to Ian is ridiculous. These Brits appear a little too dapper to be oil guys. I chuckle to myself and think about Mike's other kind of oil.

I'm hoping they're smugglers. I've never met a gay smuggler, but who else spends money like water? They have to be smugglers.

As I approach the other Brit, I see he isn't nearly as fit as he seemed at first glance. He does possess a pair of wide shoulders, yet I can see the outline of his rib cage through his shirt. His watery eyes are sunk into deep sockets in his gaunt, pockmarked face. His looks both fascinate and unnerve me.

My previous suspicions fade as my sympathies go out to this man. I've seen many skinny Pakistanis on the streets of Karachi and assume they're destitute and malnourished. This man obviously isn't destitute and at one time he might have been an athlete. What happened to him?

He stands up, his back to the window, and extends his hand.

"Harry."

I shake his cold, clammy hand. The rather intense handshake with Ian is still fresh in my mind, so I give this man only half my hand—and yet it still feels strange. I quickly pull away and an all-encompassing burst of light erupts behind him in what seems like a reaction to my handshake retreat. The scattered fires around the city merge into one blaze, turning night into day.

What the hell has just happened? I grab my right hand with my left and give it a quick inspection. It's fine. Then I close my eyes for an instant, trying to dismiss my first reaction. Despite my general fish-out-of-water condition in Karachi, I have to admit that coincidences do happen. I haven't caused this inferno by breaking my handshake connection.

When I try to refocus on Harry, I can scarcely see him. The back light has transformed him into a dark shadow standing ominously under a blazing red halo. My disorientation immediately returns and I search the room for some kind of grounding. Mike is attending to the girls and my eyes turn again to Harry's dark silhouette.

"It grabs you, doesn't it, Bill?" Harry whispers, as though uttering a revelation of life.

I don't reply but can feel chicken skin run up my back and envelop my scalp. I'm also incredulous—'grabs' me? Like the Grim Reaper grabs the dying?

Harry hasn't moved. He's still facing me, his back to the window. I wonder if he can see the firestorm outside through the reflection in my eyes.

This thought seems confirmed by his next remark.

"It's the oil tanks beyond the port."

His casual tone baffles me. Why is he so calm? My eyes continue to find relief by focusing on his dark silhouette. I can again make out his deep eye sockets and angular skull.

Harry's deep, crisp voice adds to my sense of dread.

"Is it the jets or missiles?"

I assume Harry's speaking to me as we are face to face, but then realize his question has been addressed to Ian.

"No," Ian answers. "Perhaps Canberra bombers, though it'd be a lucky hit with them. They don't fly low enough to be that accurate, even when the Hawker Hunters are flying support."

Ian turns momentarily to me.

"Hunters are Her Majesty's planes. Initially they had a flame-out problem, but the ones we sent to India were given the new Rolls Royce modifications."

Then he says to Harry, or perhaps just to himself because Harry and I are still frozen in our mutual stares, "The Hunters carry only a 30mm cannon, which is better than the 20mm cannon on the Soviet Sukhoi-7b. Bill, that's the one with the highly swept wing angle, nose intake and single jet. The Indians have been sporting those today. The model is outdated and performs nowhere near as well as a Mig-21— although the Sukhoi can be outfitted with the best missiles the Soviets make. Not a Sidewinder, mind you. You Yanks are the best at that. If these slow-footed Pakis get a few Sabre F-86s in the air, then maybe we'll have a bit of sport."

Although Ian hasn't offered any ideas for redecorating the Nasreen Room, it seems darkly humorous to me that he offers such advice to remodel an air war. This scene, however, isn't a comedy; it's more like a horror show.

Ian's monologue increases in tempo as he rattles on about the airborne military equipment involved in the city's fireworks. His words create a buzzing sound in my ears. I'm focused on the visuals outside, however, and on the meaning of his last word, "sport."

Ian's other words replay in my head, "the ones we sent to India." Does he mean the UK? Or is he referring to himself and Harry personally? These guys know more about military jet aircraft than I do, and I grew up immersed in that world.

Who are they?

Harry interrupts my inner dialogue.

"Bill," he says, "you need to examine these illegal activities you're involved in. Your numbers are ridiculous. Whatever you figure in the thousands we tally in the millions. Look at it this way: You're bouncing around all these God-forsaken countries doing the same thing we are, but at a fraction of the reward and much more risk. You need to rethink your choice of contraband."

I can't believe my ears. Harry is preaching to me? Rethinking choices has crossed my mind today but certainly not in the way he means. The recent memory of Dustin Hoffman receiving fatherly guidance in the movie "The Graduate" pops into my head, and for a moment I can see his character's incredulous face as he receives that one word of advice: Plastics. Maybe I could use some direction at this point, but Harry's attempted seduction is rubbing me the wrong way. His two bits can be reduced to one word: Weapons. Harry's bottom-line speech jolts me into a total understanding of their profession. These proper Brits are gun runners.

While Mike and I would prefer to be somewhere else, surfing, these guys are in their element; they have front-row seats in Karachi and are thoroughly enjoying their view of this super bowl of death and destruction.

Although I'm not a huge fan of either the Indians or the Pakis, watching them kill each other isn't tops on my list. My viewpoint may be disillusioned, but it's still sympathetic to the cause of peace. These guys obviously have their bets on the opposite side of the ring.

But I'm curious.

"Isn't this a little risky for you guys, being here?"

Harry turns a fraction so I can see the glow from the outside inferno spreading across half his face. It resembles the color of a sunrise I recently witnessed over the stark landscape of the Hindu Kush.

He scoffs, "Huh?" Then he thrusts his scary. pitted face near mine. His eyes have a lifeless glaze as he sighs in an exasperated manner.

"Bill, both sides are clients of ours. We deal with and sometimes support governments. Can you understand that? So the answer is no. We know where the targets are."

He emphasizes the word 'know.' My head is spinning.

"Shall we talk about risk?" he continues. "Mike has told us you live on Bali, which means you're comfortable living outside the laws of your own country, correct? Will that really work for you?"

By now my previous sympathy for him has completely evaporated. Though I'm speechless, my insides scream yeah it works great for me, you creep.

I want to talk but he doesn't allow me to begin.

"If your country doesn't protect you, who will?"

What the hell? What is he talking about? He's studying my confusion as he interrogates me.

"Mike didn't tell you, did he? You see, that's the problem with dope. You guys forget everything. You're just surf bums blundering around on thin ice, fortunate to have our protection."

The meaning of his last word thunders into my brain.

"That's right, Bill," Harry continues once again, "bodyguards, information, timing, you name it. This part of the world is a very messy place."

My chest feels hollow and I want to say something but my mind is overwhelmed. The overall volume of conversation and music suddenly make my ears begin to hum. The bar feels foreboding and dark, even in the midst of this blinding light. The only thing I'm certain of at this moment is that these two specters are the scum of the earth. I realize, regrettably, that we had to depend on someone for protection. It's obvious that Harry knows the purpose of our recent journey; his implication that our safety has been secured from his corner has the ring of truth. The worst part? I've just shaken his hand. I shudder and try to make sense out of the evening's chaos.

Harry has only been partially correct, however. The whole world, not just this little hellhole, is a messy place. Others may hide it better, but I know everyone has to carve his own way. Some do it legally, some illegally. Even though Ian and Harry are operating legally and we aren't, I know there's a significant difference between what these vultures are doing and what we're doing. Maybe it's the vision of hashish versus the vision of war that we're witnessing just outside the window.

My soul needs cleansing and I'm doing it the only way I know how—by smoking hashish. Although at this moment I'm not even sure that will work.

The spell snaps and I step past Harry without touching him and walk over to Mike, who is still attending to the girls. More coke. He's holding a line under Samantha's nose. She sniffs hard. Mike nods towards me.

"Sure you don't want to try some?"

I shake my head. My mind is still absorbed with Harry's revelation.

"I'm going back to the room."

Mike nods without looking at me.

The shower feels good but doesn't help the fact that my head is still screwed up. I'm ready to crawl into the sheets and read. Two books are in my bag, *Flashman* and my dog-eared, marked-up copy of *Moby Dick*. Though *Flashman* is mindless and fun, I'm not really in a fun mood. Melville always has answers for me. Tonight's events make me leaf through my bible.

"I always go to sea as a sailor, because they make a point of paying me for my trouble, whereas they never pay passengers a single penny that I ever heard of. On the contrary, passengers themselves must pay. And there is all the difference in the world between paying and being paid. The act of paying is perhaps the most uncomfortable infliction that the two orchard thieves entailed upon us. But being paid—what will compare with it? The urbane activity with which a man receives money is really marvelous, considering that we so earnestly believe money to be the root of all earthly ills, and that on no account can a moneyed man enter heaven. Ah! how cheerfully we consign ourselves to perdition!"

Mike returns to the room an hour later with the girls, who both have wild looks in their eyes. I'm guessing the firestorm outside has everyone on edge.

Samantha yells, "Put the Stones on."

I'm still pissed about Harry and glare at my brother. I've trusted him up until this moment, but my confidence is beginning to crack.

"Anything but 'Jumpin' Jack Flash.'"

I must sound frustrated because my words prompt Mike into annoying me. He turns on the song with that grin I know so well.

He's screwing with my head and loving it. As the song's opening lines fill the room, describing my brother's gun-running friends to a T, I take one last look out the window at the Dante-like inferno and close my eyes.

It's been twelve more days in Karachi since the air attack. Commercial air traffic has resumed and we're flying to Bali. And I'm thinking about the dilemma I'm facing.

It's always odd how people draw a line for themselves. Dad had his lines that I often crossed as a boy. One of the 'facts of life' he drilled into us was that there was only a right choice and a wrong choice. He still had me convinced that was true up until two years ago, when I was back on Maui with my parents after our first trip to Bali.

We were up at my grandmother's house in Olinda to watch the moon launch that summer of 1969. More than ten years before that summer, the Ruskies had arrived in space first. Dad had seemed crazy and pissed-off back then when he yelled at the TV about Sputnik, so I figured he'd be pretty gung-ho about this moon launch. He might even provide some in-depth detail of what was happening to make it more real than just the rah-rah BS on the news. But Dad had never snapped back to his old self after I found him with the gun. During the broadcast of the moon launch he stood in my grandmother's kitchen, intently carving a turkey without comment.

It was Mom who kept going on about Neil Armstrong being one of the Pax River test pilots. Her exaggerated response to the moon launch cheapened it for me. It felt uncomfortably like she was filling in for Dad, and I almost began missing the crazy pissed-off Dad. How could I get him to participate? Be contrary and get under his skin? So I asked Dad about Werner Von Braun, the ex-Nazi rocket scientist who was the Director of NASA. It was a question I never would have asked him before his breakdown.

"Dad," I said, "did Von Braun really care about a step for mankind when he engineered those buzz bombs that killed thousands of innocent people in London during the Blitz?"

Dad turned to me and said, in a very low, non-emotional voice, "Would you prefer that the old Nazi work for the Ruskies?"

It was chilling to discover he felt some questions were no longer right or wrong, but involved a choice between two evils. Even though I was spoiling for an argument, his answer stunned me to silence.

Now, after meeting the two gunrunners, I'm beginning to examine my own line as I try to determine what's right for me. Any romantic notions about smuggling have been dashed in Karachi. But we should make a pile of money and it's time to go back to Bali and live our surfing dreams. It better be worth it.

Chapter Fourteen

Edge City
1972

Mike and I step into his Kuta Beach home. We hoot and lay down our travel bags. He stares at me, looking a little ragged.

"Man, it's good to be back."

"Sure is."

"Wish I didn't have to go back so soon."

"I'll go with you again."

"No, you hang out here. It'll be a short trip."

He must be reading my face.

"Hey, what's that look, Bill?"

"Just feels strange with you doing anymore time in Karachi while I go surfing."

"Guilt is for fools. Besides, you're getting the surf part of our program wired. That's what we're here for."

"Cool."

"Very cool. Hey, Laverty and Barness are coming over for some of our macro chow."

Our pals show up and soon we're all sitting around, talking about boards and waves.

Laverty asks, "Hey, Barness, you were back on the North Shore a few years ago. Did you see the Expression Session?"

Joe takes a hit from a joint.

"For soul surfers? Yeah, right. Man, the waves were crap and I heard there were fights about who got invited. Wasn't supposed to be any competition, but it was weird. Only cool thing was seeing Jock. He ripped."

"Thought he got drafted."

"He did, but was stationed in Hawaii. They cut his hair but he's still the best surfer on the planet. Man, he was the only real soul surfer there. All those other guys are trying to make some dough off surfing."

"How much for that contest?"

"Two bills each."

Mike laughs.

"In a few months those dollars won't mean jack."

"What's that supposed to mean?"

"Fucking Nixon, he's pulling the gold from the U.S. currency. Man, I know. I've met guys who know all about money."

Joe says, "What's being here worth?"

Mike says, "This? All these waves to ourselves? Hell, if you can pay for it with money, it's cheap."

Joe takes another puff.

"Well, I kept my mouth shut about this place while I was in Hawaii."

Mike says, "You got that right. Why try to create a cast of characters? Central casting will provide everyone who's supposed to be here. It's better if anyone who comes here figures things out on his own."

I'm thinking that sounds cool but know Mike has brought me here. I never would have found this place on my own.

Today the four of us are driving over the washboard road across the barren dry terrain of southeast Bali towards the isolated temple of Uluwatu. The ride in this old classic car with worn-out shocks is jarring. Mike elbows me hard in the ribs.

"This is why I bought the Avon—and you guys sank it."

"You're the one who saddled us with a poly prop anchor line."

Joe and I lost the Avon boat surfing at Uluwatu last week. The anchor line apparently frayed and snapped with the force of the huge swells. It was drifting towards the line-up as I kicked out of a big wave. Scrambling into the boat, I yanked on the start line a few times, but the 50-horse outboard engine had been firing reluctantly in the last few days. A glance towards the outside set revealed a massive feathering wave. In a moment I imagined going over the falls with that big motor and had to dive away to survive. The wave broke and the Avon was in a million pieces by the time it washed up on the low-tide reef.

We hit a big pothole and our heads bang into the car roof.

"No, no, no. You guys are the fuck-ups."

Joe passes a lit joint to Mike.

"Mellow out, man. At least this shitty road will keep most people from coming out here."

The dust is so thick we can't see where we are when the rumble of our broken muffler stops. Has this classic car finally died? No, we're here. As our dust cloud settles, a mob of young boys surround our car, pleading to carry our boards the remaining two miles to the ocean. We started hiring them when we previously passed by their houses on the hike from the road to the water's edge. Now we can barely get out of the car.

Despite this frenzy, we enjoy having our hands free to run the two-mile labyrinth of trails through farmlands cultivated with tapioca. We look at it like a cross-country running track with numerous cactus hurdles to test our agility.

The locals who farm out here are very different from the other Malays living on Bali. Their lives are even less affected by modern times than the lives of those in sleepy Kuta. We see only thatched huts and barefoot people.

Mike trips jumping over one of their cactus cattle guards. We stop to take his shoe off to check for an ankle sprain. Some of the locals come out to see what's making all the commotion. It delights them to examine Mike's fancy running shoe. A beautiful young girl steps into the sunlight, naked from the waist up. She beams such incredible energy towards us and we try not to stare at her upturned breasts. In this moment, light years of cultural gap are bridged by mutual awe.

Our jog to the ocean normally ends at the cliff edge with a cheering pack of monkeys ready to watch our show from their mezzanine seats. But when I catch up to Laverty, I find him glaring at a photographer with

Bill Boyum, Uluwatu, 1972

a tripod and camera pointed out to sea. A few high-caliber surfers are ripping it up in perfect ruler-edged waves.

Bob turns to me while I'm bent over, heaving for air.

"You see? It's happening."

The photographer brags that he's working on the first surf movie that will have footage of Bali, and goes on to say his movie will be about soul surfing. But right now we're paddling out to share waves we've never had to share before.

We're back at the house. It doesn't matter what the photographer calls it. Laverty is right, when surfers all over the world see this movie, they'll know our secret and the floodgates to Bali will open. Bob's reaction to the moviemaker is to begin planning for the trip to his mysto surf spot on the southeast tip of Java.

Mike is jazzed but says he's too busy wrapping things up before he takes off again. I know he'll be heading for Kandahar.

He's nodding towards Laverty and I know he means for me to jump in. No one else really cares about exploring because there are still plenty of empty waves on Bali. I hear this cardinal rule over and over again—never leave good surf to look for better surf. No one here on Bali has even thought about East Java except Bob—and for a few good reasons.

When I first arrived in this country, Joe Galloway informed me of Java's rugged recent past with its Communist insurrection and counter-coup where millions died. Traveling is difficult in Indonesia, and this trip would be loaded with unknowns. On the other hand, Bob's enthusiasm is infectious.

I tell him, "I'll go."

He makes it sound so simple and fun. Whatever happens, I need to get out there and do something wild.

We decide our work horses will be fat-wheeled Suzuki 80s. They're used all the time for cruising Kuta Beach at low tide, and once we get to Gradjagan it should be easy enough to get across the lagoon, then continue up the beach until we find the holy grail.

It all sounds good, although I'm concerned about the overland legs on Bali and Java. Driving on this island is always a wild ride. Most Balinese motorists make up rules as they go, and we've seen plenty of motorcycle casualties on our trips from Kuta to Uluwatu. Our policy has always been to hire a driver with a big muscle car and close our eyes.

Despite these reservations, we hang our boards on the sides of the bikes and pile camping gear and backpacks high over our heads. We're absurdly overloaded. But we've seen families of five going off to the market piled onto one small motorcycle—this should be no sweat.

We leave Mike's house before sunrise to avoid the traffic and the heat. It's a stunning drive through Bali as the first light lands its magic on the rice paddies. An early-morning mist hovers over an empty road as we climb through some lower mountain passes. While we head west towards the port of Gilamanuk, the cool mountain air is invigorating. Volcano tops rise majestically out of the clouds as we travel through a

Suzuki 80 loaded up, 1972

tapestry of rice terraces, the peaceful silence broken only by the sound of our puttering engines.

I'm excited; no worries about our unknown destination are possible in the midst of all this beauty. Bob looks every bit the Viking adventurer with his long hair and beard and a rolled-up chart protruding from his backpack. I like to think we have it together.

A Malay man with long dark hair appears out of the mist, standing on the seat of his motorcycle, arms spread out into a T like a Flying Wallenda. He banks around the winding mountain road with grace while a cigarette dangles mystifyingly from his mouth below his Dali-esque mustache.

The sun rises and the cool mountain air disappears, along with all the other accompanying magic as we descend back into the lowlands. The traffic suddenly congests with blaring horns and chaos as the road funnels us to the ferry embarkation point across the narrow strait to Java.

Because of its fat wheels, the Suzuki is the perfect motorcycle to ride on sand, but in the hordes we've run into it's the worst for negotiating this heavy traffic. My bike feels small and vulnerable.

At the ferry dock a while later, Bob and I gather our documents and wait to board a relic landing craft left over from WWII. The crowd around us is a mix of people, with many of the women and girls wearing traditional headscarves. I'm reminded that Java is a meltingpot of religions, with Islam the most common.

Bob looks at me funny and asks what I'm thinking about.

"Nothing," I say, "just this question about religion. For me, you and that banged-up Brewer says it all."

"Says what?"

"That guys like us belong to no one. We're surfing nomads who worship under the shrine of the open sky."

"Yeah, sounds great. But if they ask at the border, it's 'Allahu akbar.'"

Bob and I load onto the ferry and the straits show us some interesting whirlpools before we make landfall on the Java side.

The craft lands and as we offload, a border guard stops us to inspect our documents before we can enter Java. Even though the locals in Bali know about surfing, one look at this guard and I can tell he's totally unfamiliar with the concept. He shakes my board, looking puzzled and frustrated, then sets it on the ground and points his gun at it, signaling that he's sure there is a weapon encased inside the fiberglass shell. Will he use his gun to break the board open? How can I explain we prefer the barrel of a wave to the barrel of a gun? I do some fast talking with my poor grasp of Bahasa, trying to convince him that I'm going to the coast of Java to have fun and play in the sea.

One look at his face and I think what a joke. This area is desperately poor and I can sense that both ideas of fun and play are foreign concepts or even inappropriate activities from his Islamic perspective. Added to that, Joe's info surges into my mind about the slaughter that took place in this same area just a few years ago. My take is that this guard sees everything as a place to hide contraband. Fear is his instinctive response.

I change tactics and hold my board up toward the sun with my hand behind it to create shadows. Hopefully he can see the translucent inner foam core. I repeat my mantra in Bahasa, *"Ngga tidak ada apa apa di dalam ini"* (there is nothing inside). The repetition of these words briefly brings the metaphor to the top of my mind. What do I have inside of me? I have a tendency towards introspection, but this isn't the time and I shake it off quickly.

The guard looks at me as if I'm trying to fool him with some magic trick. He waves his gun in my face. I readjust. My eyes never leave his, even when my mind wanders. I learned this growing up with a much more menacing person than this young guard.

Even though he's armed, in a moment of indecision he loses his confidence and puts the gun down. Bob pushes me forward and we bull our way through.

Bali-Java ferry, 1972

My heart pounds with each step away from the guard. Have we taken advantage of the years of insecurity instilled by white Dutch colonials? Even though I've always been good at escaping, any illusion that our quest would be easy has been dashed.

We mount our bikes and kickstart their engines. Soon the ferry crossing fades behind us as we continue our journey to the south coast of Java.

A gas stop is unnerving when a large crowd surrounds me within seconds. There are some people with medical conditions I've never seen before. A skinny man has a huge tumor protruding out from the side of his head like a rhinoceros horn. He speaks quickly and I don't recognize any of his words from my vocabulary of Bahasa. It must be Javanese. The language isn't the only difference. This Islamic culture seems edgy compared to the Hindu vibe in East Bali. The horned man is very aggressive and interested in everything I carry, tugging on a few things attached to the outside of my backpack. His appearance is a painful reminder of Dad's condition and makes it difficult for me to even glance at him to say no with my eyes. I tug back without looking. Bob's eyes say let's beat it.

After miles of teak forests we arrive at a large gate marking the small village of Gradjagan. The pavement ends and turns into a dirt road. I follow Bob as he guides his bike carefully through the path with its strong smell of drying fish.

After a while Bob stops and we're scoping out a small inlet that provides a safe harbor for fishing boats. On the other side of the inlet a finger of sand connects to a thick jungle and what we understand is a national park. No people live beyond this village.

I can hear the concussion of surf from the other side of the lagoon. My heartbeat quickens.

We're intent on exploring so I arrange for us to enter this isolated terrain. With some language difficulty, I ask a wiry boatman if he will take us across the inlet. His dugout canoe is just big enough to carry us and our motorbikes, surfboards and backpacks in two trips across the short distance of calm water. Bob goes first. After I cross, I notice the boatman glance around as I unload. When I'm done, I take a moment to check out the magnificent swells exploding in front of us.

Turning back to the boatman to offer some payment, I see he's already shoved off without a word and is stroking back to the safety of the village. From the looks of the empty beach, it's clear that the jungle and its wildlife intimidate the people of Gradjagan and keep them away.

We mount our bikes and charge off down the empty beach. The narrow strip of sand between a large marshland and the thunderous surf defines the road to our destination, which we're guessing is eight miles in the distance. It trips me out when we flush a flock of flamingoes as we break the silence of their sanctuary with our out-of-place motorcycle noise.

At first the sand is hard packed. It gives me good traction and an empty freeway for my thoughts. I gun it and feel the clean ocean air whip across my face. A surge of personal history immediately floods my mind with how I came to Bali and now to this isolated place far from Maui. So much has happened so fast.

Gradjagan lagoon, 1972

My God, I think suddenly, Dad is in a spiral of terminal brain cancer. Despite the years of fear he caused me, he's still my father. I ache that there was nothing to do but watch and grieve as his health eroded. And then events threw me a difficult choice. I chose not to hang around on Maui and be a helpless witness to his deathwatch. Being free of the draft and sadly free of Dad has offered me an opportunity to put on my own guilt-ridden wings.

Meanwhile Mike's path had evolved 180 degrees from focusing on a healthy diet to promoting the first rock group in Indonesia and falling into its associated lifestyle of drugs and debauchery. But that was nothing. Now he's moved on to international drug smuggling and, incredibly, I've signed on.

Mike always laughs when I try to justify smuggling as our gift to enlightening the masses—peace and love, brother. But he's probably right when he tells me not to make it something righteous—because it's only a means to an end. It's been such a fast-moving stream to enter, but Mike's focus is clear now. He wants to establish a financial base to ensure a lifetime of endless surfing and I want it, too. I want it bad. This trip into the wilds of southeast Java could prove to be the prize we've been searching for. The future looks exciting for me and smoking hashish obliterates any doubts.

I chase away these thoughts to concentrate on handling the motorbike. My attention turns to Bob when I observe his bike do a dangerous wobble. The consistency of the sand is changing.

My focus shifts to what we've brought to survive. Over-planning can sabotage a trip. We had to figure out what we absolutely needed in a world that would provide nothing but perfect surf. Our backpacks contain the things we hope will keep us alive. What we don't have are any medical supplies beyond a few waterproof bandages.

Now my bike does a wobble. Control is becoming sketchier in the increasingly soft sand. The fat wheels have their limitations, and there is too much at stake to risk a crash at this point. Going fast is great, but injury in this place is unimaginable. Or rather, I can begin to imagine it, but don't dare.

This reconnaissance has us out on the edge of the world. We have to concentrate. Our destination is an unknown wave, maybe one of the best on the planet. I hope I can leave all my anxieties behind. Surf nirvana lies just ahead.

The bikes aren't stable enough to continue so I signal Bob to stop. We examine the terrain, which has changed from marsh to a thick jungle. It's intimidating but we dismount and push the bikes off the beach, where we confidently prop them against a huge tree. They're sure to be there when we return. There are no human footprints on this beach.

The effort involved in pushing the bikes this short distance produces a sweat that combines with the day's travel grime. It's getting towards sunset and the mosquitoes descend on us.

I have the fool idea that the jungle will give me more solid footing than the beach. While true, this thought awakens some primal fears about dangerous animals. As a boy in the comfort of my grandparents' home, I'd read and enjoyed books about the jungle. But this is the real thing, and I'm unaccustomed to jungle smells and sounds. Added to the hum of the mosquitoes, the unfamiliar orchestra from this dark world makes me shiver with dread.

Bob nods towards the sea and we retreat to the sunny sanctuary on the water's edge. We strip and wash the day's sweat off our skin in the crystal-clear ocean. Thanks to a slight breeze on the beach and our cooler skin, the mosquitoes cease to be a problem.

Despite this success, my thin veneer of confidence vanishes without the bike. The speed had given me a sense of power up until this point. But now I'm unnerved by the prospect of proceeding on foot. I feel lucky to have a friend with me. Bob seems so confident. I wonder what introspections he deals with.

My fears are confirmed by a steady invisible thrashing noise in the high trees that parallel our march. One of a troop of baboons ventures out onto the sand to check us out without the perspective of altitude. It snarls at us with menacing canine teeth but then scampers back to its troop when Bob makes a sudden leap in its direction, his arms spread wide. I'm rattled and need an escape plan—just in case. Can they swim? I hope not.

I have to come to grips with these fears because we have gone too far to turn back. In more ways than one I'm beyond the point of no return. A glance towards a distant headland reveals large waves peeling with offshore spray. They rear up like a horse's mane, highlighted in the golden afternoon sun. Bob and I grin at each other and whoop. The destination is set and we march on, determined. All that we have is on our backs.

Our excitement fades quickly as we sink up to our shins in sand that resembles small bb-size ball bearings that have no cohesion. We move back into the jungle for better footing. As the cloak of darkness begins to settle around us, the jungle sings with a cacophony of animal noises. It's totally dark and we're still walking. I wonder for the first time what we're doing here, so far away from home. Edge City? Man, this is it.

Unable to see and weary from exhaustion, we grope our way back out to the beach, spread our mosquito nets and collapse into a deep sleep.

A loud cracking sound wakes me in the morning. It's easy to see why we've come this far. Eight-foot barreling waves spin off perfectly along the reef. Even though I know there is no such thing, these waves are almost too perfect. The sound they make has me wrestling with fears about how powerful they might be. Surfing any new place is a challenge, but we're drawn tentatively into the water. I've been surfing Uluwatu for several weeks straight, so I'm as ready for this as I'll ever be. We paddle out.

My gut is empty but soon surf stoke injects me with all the energy I need. The smooth ocean surface rises under me like a surfacing Polaris submarine. No drop is out of place. I begin to paddle. My heart pounds with each stroke and becomes the relevant form of time measurement. There it is, that moment where my board releases and my legs leap into a standing position. The board accelerates down the ever-steepening slope to the bottom of the wave. My knees bend to initiate the first big turn, gentle enough to maintain edge and fin control but hard enough to turn up onto the steep face. Every part of my body compresses into a deep crouch as tons of water pitch over me. The lip of the wave lands with a crack and the difference between nirvana and total annihilation is only a few feet. I'm in the tube. Seconds pass but I'm in a timeless state until the wave exhausts its energy and I kick out. My mind tries to grasp the bits and pieces of what just happened. It can't, but I know this is heaven.

Our mode of transportation dictated only minimal supplies and for three days we've surfed our brains out with no injuries. But we've run out of liquids and available coconuts, and with no fresh-water showers we feel pickled to the bone. Worn out from the intense surfing, we decide it's time to leave.

It's a drag to be back on a small motorbike again. On the highway Laverty's bike breaks down and he manages to hitch a ride in a jam-packed truck full of Javanese orphans. I can see the kids giggling with Bob inside the truck and marvel at the way he adapts so well. I solo on to Kuta, dog-tired but ecstatic about our trip.

Bob and I meet up with my brother and the rest of our pals in Kuta to celebrate with a great dinner at a pizza place. It isn't even necessary to lie, as most surfers do, about the quality of the newly discovered waves. The conversation is electric and Bob is playing the piano late into the evening. When he takes a break from the keyboard he says, "You guys wouldn't believe the world I come from. Money. Our family had money. But when you define rich, I count this trip Bill and I just did as the richest thing that's ever happened to me. I think the discovery of this surf spot will have a mind-blowing effect on our lives."

Back at the house I look for something to read. Some of the *Surfer* magazines are from this year but I'm craving a news update. Mike's collection of *Time* magazines is moldy and over a year old. One reads "The Graduate 1971. Where Are The Jobs?" and shows a picture of a college graduate in a cap and gown, pumping gas. I'm not a graduate and it doesn't look like I'll ever be one. I move on and shuffle through a few more issues. Another one catches my eye and I remember the uproar about it last year. There's a picture of a U.S. Army officer with the caption, "Who Shares the Guilt?" Inside, the cover story explains that a U.S. lieutenant has been convicted of slaughtering over a hundred women and children in the small village of My Lai. I was feeling euphoric after returning from my adventure but, even though this story is old news, it's a startling reminder of what's still going on in Vietnam.

Mike leans over my shoulder.

"Rough story, huh?"

He squeezes my shoulders.

"Dad died during your trip."

I slam the magazine shut but again gaze at the cover caption, "Who Shares the Guilt?" The words seem to blur and silently scream at me. I shove the magazine aside and bury my eyes in my palms. The darkness allows me to force the scream from my mind and replace it with my recent image of the flock of flamingoes taking flight when I was racing on a motorcycle down that isolated Javanese beach.

"Sad shit," Mike says. "Seemed like there was hope for the old man when he was here."

I spin to look at Mike. His eyes are wet like mine.

"I'm almost relieved," I say. "It was terrible to see the erosion of his body and mind. But man, I feel guilty about not being there when he died. I didn't think he would go so fast."

"Don't start, Bill. Let's not spin out over this. Here, have a hit."

As the hashish soaks into my body and eases the pain of losing some-thing I didn't even know I had, I decide to deal with this loss later.

Today I need to do something to distract myself, so I'm surfing at Uluwatu with Laverty and Barness, thinking maybe the surf will wash away the pain of Dad's death. It must not be working, though, because in between sets Laverty paddles up to me.

"Wow, Bill, can you believe that last set?" he says. "Joe got locked in deep all the way through to boneyards. You think it's getting bigger?"

"Uh, yeah."

"You OK?"

"Yeah, man, I'm cool."

"Well, let's see you bag one of these. How about this one? Got your name all over it."

The wave feathers up but after some half-hearted strokes, I pull back. Laverty is checking me out. The set is over and there's nothing to do but wait.

"That wave was perfect and you just let it go. What's eating you, man?"

I decide there's no use pretending I'm OK. "My brother told me our dad died while we were over in Java," I explain. "We had a rocky road with him growing up and right now I'm just really fucked up inside try-ing to figure it out."

"Whoa," Bob says, "heavy shit. I've had some dramas with my family but my dad has always been golden. I love the guy. He was behind me every step of my life and is the reason I'm shooting pictures of all these bitchin' islands instead of stuck in some nine-to-five desk job."

He smiles, slaps me on the side of the shoulder and continues.

"And going on adventures… with you. I feel like the Captain Cook of southeast Java. That was some kind of trip, huh?"

"Sure was, Bob."

"Well, you'll work things out eventually about your dad, but right now here's another set and it's all yours. This time, paddle like you mean it."

Bob's optimism somehow lifts my mood and power surges into my arms. I make the wave. When I kick out, I can see a set breaking all the way across the line-up. Barness and Laverty are too far inside and are getting worked by some violent whitewater.

The ocean flattens out for a moment and I paddle up to Joe on the outside.

"You guys got smoked by that set."

"Yeah, man, kept getting bigger with every wave. Getting spooky."

"Where's Laverty?"

"Yelled over to me that he was headed in. Saw him prone out in front of a monster. How was that big one you got?"

I'm distracted a moment by seeing whitewater smash into the jagged cliff shoreline.

"It was unreal. Hey, I think I'll head in, too."

"Well, I'm not gonna stay out here by myself. Let's catch one and go in down the line."

Joe and I ride waves all the way into a small pocket beach, where we stay put until the rapidly receding tide allows us to wade back to the entrance cave in waist-deep water. Just before that entrance there are two large rocks that are V-shaped, like the prow of a ship. I spot Bob's board floating in between them.

"Look, he lost his board."

Pulling up the leash, I stare in horror as Laverty surfaces. There's a gash in his forehead and his body is already blue. I can feel the heavy pulse in my head and can't believe what's happening. We're not willing to accept that Bob's dead, though, and Joe and I give him CPR for an hour. Tears flood our eyes as we look at each other and admit it's over. I had the trip of a lifetime with this Viking—and now his blue body is all that is left.

The Bali police are asking questions about Laverty's death. Mike had planned on flying to Karachi in a week, but hurried his departure and split yesterday when a rumor spread about a passport check. He, along with all our pals, would rather not speak to the cops. I've had to deal with them by myself.

Despite all the effort we'd expended to find solitary waves on Java, Bob and I will never surf together again. Lonely and sad, I decide to find a phone and call Mom. If I feel this bad, how has she been feeling since Dad died?

Silence. The phone hangs in my hand like the dead feeling inside me. I've driven to the other side of Bali to use what I hoped would be working phones. But even though this is the best hotel on the island, my attempts to reach Mom the last several days have been unsuccessful.

Each time, the line goes silent after minutes of waiting and listening to various noises. Nothing works on Bali. Being out of touch and on The Edge isn't working for me anymore. I should go home.

The phone comes alive.

"Mikey? Billy?"

I hear sobs on the other end.

"Mom?"

Silence again.

"This country is so fucked up!"

God, I'm yelling at a disconnected phone. At least now there is no doubt about what to do next.

Eating one last durian on Bali before I jump on the plane to Hawaii makes me contemplate a game. I'll smuggle some of these durian seeds through U.S. customs in Honolulu. Maybe durian will grow on Maui. Smuggling a seed is a risk I can take.

Landing in Hawaii, the game is on. Honolulu Customs confiscates the seeds. I lose but there's no penalty. The agent sees I'm a resident of Maui and tells me he'll let me go to the bathroom and get rid of anything else I may have. That seems like a nice gesture, but is it a trick? I tell him no need and he rummages through my bags with a fine-tooth comb. After a fruitless search I'm allowed to pass but I'm a little shook up. How could anyone sneak stash through this airport? The Customs officers sure spotted me quickly enough.

Jumping on an Aloha Airlines flight to Maui, I'm happy to leave the tension of the Honolulu Airport. Mom is there to pick me up. It's only been six months since I last saw her but she's aged. Her eyes are puffy and I can see more gray around her temples. We hug and her body feels frail. She keeps telling me how happy she is that I'm home, but I know it'll be some time before I can cheer her up. Words stick in my throat.

Alone in my room, I think about my search at Customs and am relieved I haven't done anything stupid. What a long trip. I throw my bags on the bed and *Moby Dick* slides onto the floor. A book-sized slab of hashish slips out from its pages. My heart skips a beat as I remember that a friend of Mike's had placed it there during my time on Bali. A case of stupid forgetfulness and I've barely missed going to jail.

Mike struts in Mom's door sporting a safari jacket, a tight-fitting flowered shirt with a large collar, styled Rod Stewart hair and some snazzy oversized movie-star sunglasses. It's only been four months since I last saw him and now he looks like he's bought the flashiest clothes in L.A. The sorrow Mike felt on Bali after we heard about Dad is long gone. He's nodding with his mouth tightly shut, as if something is going to erupt from his insides.

"Got popped. Taped some condoms full of hash oil under the metal hatch plate of the seat in the upstairs shitter of the 747 and another under my seat. Planned to clear Customs in Honolulu and then re-board the plane to L.A. Got back on, grabbed my stash—then told them I changed mind and wanted to get off in Honolulu after all. I was stowing the oil in an airport locker when I realized I'd forgotten one of the stash spots on the plane."

Mom and I can't believe what we're hearing. I've always liked it when Mike lets me in on stuff, but this time he's too animated and is talking faster than ever. Words flood from his mouth and I'm checking Mom out to see how she's taking this.

"What a screw-up. Shoulda stuck with my plan but instead I flew to L.A. to track down my original flight to get that last bag. Found the plane, grabbed a stew and told her I needed to run back to my seat to find my shades. She told me no but said she could go look for them. Thought she was cool so I let her know what it really was. Waited in the boarding area until I saw it take off—with my damn stash. So bummed. Stuck around for about ten minutes feeling pissed that I'd lost so much—and was still sitting there when Customs officers walked up. Fuck. But made bail and have a dyno lawyer. You know, it's kind of fun in L.A."

Mom asks, "Did you get to see your cousin Tom while you were there?"

Cousin Tom? Didn't she get it that her darling son was just busted? And is she actually smiling?

I grin at Mikey.

"Oh, man, did you ever fuck up."

Mom's eyebrows shoot up.

"Billy, you're talking like a sailor."

She's worried about my language?

Mike pokes me in the ribs to rub it in. I get back to business.

"Did you get what you stashed at the airport?"

"Yeah, of course. It's right here. Let's bust it out."

Mike's so radical. Everything I think would be intuitive, like not going back for that stash, he throws out the window.

Mike and I go to Mom's kitchen to heat up the condoms.

"Hey, Mike, you know it's wild," I say, "Mom hasn't been happy since I've been home—and I get that—but now that you're here she seems on top of the world."

"Dig it. She's been grieving this whole time since Dad's diagnosis and now that he's finally gone, it's like a weight has been lifted. She's stoked to have both of us at home."

That might explain it, but suddenly I'm thinking about the time Mom stuck her head in our room during the Dodger's World Series run with the Yankees when we lived in Coronado. She asked Mikey if Maury Wills had stolen any more bases. We were intently listening to Vin Scully call the game and it bugged me that Mom was faking interest in baseball just because my brother was so jacked up about it. We always got infected by Mikey's enthusiasm, but Mom more than anyone.

Mom walks into the kitchen. I try to distract her in conversation, but she knows something is up and has that old twinkle in her eye. She moves around me like a cat and examines the pot. Mike smiles at her and explains everything he's doing like he's reading from *The Joy of Cooking*. Instead of being upset, Mom seems tickled and proud that her son has turned into such an enterprising young man. I'm thinking it's just like when we were kids when she would jump on any interest we had and expand it into our career choice. She ends up helping him with the hash oil processing.

She tells us, "We mustn't lose a drop."

It's bizarre. I don't know what I expected in the wake of Dad's death, but this isn't it. Mom has become completely unleashed now that Dad is gone. Far out.

But she is concerned.

"The district attorney in Long Beach called before you came home and you're supposed to report for sentencing in two days."

How's Mike taking this? He's had a wild ride this year—from the firestorm in Karachi to the impending reality of his possible prison time. Right now, though, he's waving off the bad news as if it were bad weather.

Mike is already back from L.A. with Mom and me on Maui.

"The judge says it'll be thirty days in the can, six months in a halfway house and probation."

"Wow, what a deal."

"Probably the best I could expect, but I don't have to go inside for another month. Plenty of time to check out that surf spot you and Laverty found."

"You don't have to stay in L.A.?"

"That's probably what they expect but nothing was spelled out to me."

Mike turns to Mom.

"If the FBI or DEA calls, please don't tell them I'm on Bali or anywhere out of the country."

"I'm sorry, Mikey. The last time they called they didn't say who they were and made it sound like they were worried about you, so I was, too."

"Mom, these guys are sneaky bastards. Just remember less is more and nothing is best. Just play dumb."

Chapter Fifteen

Heaven's Door
1973-1975

As we board our flight to Bali, I grab a *Time* magazine to help me fall asleep. Mike's in the seat next to me. This is fantastic; we're flying to Bali again, loaded with new boards. Mike's a wild man. Who else would try to fit in a surf trip before he goes to jail? But he is, and I'm going with him.

It feels like we've been on airplanes as much as anywhere. I thought we moved around too much when we were growing up, but that was nothing compared to what we're doing now. Only now we dig it.

"Hey, check this out."

I shove the magazine cover at Mike. "Gang War: The How and Why of Murder."

"Hey, Mike, they're a little behind the times, aren't they? That looks like a Mafia guy from the '50s. It's not like that anymore, is it?"

"You think all I deal with are surfers and flower children?"

I check the seats behind us. They're empty and we're out of the U.S.

"Well, yeah."

"Maybe at first it was. But this last trip was a tad crazy. The more money you deal with, the more high-strung people can get."

"What happened to 'California Dreamin'?'"

"Man, you got some uptight motherfuckers in L.A. First time I've seen guns around a deal. They blindfolded me and took me to some outrageous pad. But yeah, in the end they were still surfers and they'd never seen honey oil before. Loved it—paid big coin."

Mike swats me in the chest with the back of his hand.

"And get this, Bill. They're joining us on this surf trip. Paying big coin for that, too."

We're sailing across a fifty-mile stretch on the Bali Strait from Kuta to our new discovery on Java. There are six of us on this comfortable trimaran and we're running with the wind. The hulls begin to hum and our speed accelerates as we drop into a long smooth trough. I've got a firm grip on the bow rail and my legs are flexed. One of the other surfers gives a loud hoot and points. Five porpoises leap in front of us. The swell was building when we left Bali and now our anticipation is off the charts.

I understand what Mike means by having a fat war chest to get everything we need. Even though this is Indonesia, we've spent a big wad for this adventure. But that's what the trip to Bananastan was about and now we're looking tight. We should be able to stay for a few weeks.

Anchored off of our private paradise, all our surf dreams are coming true. Mike's new buddies tell me they got into surfing to get away from the edginess of the workaday world. We all know that surfing in a crowd is a competitive experience when there are more surfers than there are waves. Our efforts to set ourselves up in this surf utopia have solved this supply-and-demand problem. There are many empty waves that spin away towards oblivion, and we like it that way. Added to that, the quality is absolutely flawless. The wall of this wave lines up like the racetrack for the Daytona 500.

Our training pays off. We surf for hours and Mike's deck crew has a macrobiotic feast waiting for us when we paddle back to the boat.

Mike charges a hundred bucks a night and no one is blinking. The cost to live on this boat includes the best of everything possible in Indonesia.

All these guys are capable watermen. None of them is famous. They're hardy adventurers off the beaten path. They have to be fit because Mike's prerequisite for anyone who goes with us is to pass a physical test—a swim out and back to the outer reef off Bali. We always join them just to show we aren't pricks. This wave is powerful and dangerous. We don't want to deal with any unnecessary casualties.

Anyone who makes the cut enjoys the ultimate pay-off for leaving his hometown crowds behind. We never ask where that is. None of these guys wants to answer any personal questions, and business is never discussed.

It's been twelve adrenaline-filled days on the boat, but the combination of surf fatigue and bobbing up and down on huge swells is making all of us a little weary. I elbow Mike and point towards the beach.

"Next time I'm bringing a tent. I like solid ground."

"Oh yeah? Did you know that European hunters pay fifty G's to come here and bag tigers and panthers prowling around in that jungle? And that's just for starters. There are also green mambas and every poisonous insect in the book."

"Bob and I did it before and nothing got us."

"You were lucky."

I have to admit to myself that I heard some very intimidating noises on that first trip.

"Well, we could build sleeping huts on stilts off the ground, like Robinson Crusoe."

"Robinson Crusoe?"

Mike laughs and looks at me like I'm crazy.

We wake up excited about huge swells rolling under the boat. The excitement about our day of big waves turns to panic, however, when we discover our anchor has been dragged overnight towards shore. We're near the impact zone. Our boat barely crests a breaking wave. Twenty feet inside of us, the offshore wind rips off the top off a wave and drenches the boat. The wave explodes. We stare at each other and in a moment know the next wave can be the one that sends us crashing onto the reef. One of the crew starts the engine. Mike slices into the anchor line. The last strand snaps. We're free.

We move out of danger and begin to relax. Mike informs us that despite all the planning and supplies he bought, an extra anchor is what we don't have. There's relief that we've avoided disaster but disappointment as we sail away from epic waves.

The beat into the wind back to Bali is rough. I'm sensitive to choppy seas and still have the same tender stomach I've always had. There are others who are also sick. Mike watches me throw up over the side and rubs my back.

"Robinson Crusoe, huh? Maybe it's not such a bad idea."

I'm on Maui, hanging out with Mom and surfing winter swells. Mike has had his taste of paradise and returned to L.A. to serve his time at the halfway house in Long Beach. He left me in charge of writing letters to officials in Indonesia about the feasibility of operating a surf camp.

The phone rings. It's Mike.

"The letters?"

"Yeah, yeah, I did all that."

"Hey, how about finding me some magic mushrooms?"

"Fuck, no. I don't want to end up in there with you."

"Bill, they're legal."

"Maybe they are, but the answer is still no."

"No worries. I can probably find them here."

"You're nuts."

"And you love it, don't you?"

I hang up and know he's right. Even though he seems crazy, things are coming together in Indonesia.

Mom has the TV news on. The report is that there are peace talks in Paris. This year might be a good one.

It's been six months since Mike went to the halfway house. Mom and I are in the kitchen when he charges in the door and gives us both bear hugs.

"I thought you had to stay in L.A. for a probationary time?"

"No sweat. I've arranged for someone to pretend they're me and call my probation officer for my monthly check-ins. If it doesn't work, screw 'em, maybe I'll never come back to the U.S."

Mom looks like she's going to cry.

"Mikey..."

"Don't worry, Mom. I'll bring you out there. It'll be great."

Mom cheers up a little but my head is spinning. It blows my mind how Mike is willing to cut off his options so quickly. I still want to spend some time in the U.S. in the future and would hate to lose that option.

Bali. We're back on Bali. It's going to be a groove to hang out in one place for a while.

Mike has bought a Radon motor boat in Singapore and we're using it to cruise the fifty miles across the Bali Strait. It's faster than the trimaran and the run is smoother in both directions.

We have two anchors now but a safe anchorage is still a problem. The Radon is smaller than the trimaran and the cramped quarters are getting old fast. Our trips have been only a few days long, then back to Bali to recharge and resupply. If the camp comes together, we'll be able to stay much longer. The Radon will change from being our sleeping quarters to being our supply ship.

There's a rumor that the electric line will be brought all the way down the Kuta Beach road close to the ocean. New *losmans* (motels) and *warungs* (restaurants) are popping up along the ocean front to handle Western tourists coming to Bali in greater and greater numbers.

We see more surfers each time we return to Bali. They're walking the narrow pathways and eating at the warungs around Kuta Beach. I hear Bob Dylan playing "Knockin' On Heaven's Door" on a scratchy sound system and smile. We think this place is heaven and now it looks like many others are seeing Bali the same way. The buzz is that the surf movie, "Morning of the Earth," along with various surf magazine articles are putting Bali on the map as the new surfing mecca. Guys we've never met are showing up at Benoa Harbor, trying to get on our boat to wherever we're going. The story is out.

High-profile surfers from Hawaii and Australia are among this new wave of travelers. They talk like they're into the soul thing, like the first groups who went with us to Java. But these guys are the first ones I've seen trying to make a living off the sport. Photographers are also showing up to shoot pictures of them in this newly discovered hot spot, in order to sell imagewear back in the U.S. and Australia.

I've always thought of surfing as the sport for rebels who didn't fit in the nine-to-five world. But that straight world—in the form of sponsored surfers—has shown up at our door, way out here on The Edge.

Many of them are stoners and they might laugh at my calling them straight. But the way I see it, they're here to have articles written about their discovery of new waves they claim to have found in this place we wanted to keep secret. I shake my head as I think about Laverty's prophesy. He was right on when he said how the crowds would follow in our footsteps—and that it's impossible to keep secrets. Thanks to his foresight, we fortunately do have a sanctuary. Even if surfers were able to do what he and I first did, they wouldn't be able to hang out long in the jungle without the logistical support of shelter, food and water. We know that's going to stop most of them. Conditions at our new oceanic citadel and the travel to it are just too harsh.

How to exist on the edge of the jungle is our main concern. Living on boats presents too many problems—like anchors. Mike digests my Robinson Crusoe idea and we decide that building a surf camp, and the logistics to supply it, is the way to go. No one else has ever done this anywhere—and the idea is turning us on.

It's November. The winds have turned onshore and the waves are sloppy. So our focus has shifted to forging all the connections necessary to wade through red tape with the Indonesian government. Our goal is to secure a permit to build our camp. No one has ever applied to do this in the remote national park of Plengkung on the Blambangan Peninsula. What Mike's doing is impressive but it's becoming obvious we will need more cash to pay off officials and build our Robinson Crusoe-style treehouses.

Mike tells me he's made some connections with some former U.S. Rangers in Thailand to buy a load of Golden Voice Ganja. His hash operation in Afghanistan is too well-worn and it's time to change product.

We're flying to Manila to hire a large cargo vessel to make the pickup in the Gulf of Thailand. I feel pretty relaxed—we aren't doing anything illegal yet. What can happen?

Waiting in line for Customs in the Manila airport, I can smell the durian that Mike is trying to smuggle in with us. He has wrapped it in a million layers of plastic but the smell is radioactive. It's our turn and a bald-headed customs officer struts up and gives us a menacing leer with our passports in his hands. He looks like a Filipino version of Telly Savales in "Kojak." This Filipino Kojak hasn't given this treatment to any of the other passengers. I'm guessing he's one of the many people in the world who hate durian.

Mike grabs the back of my hair and gives it a quick yank. He's silently letting me know he thinks my long hair is the reason for our shakedown. I want to smack him but don't want to make a scene.

Kojak is directing his minions to empty out all our belongings onto a table. There's the package of durian, which isn't sparking any interest from them.

I'm surveying our stuff. Have I forgotten anything, like the slab of hash that jerk on Bali put inside my copy of *Moby Dick*? Every item that I packed checks out clean in my mental inspection. Let them rip me apart.

I glance over to Mike's stuff and right off notice his spray can of Right Guard. Shit. I know he doesn't use it as a deodorant but as a secret stash spot to smuggle small amounts of weed or hash, just enough for personal use. Does Mike have any dope in it right now? Fuck. If Mike goes down, I go down with him. Do the Filipinos have the raps of cane?

Kojak has his back turned to us as he's yelling at his subordinates. When he returns his hostile look to us, he directs his men to begin searching our baggage. They're zipping, unzipping, pinching, squeezing and examining everything we have. Kojak picks up the Right Guard can and puts it aside on the table. Uh oh.

The search is over and Kojak's men are shaking their heads. In a dramatic way Kojak puts his hands up for all the men to take notice; school is about to begin. He dramatically grabs the can and glares intently at us.

Can he see my heart pounding through my shirt? He grabs the bottom of the spray can and gives it a healthy counterclockwise twist. He's apparently seen these containers in his training and is about to crack this case. The bottom of the spray can doesn't twist. With a slight smirk, Mike points to the nozzle. Kojak glares back and twists again with added force. Nothing. He sets the can down and turns away, the strut gone out of his step.

My heart is still pounding when we get to our hotel room.

"Do you have stash in there?"

"Of course I do. Can you believe that guy?"

"Fuck. I can't believe you. Goading the sucker with that arrogant grin."

"That was on purpose, pal. Piss off a guy like that and they want to solve everything with more power. Thank God for reverse threads."

I'm shaking my head. Mike has taken an absurd risk despite knowing we would disappear forever in the black hole of a Filipino jail if we got caught.

Mike is laughing, but I'm not. My confidence in his judgment has just gone over the falls. I need a break from him and decide I should return to Maui for the winter to check in on Mom.

Chapter Sixteen

Marriage and Divorce
1974-1975

It's 6 a.m. in Kula and the shadow of Haleakala is still blanketing the valley between east and west Maui. I'm in the kitchen making some hot tea for my girlfriend, Candy, who's eight months' pregnant. While the water is heating, I'm checking out the latest issue of *Time*, with Jack Nicholson on the cover. He has the same this-means-trouble grin as my brother's. Leafing through the inside, I see more news about Nixon's slide. Nixon. The guy just won by a landslide and already many people think he's a cold, calculating criminal. So far 1974 has been all about him. The nine years before were all about Vietnam. U.S. troops pulled out last year and now the South Vietnamese army is trying to cut it on their own. Without the huge distraction of the war, everyone started scrutinizing our president a little more closely. Radical changes in the world.

Wow, someone's knocking on my door this early? Looking out of my window, I see two men with sidearms. I recognize the larger man. He's the infamous vice squad cop Solomon Lee.

I flash to the marijuana plant I'd been growing in the back yard. It was a ten-foot beauty and had just started to bud. I had been trimming off the sun leaves to allow the buds to maximize their potential. Candy insisted on saving those leaves because buds are too strong for her. I've told her many times to keep the bag of leaves in the bathroom by the toilet.

I call out, "Honey, the police are here."

I hear the toilet flush. She knows the drill. I open the door.

"We have a warrant to search your premises."

"Sure. Come on in."

I can afford to be cool, knowing someone ripped off my plant yesterday. I was furious then but now that the cops here, it looks like that was a lucky break.

One of the vice squad officers goes around to the back of the house and then enters through the back door, shaking his head.

"No mo."

"Da buggah wen' wackem. Reep da house."

They rifle through all the rooms and can't find any pot until they search Candy's drawer and find one joint that she's hidden in her bra for after the birth.

"Whose is this?"

Candy says, "Mine."

They prepare their handcuffs for her. This has got to be a joke.

"You know how to deliver a baby? You better take me."

After a long moment, Lee nods.

The other officer comes out of our spare junk room with my grandfather's Colt .45 in his hand.

"Is this weapon registered?"

I'm staring at that fucking gun. It had been packed away with the rest of my parents' belongings, out of sight, out of mind. Mom had left it with me when she moved to Lahaina. Now here's the damn gun, surfacing one more time to cause me grief. I've never owned a gun and know nothing about registration.

I shake my head. The answer is no in so many ways.

"Then we'll have to confiscate it until you do."

The marijuana charge is a minor deal and my hang-gliding partner, Dave, follows the police cruiser down to the station to help me pay the misdemeanor fine and then bring me home.

I drive home with him an hour later and relate the whole tale.

Dave asks, "What about the gun, Bill? That thing is worth some big coin. You gonna get it registered?"

I don't even give it a second thought.

"Nope."

That's it. The cops can keep it. That cursed gun is out of my life forever.

Mike's back on Maui, staying up at a friend's house in Olinda. I wish he were staying with me but can understand his not wanting to listen to a screaming baby. I have a fine healthy son, Nat, born this last Veterans Day.

I drive over to visit Mike. We talk alone.

"A kid, huh? Wow, Bill. What were you thinking?"

I glare at him. Man, he can say things just the right way to make it hurt the most.

"These things happen with girls."

"Yeah well, a chick is one thing. But a kid is another."

"Just come over to my pad and check him out."

Mike walks into my garage and is running his hand over my glider bag.

"You're fucking doing what?"

"Flying. Gliding and soaring. No engine."

Mike squeezes his eyes shut like I'm crazy.

"You got to come back to Indo with me. The camp is up and running now, just like you imagined. Robinson Crusoe-style."

Candy brings out the baby and Mike's hard stance melts. Immediately he's Dr. Spock.

"You have to breastfeed for at least two years. Most Americans quit too early. And when you start feeding him, no sugar. Never start. Carrot juice is the sweetest food you want. And when you start adding solid food, be sure to pre-chew the brown rice for the kid."

I'm staring at Candy, who seems overwhelmed by Mike's strong, know-it-all advice. I'm holding the baby in my arms and we're marveling over his features when a stream of pee arcs up and hits me in the chest.

I've been surfing the North Shore with Mike and some of our pals this last month. It's been like old times—but now he's getting ready to fly back to Bali. We talk on my front porch overlooking West Maui.

"You know, I had to spend a lot of dough on my legal problems and building the camp. I'm tapped out. But I have a huge deal coming up. If you want in, it'll be an eight times return."

"I don't have very much."

"You got this house. Come on. You're not going to live here. It's time to head back. Can you believe it? We have a spartan camp now—bamboo huts have been built high off the ground for good air circulation, tanks of LPG for cooking and Igloo ice chests for refrigeration. I've made arrangements for a daily supply boat to bring fresh food, ice and bottled water. Now we can hang out comfortably the whole season."

Mom has deeded me this Kula house. She had already given Mike his inheritance in stock, which he sold to travel the South Pacific. This house is my share from the trust my grandparents set up for me. My life here is comfortable but Mike is right—I'm destined to live in Indonesia.

"Now it's more than just me."

"Yeah, I know, but it'll be easy. She'll have childcare and she'll never have to do any laundry or cooking. That kid will become a champ under our guidance." He's grinning at me the way that always sucks me in.

God, everything he's told me sounds so good. I love hang gliding but I have missed surfing and especially our tube sanctuary on Java. I dream about the place. Everything is coming together for our camp. It will be so much more comfortable than living on a boat.

Mike has even considered my family situation. It takes a lot to care for a young kid and I'm thinking that cheap help will be fantastic. If someone is watching him then I'll be free to go surfing with the gang. This whole parenting deal has been pretty consuming so far, and I could use a break from Candy's bugging me about flying too much of the day. She'll be able to walk to the beach on Bali. She'll love it.

Mike fills me in on the details of his scam and finishes with my part in it.

"You say you can get sixty for the house. Great. Keep thirty for your own expenses and invest the other thirty in the scam."

It sounds really good. I can make a bunch of money and be surfing at the camp simultaneously.

Candy has always been adventurous so moving to Bali appeals to her, especially after I tell her about the childcare. But I still have a lingering seed of doubt from my experiences with Mike in Karachi and Manila. After I weigh the pros and cons, the pull of the life we could live on Bali is just too strong to resist. I sell the house and wire all the money to Mike.

As I'm flying to Bali with my small family for the 1975 surf season, I think maybe this is it. Maybe we'll stay in Indonesia forever.

After we land I get Candy and Nat settled into one of the rooms at Mike's beachside bungalow, where they'll live while I commute to the surf camp on Java.

I have just come in from surfing at what the rest of the surf world is now calling G-land. The ocean water is cool—warmer than California but cooler than Hawaii. After I shower with a black solar water heater bag, I ask Sunar, one of our camp workers, for an ice-cold juice from a young coconut. The sun is blazing hot.

"Minta kelapa muda."

I retire to a raised gazebo with a palm frond roof. The cool offshore wind blows through while I read a book, glancing up occasionally to watch one of our pals ride a wave. I can smell garlic cooking from the

The G-Land surf camp – Don King photo

Mike Boyum and his bamboo bungalows

Mike Boyum, Speed Reef, G-Land

Mike Boyum camp manager

nearby kitchen area. It won't be long until dinner. I adjust the mattress and settle in for a catnap.

One eye opens when the sound of an edgy voice interrupts my dream state. I spot George, one of our guests, holding his surfboard. His foxy Australian girlfriend, Lulu, argues with him on the beach.

Why don't they step into some shady spot to talk?

"Is this how it's going to be? You surf all day, I lay in the sun and brown my tight little buns for you to hump until you pass out?"

George's tone is soft. He's looking around, which I think means he's not happy to be having this discussion within earshot of anyone.

"I thought you wanted to come here. You said you were tired of Bali. What about peace and quiet?"

"For a few days, sure. For a lifetime? Are you crazy? Is this what you want?"

Jack McCoy, Gerry Lopez, Mike Boyum

"Baby, I'm living the dream. Like I told you last night, this camp is the ultimate. Mike is going to let me invest here so I always have a place in the line-up."

"So you just want to surf for the rest of your life?"

I see George nod enthusiastically even though I'm guessing this might mean the end for his sweet nights with Lulu.

"You know it, baby. This is the place and I have the means."

So that's it. George is a smuggler. His biggest concern: How to spend his money in the ways he wants without attracting attention in the U.S. or Australia. And Mike has answered that question for him. Once Mike shows the camp experience to a pal, there is no doubt about his return. Our camp is any surfer's dream come true—and Mike knows it.

Unfortunately, non-surfing women really don't have much to relate to in this jungle. A few guys tow their girlfriends out here in order not to leave them to the wolves in Kuta, but it always spells doom. The camp has become our monastery of sorts. We're surf monks; we eat terrific food, do yoga and have incredible adrenaline-pumping exercise every day. Women aren't supposed to get in the way.

I'm looking around the camp, thinking how Mike had enticed me with Robinson Crusoe. We can check out the waves from our huts by simply lifting our mosquito nets. This is like a magical childhood dream

Bill Boyum, G-Land

that usually never comes true. But it has. We've found our treasure where X marks the spot on a tropical island.

At dinner Lulu glares at Mike.

I can tell she doesn't like being in second place with George, and I'm really glad I have Candy on Bali feeling comfortable. My family situation is just fine.

Back on Bali, I'm sleeping in the pre-dawn hours with Candy and my infant son. Mike sneaks into our bedroom and gives me a shake. We're going surfing.

It's 4 a.m. when we drive out of the morning mist towards the wave at Nusa Dua in Mike's new yellow VW bus. I can barely contain myself.

"I could hear the waves all night. Should be huge."

Mike turns around with a pile of white powder.

"Here, snort this."

Mike's lawyer had brought a couple ounces of cocaine with him from L.A. I know how much Mike likes it, but I've never felt the urge. Now here I am with a mound of coke in my face.

I'm so excited about the surf and this time I figure, what the hell.

"What the hell? My nose is burning."

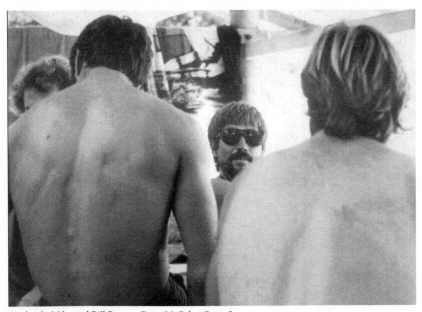

Reef rash, Mike and Bill Boyum, Peter McCabe, Gerry Lopez

"Peruvian flake, man. It's da kine."

Mike looks like he's trying to smile but parts of his face aren't working.

Soon an incredible feeling of euphoria overwhelms me and I'm babbling like a mynah bird about any idiot thought that enters my head. Mike passes me more.

The waves are big. We catch a few but my throat is numb and I can barely breathe. My timing is horrible. Every wave I take off on closes out.

On the way back to the house we try to mellow out by smoking several high-powered joints of Thai pot.

When I return to my room, Candy's on me.

"I can't stand these beach vendors. They just won't leave me alone."

"How can you whine? You've got all the help you need."

She's giving me the stink eye. Suddenly I feel so impatient I'm about to explode. My life here should be unreal, but something is wrong and it isn't Candy. I'm just too stoned to figure it out.

Since Candy and I have been on Bali, I've had no time to talk to Mike alone. He seems stressed and when I do say something to him he trances out. He must be dealing with logistics of one kind or another. But he's even worse when we're at the camp. The camp was supposed to be our sanctuary. I'm digging it, but it doesn't look like it's working for Mike.

He's here now and I grab him by the arm. He looks at me like I'm a stranger.

"What's up?"

"I want to talk about money."

"Bill, you don't talk about money. You're either making it or spending it."

"OK, but I'd just like to check in to see how things are adding up."

"They only subtract, pal."

"You know what I mean."

"No. And I don't even think you know what you mean."

"Wow, man. I just want to be kept in the loop."

"The loop? Man, the fucking loop will just hang you, Bill."

"Fuck, you're talking in circles. Can't you be straight?"

"Can't you be anything but a drag?"

I spin around to walk away, shaking my head.

"OK, what do you wanna know?"

"Seems like we're spending money on shit we don't need."

"That's not a question."

"Well, for starters, why did we buy that yellow bus?"

"To get us where we want to go."

"But we were doing fine without it. How much did it cost? I think we should tighten up until the scam pays off. It's extravagant spending."

He glares at me.

"So you want to be in charge? Do you know what we need and don't need? You handling food and beverage?"

"Hey, take it easy, man. I just want to keep track of how much is going out."

"Right. After all this time you suddenly want to make sure the balance sheet is perfect since you put in your measly chump change. Well, it's never perfect, Bill."

"But you've sent all of my thirty G's off to the scam, right? And I still have the other thirty for my expenses?"

"Wow, Bill. You want to separate everything into checks and balances? You don't like the way I'm handling things? Are you clear on the big picture here? Do you want in or not?"

He's on a rant. I know the big picture is a life of surfing and time to enjoy it. There are many complicated parts of this puzzle that he handles here in Indonesia, and I have no idea how they're accomplished.

"Of course I want in. I just…"

"Hey, haven't I always looked out for your best interests? Who's turned you on to everything fun you've ever done? Haven't I always come through? Haven't I always been there for you?"

"OK, OK. Sorry."

"I know you're trying to keep it real, but don't worry about dough. We're gonna be rich."

I'm trying to sleep but some *gamelon* music is drifting through the night air along with clove-scented cigarette smoke. With the amount of exercise I've done today I should fall right to sleep, but maybe it's the coke or the ton of pot I've smoked to mellow out, because my mind just won't stop spinning.

A half sleep sets in and Mike's voice drifts from the present to the past.

"Hey, don't worry about dough. We're gonna be rich."

In 1959 Mom had washed Mikey's favorite aloha shirt with something red. Dad beat the crap out of Mikey after he said, "You just want me to look like a grunt." Sean Flynn told us that soldiers can go nuts long after the fighting stops and maybe Dad was nuts, but back then we didn't know what he was. He was just scary.

Just as nuts was Mikey's persistence about looking sharp in spite of

Dad. Somehow he got some money, probably from Mom, and bought a pair of canary-yellow slacks. He showed up at breakfast dressed to impress. Dad wasn't.

"You god-damn nigger pimp. Where did you get the money?"

Dad shifted his attention to Mom, then back to my brother. He was on his precise schedule to be at work soon and was already in his starched tan uniform—in no position to go at Mikey with the fury he had locked up inside.

"There'll be hell to pay when I get home from work."

Mikey decided not to be home when Dad returned. He ran away. It wasn't the first time. Mom called the cops after he took off. They easily spotted him with his distinctive yellow pants, playing pinball at the Greyhound station.

Child Services asked for a family counseling session. Mom made up some excuse about Dad's work keeping him away. She blubbered tearfully to the counselor and tried to justify Mikey's behavior.

"He has a strong will," she said, and, "He's a high-spirited boy."

After Mikey told his side of the story, the counselor told him he had a choice: Go home and work things out with Dad or go to the juvenile home for boys.

He told the counselor, "Sure. I'll go to juvie."

That brought Mom to tears again and she had to make many promises to the counselor to ensure that she and Dad would be better parents.

Dad's idea of better parenting was for Mikey to take boxing lessons on the base.

"If he thinks he's so tough, let a real fighter take some sass out of him."

So Mikey began taking boxing lessons at North Island and I went with him. Right from the start he was a natural scrapper, with the viciousness to be good at it. He took a punch and kept on fighting. I cringed.

Mikey wrapped his arm over my shoulders as we were walking home from the gym.

"Don't you want to box?"

"Does it hurt? It looks like it hurts."

"Yeah, it hurts."

I shook my head.

We were silent for a while. Mikey had his lower lip pushed up into his upper lip with an intent look in his eyes. He jabbed, punching at nothing. Each jab was timed with a strong loud exhale.

"I wish you weren't mad."

He shrugged and kept shadow boxing.

"You gotta be tough to survive."

"What are you doing, Mikey?"

"Getting ready. I'm gonna do big things. You can come with me."

"How are we going to get money to live?"

"Hey, don't worry about dough. We're gonna be rich."

My eyes open and my sheets are soaked with sweat. I was just a kid then and Popeye was my hero. Now I have a kid, and Bluto died four years ago.

I've been doing these coked-out surf sessions for the last month and the result is always the same—high expectations and dismal results. The euphoria I first felt with coke never happens anymore. I only feel irritable.

I have to smoke massive amounts of pot in order to come down off the coke, just like I'd seen my parents drink to take the edge off. I'm unprepared for the chaos of this strong stimulant. Coke drives me nuts. It rattles my body and upsets my mind. Where's the good part? Why do I keep doing it? Mike has been doing blow like it was some kind of ritual, and taking part in that ritual has been my way of trying to regain our brotherly bond. The fact that it hasn't worked hasn't kept me from trying. Until now.

The mystery of my interrogation by Harry, the gunrunner in Karachi, floods back into my memory. He and Ian had speed-rapped like Mike and I are doing now. I'm disgusted that cocaine has made me anything like them. Other things that I've ignored come roaring back into my consciousness. The cocaine habit, along with the world of drug smugglers, is getting sleazier all the time. It's a world of lies.

I don't want to do this anymore.

The outright hedonism of our existence is weighing against the overwhelming enormity of my recent fatherhood. I look at myself through the eyes of my new son. What does your daddy do? Nixon's face keeps popping into my inner dialogue.

I am not a crook.

Candy isn't grooving, either. I thought I was providing her with everything she needed. But now I can tell she's destabilized by my lack of attention. I'm gone all day and come back so blitzed that she really doesn't have anyone to connect with. I have to admit that she's lonely.

My toddler son fell from the steps of the house a few days ago and cut his head on the coral rocks surrounding Mike's magic mushroom patch. The next day boils erupted all over his body. I imagined infection everywhere—a metaphor for my situation. Luckily a visit to a doctor resulted in some medicine for Nat, but now Candy is even more disillusioned with this tropical paradise.

Driving to one of our recent coked-out surf sessions, I overheard Mike talking with the other guys about the progress of our scam—and realized he had brought them all into it as well, with the same enticement. If any money ever comes in, there's going to be a long line of open hands. If... ever.

I feel an urge to change my priorities. What should I do? Any option will take money. I attempt to be upbeat when I enter Mike's room.

"Hey, Mike, any good news about our money?"

My brother glowers at me and his tone is agitated.

"You think I'd keep any good news from you?"

"Wow, man. Take it easy. Just wanted to know what's up."

"Here you fucking go again. OK. I'll tell you what's up. Someone has split with the dough. Wait. Don't ask me why. You don't get to ask why. Guys get desperate and bolt. Who knows? Don't worry. I'll take care of everything. It's all gonna be OK. Just be patient."

But I'm not patient. When I consider his track record and extravagant spending, I realize there is a strong potential for his schemes to unravel.

I'm shaking my head.

"Man. This isn't working for me. Just give me my other half and I'll hit it."

Mike laughs.

"You're just going to hit it, huh? Half? What about your expenses, pal?"

"How much?"

I've been in a poor Third World country for three months. How much money could we have spent?

"Ten G's, Bill."

Inside my head these numbers aren't even close to adding up. Ten G's? How? I'm staring at Mike and feeling pretty bummed out. I know guys that spend three hundred a month here and live high on the hog.

This is so fucked up. Mike has all my money. There's nothing I can do. Arguing isn't going to accomplish anything, even if I could stuff my anger to manage a comeback.

He takes in my red face and scoffs.

"I knew you'd screw things up by getting involved with a chick. You didn't even pick a good one. Yeah, why don't you hit it? I can give you enough to fly back to Maui. You'll have to wait for the rest."

I storm out of the house and tell Candy we'll stay in a hotel until we leave. It's too uncomfortable being around Mike anymore; time to start a separate life with my new family.

Before we leave, I think I'm calm enough to get an explanation from Mike about the 10G figure.

"Did you think all that blow was free?"

Right away I lose my cool. I wasn't keeping track and have no idea how much coke costs. As far as I knew it was just another drug like weed, which over here on Bali is very cheap. Now he tells me coke is very expensive. When he first offered it to me I hadn't even considered I would be paying for it. He was sharing and I said yes. Money was never mentioned. Suddenly I'm seeing him in a different light. Pusher.

Mike's attempts at purifying himself with different drugs have turned him into a Mr. Hyde. When I first read that book I thought Dad was the reincarnation of Mr. Hyde and that Mike had wrestled me away from that fiend. But Dad is gone and right now it's Mike who's freaking me out. I can't be his little brother anymore, trusting him with all I have. He's become a cold, calculating criminal. A fair outcome in a partnership is impossible in the criminal world. And that's what I'm dealing with now—a broken partnership. But worse than that, my brother has broken my heart.

I gave Mike control of the money when I sold my home and now I'm going back to Maui almost broke, with no home, and the responsibility for two other people.

"What is it, Bill? You got something to say?"

I shake my head and exhale.

"Yeah, didn't think so. See you in the next world."

Chapter Seventeen

Invisible Wounds
1980

Grabbing *Newsweek* as I board a plane alone, I'm astonished when I buckle up and check out the tank on the cover under the headline: "A New Cold War–Soviet Armor in Kabul." I can't believe it—the Ruskies rolled into Afghanistan last week. Haven't they read Kipling? Nobody has ever won invading that country. The Soviets say they're concerned about Islamic Fundamentalism spreading over their borders.

I land in Kahului and put the magazine away.

I'm returning from Bali and instead of calling Candy for a ride, I'm grabbing a cab from the airport to my home in Kula. My thoughts drift on the drive up Haleakala Highway—so happy that I'm far from invading Ruskies and about to see my two sons, Nat and Cyrus, who are five and three. I can't believe it's 1980. What will the '80s be like as they grow up? It concerns me.

I'd hoped to leave the dope world behind when Mike and I fell out in 1975, but I haven't. Growing weed is the only thing I know how to do well enough to support my family.

And pot isn't the only thing I haven't left. Mike and I have had a reconciliation of sorts. He felt bad about the way things went down when we had our big blowout on Bali, and has been enticing me back to the camp every year with promises to repay the money he owes me. Each time he's found some excuse for not coming through and this time was no different. His answer is always the same and his cheap cliché is getting old.

"Hey, Bill, you can come back to the camp next year. How much is that worth? If you can pay for it with money, then it's cheap. Only you're the only one who won't be paying."

But I know I keep paying each time I return to Candy empty-handed.

I hope she isn't still pissed at me. She called me an adrenaline junky before I left after I spent too many days hang-gliding off the slopes of Haleakala.

But she really scoffed when I brought up going on another trip to Indonesia—using Mike's promise. Candy has called bullshit on me each time, saying it's just an excuse to go surfing while her job as mother has doubled since 1976, when Cyrus was born.

Maybe it'll take the edge off when I tell her about the container of furniture I shipped here from Bali. I'm hoping that the money I make from this trip will justify all the times I've left her alone at home, guarding my marijuana patch and taking care of our kids while I fly or go on surf trips. This time I'll make it right.

What a surprise it'll be when my family sees me.

The taxi rolls into my dirt driveway. I inspect the health of the avocado trees I planted three years ago. They look fantastic, but my attention quickly turns to seven teepees set up around my yard. They can't be for Nat and Cyrus—too elaborate. What the...? I enter the house and call out to Candy; she'll know why our two-acre lot looks like an Indian reservation.

Strange. No one answers. The fact that she isn't home reminds me we haven't been able to do anything together away from this house for years. Marijuana cultivation is a never-ending cycle of planting, trimming, harvesting, drying and selling. Even though it provides for our needs, it's been a kind of ball and chain, especially for Candy. I need to find a legal way to make a living.

Candy's car is here. Where could she be? A look around my bedroom reveals many items and clothes... that obviously belong to another man. His accessories include tarot cards and crystals, and his crushed velour clothes hang in my closet. I can feel my heart pound and my face flush. My stomach is in knots.

I try to count the ring lines on the slab of monkeypod wood that is my kitchen table. Someone, probably one of my sons, has picked at the dark core in the center and the protecting veneer of resin is gone. My fingers loosen a chunk of rotten wood from what was the core of an old tree.

A glance at the clock. It's been an hour.

A giant cloud of fine Kula dust fills the air. When it settles, I see a convoy of beat-up cars roll into my yard. People—no, freaks—almost fall out of the open doors. Hippies have invaded my home.

These last ten years I've always considered myself a hippie of sorts. I smoke and grow dope, have long hair, say 'far out' too much and eat avocado sandwiches with wheatberry bread and sprouts.

But these guys and gals don't look like me as they spin around the yard. One has his arms over two women and they are looking at him as if they are both his lovers.

My wife strolls across the yard arm in arm with a bearded, Rasputin-looking guy. She's dressed like someone from "Hair" and there's stuff in her braids. The guy at her side is wearing a purple suede jacket. His hair and beard are completely gray and he looks to be in his early fifties. Candy and I are thirty. What is this old man doing hanging out with someone our age? Emotions from anger to outrage to hurt are ripping me apart. I'm speechless.

Another hippie tries to hold both of my sons' hands as they walk across the yard. The boys resist. When they spot me they break free and charge into my arms. I set them down and they run into the house while I remain standing in front of the door.

Candy is smiling and looks composed as she casually introduces her new friends to me as if I'm a visiting neighbor.

"This is Lilly, Butterfly and Arrow."

My mind tries to digest these names. Butterfly? You've got to be kidding me.

One of them introduces himself as Bodhi and attempts to hug me. My body is rigid and I push him back. He has taken a patchouli oil bath that doesn't cover up his stench.

"Hey, brother, I'm feeling your heavy vibes. You need to move out of your lower chakra."

He uses the word 'brother' so casually.

Candy spots my clenched fists and tenderly squeezes this jerk's arm.

"He just got off the plane from Bali. Can you imagine the jet lag? Give me some time alone with him."

She cares so much about his feelings. What about mine? What's happening here?

The strange ones leave and Candy and I sit in the kitchen. Both of my sons jump into my lap. She looks at me and her tone turns serious.

"You're back earlier than you said."

I sit with my arms around both of the boys. Tears stream down my face as I stare at their mother.

"What…?"

I can't even form the question; the answer is all too clear.

"I can move out into the yard. Charles and I have set up our own teepee. That way you can be around the boys."

My God, this is real. I can tell by the sound of her voice that she's already made up her mind. She's offering this solution as if everyone would win.

"No!"

The word roars out and my whole body is shaking.

"The kids stay. Everyone else has to leave."

She isn't smiling anymore.

"If I go, the kids are going with me."

The boys are crying. My mind goes back to the trauma I witnessed growing up where kids were caught in the middle of their parents' split. They got hammered in the tug-of-war for possession. I feel possessive of my sons right now, but when I see their faces I know that if I fight about this with Candy their pain could be even worse. They seem so fragile. I know I am.

"Where will you live?"

"Nahiku, on the way out to Hana."

She has all her options ready. I have none.

Mimi's voice chokes up when she calls—she needs to come over. What could be upsetting her? Mom? No, it couldn't be. Before I took off to Bali Mom had been diagnosed with colon cancer. The doctors had said the chemo would work much better than it did for Dad eight years ago.

Mimi arrives and tells me Mom died while I was in Indonesia. They had given her chemo but her liver was so damaged from drinking the chemo pretty much finished her off. Mimi had held her hand as she died. Thank God Mimi was there. But I wasn't, again.

Mom had been talking about her imminent death so much since Dad died that I had become numb to it. I didn't think this could happen. She loved Dad so much and needed to adjust to life without him. But I guess she never did.

I can see that Mom was Dad's only connection to love and happiness during his adult life. That was her role and since Dad's death she hasn't taken care of herself. Maybe Mike and I could have helped her, but we left her to cope on her own. Our desire to leave Dad's tense world spun us out of an orbit that should have included her after she lost Dad. She must have felt so lonely. Grief feels like it wants to explode inside me. Mom has died and I can only see my sons on weekends.

Dad's niece, Chubby, is here to visit me from Oregon. She's two years younger than Dad and grew up with him on Maui. Chubby has come to Maui to see Mom but, like me, she's too late. I reminisce with her about Mom.

"I loved the twinkle in her eye when she got on us about eating carrots," I said at one point.

"So did you eat your carrots? They say it improves your night vision."

"Oh, yeah. Tons of carrots. My brother and I drink gallons of the juice just to stay healthy. Maybe if our parents had drunk less booze and more carrot juice, they might not have died so young."

"But your Dad was a great night fighter pilot. He must have been able to see in the dark very well."

"It's funny, but the Germans in WWII thought all of England must be planted with carrots since RAF pilots were shooting down so many German night bombers."

"So there, you see it's true."

"No, Chubby. The English pilots drank beer and had a secret technology at that time called radar. That's how they saw at night, and that's how Dad saw in the South Pacific."

"Oh."

"Don't worry. That's what Mom always thought, too. I'm sure Dad never briefed her on how radar worked."

Chubby sighs.

"Oh, Bill, your parents were such a lovely couple. You know your father was an exceptionally handsome young man."

She sounds like Mom when she says that, but I need some answers.

"Did you see him much when you guys were young?"

"Oh, yes. At Maui High everyone loved him and he was so brilliant. Jack was friendly to everyone, a real island boy."

"Did he get along with his parents?"

"Oh God, yes. He was your grandmother's golden child. She adored him."

"I'm asking you this because I'm trying to figure things out for myself. Did you know how he beat us?"

Chubby's face contorts and I can tell I've hit a nerve.

"Yes. You know, your mother told me in private about that. My God, Bill. He changed so much. It was about a year after the end of the war. I was a few minutes late for some get-together we were supposed to attend and he flew into a rage, completely out of control. He had a malevolent look in his eyes that really scared me."

"Well, he scared me most of the time."

"You know, Bill, it was the war."

Chubby and I share a long moment with tearful eyes. I kiss her goodbye.

This conversation with Chubby reminds me of the talk I had with Sean Flynn before he left Bali to go back to the Vietnam War. It's been seven years since Dad died and I'm still trying to get over my anger with him. But the way my life is going, I'm pissed off with myself most of all.

My friend Dave and I are driving a small cement truck to pour a sidewalk. He hires me to help him with these jobs, but it's not steady work. Our steady job is still growing dope. Our truck is rumbling along with rattling sounds from the many loose fittings. There's no music but it doesn't matter. We're puffing on a big fat doobie.

Dave says, "Man, I can't believe it's 1980."

I glance at him and smile.

"Yeah, this year has to be better than last year. In four more years it'll be 1984, like in George Orwell's novel. Big Brother. The future is almost here."

"Yeah, Bill. Changes."

"Divorce, my mom and just to kick me when I'm down, those cowboys ripped me off. Yeah, I guess that qualifies as changes."

"Cowboys, huh?"

"Yep. Heard it was Bully and his boys. They cut the wire and just barged though my wall of vines and branches. Guess they could see over it from their horses."

"Did they leave you anything?"

"Two plants. Nice touch, huh?"

Dave shakes his head but we're not angry. We both know this drama is a part of the movie of being in the pot business. We're high and right now we're smiling.

"You going to grow somewhere else this year?"

"I don't know. Kinda seems like the end."

"What're you going to do?"

"I don't know. The kids ask me when they're going to move in with me every time I go out to see them. It fills me with hope and guilt at the same time. Some day I figure I'll have them and when I do, I want to take them on a trip to G-land."

"You'll need money for that."

"I know. My furniture import thing hasn't worked out. It was much more complicated than I reckoned. Every contract and agreement that I've seen people make in Indonesia just falls apart. No wonder my brother is having bureaucratic hassles running the surf camp. You work things out with one official, he moves up or down the ladder and you're faced with repeating the process all over again. You gotta pay beaucoup baksheesh."

"What about a straight job on Maui?"

"Like pouring cement?"

We laugh.

"Every time I see Fred, he's talking about selling real estate. But I know if you don't sell anything you don't make money, and I'm fed up with risk. I've never been much of a salesman. That's my brother. Selling land feels like selling dope to me, only some realtors make way more money."

"Pot or land. And you need the land to grow the pot."

We laugh again.

"Even if I wanted to go back to growing, times are changing. If it ain't horses it'll be those green harvest helicopters. Those guys are getting good. You notice how all the large crops are destroyed or ripped off? I think the dope business is fading out."

"You think?"

"Yep, and people on Maui aren't firing up a joint every time you drop by someone's house."

"An island full of straight tourists?"

"Straight?"

"Well, as straight as a mai tai. Hey, you could wait tables."

"Tried it. That's not me, either. Man, when you've seen money made the way I have…"

"Well, what are you going to do for dough right now?"

"Candy wants some cash. Guess I'm selling the house."

"Didn't you listen to yourself about real estate? You know the part about way more money? You're crazy to sell."

We arrive at our job site and start pouring the sidewalk. The hard work is a welcome relief from my endless inner dialogue.

It's been a long day and I'm beat after the cement pour. Home alone, I'm ready to kick back in my porch chair, light a joint and soak up another spectacular sunset light show over West Maui—hippie TV. I need some kind of distraction. What Dave told me about selling my house has made me uptight. Everything he said is true, but I also know my house represents my old life. I need to change. If I sell it, the money will keep me afloat while I figure things out.

Pot smoke settles into my lungs from another long inhale. Trying to work out how to make a living fades away. Fantasizing about a hang-gliding flight or a surf expedition is perfect while feeling this stoned.

284 / Journals from the Edge

My sons have told me what a drag it is living around stoners, so I'm not getting loaded before I drive out to see them in Nahiku.

The boys and I are having weekend fun. Just a short walk from where they live in the Nahiku jungle is a beautiful stream-fed pool. They swing from a rope, let go and fly into the water. Nat shows me how tough his feet are getting by walking on sharp rocks. Cyrus swims like a fish. The water is chilled from its high-elevation source and Cyrus shakes the way I used to in Coronado when I was learning to surf. I'm toweling Cyrus to warm him up. He's looking up at me, smiling.

"Dad. You told us last time you came that we could move in with you very soon. Can we leave with you today?"

"Not yet. I'm still working on it."

His smile disappears and tears well up. My guts are knotting. I wince at his silent accusation, yet I know my life isn't together enough to take them. My house has just sold and I haven't even figured out where I'm going to live.

I'm driving home, without my sons. My rusted-out Datsun pickup rattles around each blind curve. Even with the hazardous cliffs and narrow sections of the Hana road, my intense focus isn't enough to bury my guilt. Man, have I screwed up. I screwed up bad. I've been gone just like Dad was gone when I was a kid, and this divorce will mean that I'm away from my kids even more than my dad used to be. I'm worse than my dad. My addiction to surfing has cost me so much more than the money I've lost.

The emptiness of my house stabs me as I enter. Soon, even this place will be history. I'm alone and there's no need to be straight any longer. I roll a joint with the last bit of my stash and inhale hard.

Only the stub of a roach is left and although the pain is gone, I don't feel happy, just numb. Maybe another joint might do the trick.

I drive over to one of my flying pals to get some more pot. We talk about the newest high-performance gliders while we smoke.

"Wanna make some money? I need to send a load of weed to Alaska."

Even though I know subjects can change in an instant when you're loaded, this is coming out of left field. Our stoned conversation has turned from gliders into something much more serious. I don't have a crop in the ground and have little hope of any income in the near future. After agonizing over how to change from making a living my old way, it's uncomfortable to consider what he's offering. But I'm worried about how much I've been spending these past months. Goofing off has been fun and distracting but at this rate, I'll be close to broke in a year. Then what? Having the kids live with me seems further away than ever. Maybe this deal is an opportunity I shouldn't pass up.

I'm in the slammer.

This smuggling operation wasn't even mine. My role was minor but my exposure was major. How could I be so dumb to trust guys I barely knew? There was a point when things didn't feel right and I ignored those feelings. My activities of surfing and flying have depended on instincts. Why did I ignore my gut this time? Even though I never touched any product, I did arrange a shipment of pot to be sent on an air cargo plane—so here I am, staring at the light above my cell. It's on twenty-four hours a day. I have no idea what time it is or how long it's been since I was busted. I could go crazy in here. I wish I could sleep.

On one side of me is a Hawaiian guy who screams about not being able to call his wife who has just given birth to his child. He wants to give his baby a name. The guy in the cell on the other side of me is the son of the mayor of Honolulu. He's inside for stealing his father's wine.

We're trying to calm down the screaming Hawaiian, who's twenty years old. I'm ten years older, yet I haven't learned anything more than this inexperienced kid. We're here in the same hell.

The guards tell him again that he can't call and that he'd better shut up. The Hawaiian responds like a caged animal, with intensifying screams.

What harm would it do for him to talk to his wife? Should I try to reason with the guards? I'm calm and maybe they'll listen to me.

Oh shit. It's too late. The guards charge into his cell and beat him with clubs. I can hear his screams and see blood flying out from the bars next to me. This beating shakes some painful memories loose. I feel more vulnerable than I have in many years. The guards leave his cell and his low moans torture me.

With no outside drama, my inner inquisition returns. Since Mike and I went separate ways, it seems my attempts at carving my way in the world have been going downhill. He would have known that this operation was bound to screw up. His voice inside my head tells me how stupid I am to get busted in this small-time dip-shit scam after all we've been through overseas.

But then I feel indignant and remember Mike did a little time in the pokey for his stupid bust in L.A. He's had his share of screw-ups. God, I took so many risks with him and miraculously escaped. What would it have been like to go to jail in Manila? Probably worse than what I just heard with the Hawaiian.

Ten years ago I adopted Mike's justification for his illegal activities: "When you fly jets, you don't have to live like the rest of the jerks in the world." I remember thinking it was a great argument for what Mike was doing. It's taken these last ten years, but right now the only jerk I know is sitting in this cell.

The world is reversed in here. My awake moments are nightmares and I want to escape to sleep. What did Mike do to sleep when he was in jail? A gentler voice from my brother tells me to do handstand push-ups against the bars in order to wear myself out. We used to do them on Bali during sleepless nights and the exercise usually worked.

My inner torture continues when I wake up. I'm glad neither of my parents will ever know about this. But even without their scorn, there's no relief from my own.

God, I'm hungry. Some good food might distract me but the food they serve here is inedible and even the water tastes bad.

The guard says it's been three days and ghoulishly reminds me that without bail, I'll soon be sent to the state prison.

It's not like a TV cop show in here. I asked about a phone call when I was first arrested but they told me I wouldn't be allowed to call anyone for my first seventy-two hours. They don't want to compromise their investigation. What that means is that I will finally get my first call just as I'm due to be transferred. Whoever I can get in touch with will have to take at least a day to raise bail and I'm facing the horror of the state prison, where even an hour could be life-threatening. The guard tells me I have it easy in this holding cell where I can sit in the safety of my own room. My shame turns to fear.

Mimi shows up out of the blue. I feel a little disappointed that it isn't Mike. He's on Maui. Why didn't he come? Mimi tells me the word got out on the coconut wireless from my friends who saw the cops asking questions at airfreight on Maui. I feel so lucky to avoid the horror show at the state prison. Mimi sounds like a warrior.

"We're not messing around. We'll get you the best lawyer in Honolulu." She sounds tough until she bursts into tears.

I'm sitting in a church-like pew during my motion hearings, but unlike in church when I was a kid, I'm listening. The facts aren't good and my defense doesn't seem strong. The prosecutor points out that I used a false name when I signed for the shipment. I shudder and think about more jail time. My attorney asks for a continuance.

Today a different prosecutor takes a new line of attack. He calls for the testimony of a Honolulu cop, who tells his story of my arrest. The cop leaves the courtroom and the prosecutor calls in the DEA agent who was also on the scene of the arrest. This agent gives an entirely different version of events. My attorney points out to the judge that someone is not telling the truth.

This is the third prosecuting attorney the DA's office has used in my motion hearings. He's combative and ends up attacking my attorney's sexual orientation. He swears at the judge. It's my head on the block in this courtroom drama, yet things are going so much my way that I'm able to enjoy the theater as a spectator.

It's been a week since those motion hearings and today my lawyer tells me my case has been thrown out. He's the best criminal attorney in Honolulu and now I know why.

An IRS agent tells me he thought I was lucky during my hearings but apparently someone was pissed off enough to pass my case onto him at the IRS Criminal Investigation Division. He tells me my profile doesn't look good on paper; no tax returns ever, no significant job and lots of travel to the red zone areas of the world.

I won't go to jail, but I owe fines and capital gains taxes on my house sale. The cost is huge for this bust; the horrible jail experience, the cost of a good lawyer and the IRS settlement. The remaining cash I have from my house sale is just about zero. There has been no backup from the other guys involved. I realize that when the going gets tough, the guys who always acted so tough hit the road.

It's cold up here at an elevation of ten thousand feet, but I know there will be nothing like a flight to wash away my prison experience.

Haleakala summit, 1980

Launching off the Haleakala summit, the wind is strong in my face. Fantastic. Two steps and I'm off the ground.

Crap. My harness is stuck and doesn't allow me to rotate prone. My body remains in the launch and landing position—upright, creating drag like a wing walker.

This is terrifying. In my pre-flight I checked all my lines before I launched. How could this happen? In eight years of flying it never has.

My glider weaves wildly as I twist my body in an attempt to release the rigging. Nothing works. The combination of extra drag and lack of speed limits my control but, worse than that, I only have half my glide ratio and double my sink rate.

My original intention was to soar above this ridgeline and land on my well-known turf in Kula, but with my glider's limited performance I'm headed over a black lava desert that extends all the way to the ocean. The Alenuihaha Channel, between Maui and the Big Island, is a raging tempest of huge whitecaps today. The wind must be gusting over forty. If I continue to fly towards the jagged lava coast, I will die.

I have to land now before I hit the stronger lower elevation winds. I spot an isolated rocky jeep track high up on the slope. Perfect for me, it's lined up into the wind. It looks flat. I'll land there.

I'm set up for my final approach. Uh oh, the ground is not flat. A *pu'u* (cinder cone) is upwind of my approach. I'm going to be in deep shit when I hit vortices of falling air. Should have known but committed now.

Speed too slow. Glider vibrates. Stall. Falling. Twenty feet, five feet. Crash. Shoulder slams. Pain. Deeper pain. Shoulder separated. Hot. Blast furnace-hot. Searing pain. Anger. Eyes close. Danger. Wreckage lifting. Fear. Need to unhook. Unclip D-ring. Stumble. Collapse. Mind cloudy. Don't lie down. Might sleep forever. Brain boiling. Jump up. Yank off gouged helmet. Numb fingers explore face. Blood. Mouth, tongue sticky. Breathing strained. Altimeter seven thousand feet. Water. Need water bad.

Wind whistles across this barren black landscape. My head is pounding as I stare down the steep volcanic slope. Miles of very rugged terrain lie between me and any potential rescue. Whatever that distance is barely defines how alone I feel at this moment. Can't think about that—I've got to pull myself together. I know how to dismantle the glider. I'll start there and hide it out of sight. I'll come back with a four-wheel drive and retrieve it when I feel better. Maybe. Maybe not.

My thirst is getting more intense. I have to make a move but it's hard to think clearly with my head throbbing. The horizon tilts forty-five degrees with each heartbeat.

I try to center my focus down this steep volcanic slope. Is that the way? My route would be downhill for four thousand vertical feet but sharp lava flows intersect the path. Even if I make it across that black desert, what will it get me? There is only one isolated road with little traffic to an area of the island with few inhabitants. Who would risk picking up a bloody and tattered long-haired guy in the middle of nowhere? No, my best path to help will be a two-thousand-foot climb up this loose cinder to the ridgeline of the summit, and then down a dirt road four thousand feet to my home in Kula. I convince myself I can make this ascent uphill. I have to.

The footing is unstable and I feel wobbly from the injury. Falling, I roll backwards. White-light pain knifes through me. I struggle to my feet and concentrate on each step.

Tears from so much more than the pain run down my face. Divorce, death, imprisonment and now this? The waves of my life are drowning me. It's like being caught inside by monster surf. The end of the '70s hasn't magically changed anything for me just because it's a new decade.

I have to do something to change course.

I reach the summit and gaze down at the shady forest above Kula. There's a road I can use. I've made it.

The sun is about to set when I stumble into the house of my friend Rick. After gulping down some water I try to explain what happened.

"Your harness got tangled?" Rick asks.

"Yeah. Well, it was more than that. I was twisting and turning with everything I could give it to get out of the mess I was in, but I couldn't see what was wrong, so... I just couldn't fix it. And get this, after the crash I was hanging there like a god-damn string puppet in my wrecked glider and all of a sudden my harness released to how it should have been all along. It made me crazy not to be able to see what caused the tangle."

"Well, let's try to untangle your body and see what we find."

Rick is a Rolfer and has been doing body work on me for the last several weeks. I can't believe how painful it is. He says I'm holding emotional trauma in my soft tissue—a syndrome he calls invisible wounds. These two words boom out of the past and rock my equilibrium. If he had told me this before the crash I would have laughed at him, but now I'm listening. It's scary putting the pieces together but my experience on the mountain has opened me up to looking deeper. It's more than just the events of the last few years, it's my whole life.

Rick tells me more about massage work. When I go home, I start to think about doing massage therapy for a living. It feels good and helps people... and it just might help me.

～

I rub my left shoulder and wonder if it will ever heal. It's been four years since my hang-glider crash. I've never spent this much time inside air conditioning and it seems to awaken old injuries. But this is my new job. For the past year I've worked as a massage therapist at the Hyatt on Kaanapali Beach. I commute across the island every day from where I live in Haiku.

My receptionist points to the appointment book and says I have a cancellation. There's plenty of paperwork to fill my next free hour. I shake my head every time I write 1984 on an invoice. The dreaded George Orwell year is finally here. But instead of the Orwellian world where Big Brother is watching me, I'm finally free from the paranoid world of criminal activities. It's great not having to worry about any unwanted knocks on the door at 6 a.m. My new friends all work straight jobs five days a week and I've dropped the old pack of pot growers.

In my free time I've joined an athletic crowd in windsurfing, a new way of playing in the ocean. The only flying I'm doing now is jumping over waves with soft water below me. Yes, life is good.

My next client enters the massage room. He's an old man with a bright-eyed smile and a firm handshake.

"Can you make me new again?"

I look him straight in the eye for a moment.

"Probably not. But hopefully I can ease the pain."

"Alright, son. Do your magic."

I begin working on him and after I learn his age, I ask him if he served in WWII.

"Fighter pilot on the Essex, Air Group 15, 1944-45."

That ignites a conversation. I know that the Air Group on the Essex was the most decorated in the Pacific Theater.

"Always ready to go out on missions?"

"Oh, yeah. We wanted to do our part. After a good night's sleep we woke up ready, willing and fired up."

"My father was a carrier fighter pilot on the Wasp, Air Group 14."

"What's his name?"

"Jack Boyum. He was a night fighter."

"No, didn't know him. But I didn't even know the night fighters on our ship. They were a secretive bunch and were never allowed to ruin their night vision in sunlight. Of course we never saw them because we slept at night."

"And they slept during the day?"

"I suppose. But I always wondered how they were able to sleep. I guess you can sleep standing up if you're tired enough. But ship operations were very loud during the daytime. We had to maintain constant combat air patrols over the fleet, which meant the steam catapult was working non-stop. That and other daytime noises were very loud. I don't know how they slept."

"How's life been for you since the end of the war?"

"Nothing a stiff drink won't cure. Most of my buddies who survived the war died of bad livers."

"Do you have a family?"

"Oh gosh, no. No one could live with me."

The old fighter pilot finishes his appointment and gives me his firm grip as a goodbye.

"Where is your father now?"

"He died of cancer in 1972."

He pats me on my shoulder and steps out of the room. For a moment I think about the sound of a steam catapult as I turn off the New Age music.

This work routine feels fantastic after the emotional roller coaster I rode in the '70s. Massage therapy is opening me up with strangers like this former Naval fighter pilot. I never would have met him and heard his story if I weren't doing this work.

I've lived my whole adult life in a world of lies and have kept the truth of these last fifteen years secret. Talking to people on the massage table is breaking me out of that. I'm getting therapy for myself while I work and operate legally. I'm also paying taxes for the first time. I've finally made the transition from the world of crime at the age of thirty-four.

Mike isn't paying any taxes. I've just received a letter from him describing another botched boat scam. He writes "not to worry" about my money. He has another scam in the works.

I don't think he's a good smuggler.

I'm saddened by what he writes about the camp. He won't be allowed to continue running it and is going to turn it over to our good Balinese friend Bobby. He writes that letting go of the camp will be for the best. We'll be able to go back and enjoy it and not have to watch over the relentless needs of all the guests.

Somehow I know the camp won't be the same without Mike's management, and his not being there makes me feel sad that he's moving from what he does well to what he screws up.

Right now, though, I need to get back to work. Who will be next to walk into my room?

I'm home and get a call from my ex-wife.

"Hey," Candy says, "the kids have worn me out begging to live with you. You ready to take them?"

"Absolutely."

The boys have moved in with me and my life seems complete even though I'm a single parent. My massage job is great work because I complete it every day and can come home to my sons with an uncluttered mind, ready to devote total attention to them. My only worry now is that my brother has dropped off the map, again.

Chapter Eighteen

Home
1985-1990

It's been one year since my two sons moved in with me and I'm reminded of one of Dad's favorite sayings: "There are none so enthusiastic as the
newly initiated."

Cyrus, my nine-year-old, is crying.

"Nat punched me."

"You're a retard. Don't touch my stuff."

Nat is only two years older than Cyrus, yet his size difference appears
greater. I shake my head and point to their rooms.

Alone for a moment, I can exhale while I enjoy the view from my
living room window. Pukalani, where we live on Maui, is a small suburb halfway up the slope of Haleakala. But right now it doesn't feel
like suburbia. Our house is overlooking a sugar cane field that pulses
with the wind. These moments of peace revitalize me whenever I can
grab them.

God damn it. Someone is pounding a fist on my front door. Haven't I
scared off most of the wackos who stray to the bottom of this dead-end street?
I rip the door open and struggle to let go of my irritation. It's my brother.

"Jeez, Mike, you look like shit."

"That bad?"

"Yeah. What the fuck? You haven't written in two years."

The boys charge out of their rooms and jump into Mike's arms.

"Uncle Mikey!"

I make everyone a smoothie while the boys ask him a million questions. When their attention span fades, we talk.

"How am I doing? I'm fucking broke and still owe you and everyone else."

"So, what's the plan?"

"I've found some unbelievable places for another surf camp, Bill. I
just need to get them rolling."

"Are you back here to find work?"

"Bill, do I have to explain that again to you? I need big bucks, not hourly wages."

It's discouraging to hear my brother still stuck in his lifelong fantasy of fast money. But he's not going to be open to anything I say.

I glance at the clock and yell to the kids, "Get ready for soccer practice."

Looking back at Mike, I can see he's staring at my latest *Time* magazine cover. "COCAINE WARS: South America's Bloody Business." Two automatic weapons are crossed over a pile of white powder.

"Hey, check out the article in there about how the Chinese are taking to capitalism. Funny world, huh?"

Mike lifts his eyes to me, but they are distant and empty.

"What's wrong, Mike?"

"Nobody wants to invest money in a surf camp anymore. All you guys are settled down here on Maui with kids, wives and houses. The chicks are calling the shots now. Guess I'm on my own."

~

It's been four months since that short visit with Mike, but now I've got a letter in my hand from Noumea, New Caledonia.

He's in prison and his words wear me out.

Bill,

I left Maui for Brazil. Scored some blow and flew into Noumea, where I planned to smuggle it into Australia by ferry.

Someone tipped off the French authorities and they moved in for their big grab. Made a run for it and jumped out the window of our hotel. Escaped into a foodless jungle for over thirty days. The Gendarmes were easy enough to hide from, but I was drinking crappy stagnant water and knew I would die if I stayed out there any longer. I just didn't have any more energy, Bill, and couldn't figure out how to get off this goddamn island. Finally I just sat there and let them catch me.

This prison is near the ocean and we've got pleasant tradewinds here, like Maui. The other inmates are local Kanakas involved in their independence movement from the French, or guys that have committed crimes of passion like catching their best friend in the sack with his wife. I'm getting along fine with everyone but I need real food. Right now I'd give anything for some medium-grain brown rice and umeboshi plums. I'll check and see if I can receive any food from you. If I can, please throw in some roasted sesame tahini.

Mike

~

This French Customs office, sitting on a high point above Noumea, has seen better days and the only thing to stare at on this moldy stucco wall is the 1987 calendar. It reminds me that I've been sending Mike his macrobiotic food for the last two and a half years of hisimprisonment .

I just came from the prison, where I had a short visit with him. Even with the care packages I've sent, he looks like the people in the picture Mama Marcelle showed me of our French cousins after they'd been released from the concentration camp. Mike told me he's done two thirty-day fasts to purge his mental state and cleanse his body; the soul centering he had failed to do with drugs, he's attempting to do with fasting.

His soul? All I know is you need a body to contain a soul and his has wasted away. I walked away from him with tears flooding my eyes.

Now I've stuffed the tears inside. It's time to see if I can spring him out of here. I've been waiting in this office six hours to find out how the French Customs officers will respond to my request to free my brother. It pisses me off that I have any French ancestry running through my blood. These French colonials are taking some kind of sadistic pleasure in making me wait and sweat, robbing me of the only thing I really have in life—my time. Sitting here makes me remember my short stint in jail. How did Mike last so long?

I need a distraction so I go to the window and check out the fantastic view of the glassy ocean. There's a white line of a surf break over a mile away on a distant outer reef. Man, I wish this were another surf trip.

298 / Journals from the Edge

But it isn't. The official I'm negotiating with is talking to his superior about my offer. This feels so sleezy, like making a deal with a used car salesman. Before the Customs man went into the other room he told me it's money or time for trafficking in 'stupefying substances.' It feels like ransom but I know it's a fact of life. They only care about the dough and the question is, have I brought enough?

The official returns, lights a Gauloise, stares at me a few long seconds, blows smoke in my face and then nods. The money I have collected from Mimi and a few friends, added to my meager savings, will be enough to cut Mike loose.

~

Mike was right about chicks calling the shots. My bachelor days with my two sons have grown old and my new girlfriend wants to get married. Mike is back on Maui from New Caledonia just in time to attend my second marriage.

But this return isn't a great homecoming for him. He's penniless and still in debt to a lot of his old friends. The extreme fasting and jail time have aged him. His face is gaunt. Whenever he smiles, severe gum recession adds to his grim looks. His tone of voice often sounds bitter. But I'm happy to have him home and living with me. Hopefully I can cheer him up.

I take Mike and my sons to the new Tom Cruise movie, "Top Gun." I'm thinking I can inject some pride into the boys and maybe into Mike about our father's time as a test pilot.

Cyrus enjoys the jets in the movie but Nat and Mike are disinterested. Tom Cruise isn't like any of the real test pilots we remember at Pax River in the '50s. Looks like Mike has lost that loving feeling.

We're all back at my home. My new wife, Susie, gives me her look that says she doesn't like Mike's brown rice and heavy garlic cuisine.

He glares at her when she reminds him to clean up the mess he's made cooking a macrobiotic feast for all of us. I know he figures a little help from her on the clean-up would show some appreciation. But Mike's black cloud is too much for her to handle.

In our bedroom she's frantic.

"He's freaking me out. I can't live like this."

Mike and I go for a drive.

"Hey, Mike, I got a problem."

"Yeah, I noticed. You got to work it out, not me. I can stay at Gino's."

"Thanks, bro."
Faced with an ultimatum, I don't want to fail in my second marriage.

Mike's living in Gino's guesthouse. He's a slightly younger friend of ours and his nickname comes from his good looks and Italian ancestry. Mike knew him from previous years on some smuggling scams. A few years ago Gino began to settle down on Maui to raise a family. He laundered money with his expensive backhoe business to cleanse his account and image.

He told Mike and me that his father had been a combat veteran Marine from WWII. It was rough for him and his older brother growing up, and they both found an outlet in surfing. His father also died young and Gino followed his brother's footsteps down the path to smuggling. His life paralleled ours.

In contrast to many others I've known, Gino has never been busted. He's one of the few success stories in the small world of pot smuggling.

We don't know how much money he has, but it's certainly in the millions. He has a beachfront house on the North Shore of Maui, another on the north shore of Oahu and we suspect homes in other vacation surf and ski areas. He has every toy in the book, from snowboards to motorcycles to surf gear, and is very willing to share them with our group of friends. His wife is a great cook and often invites us over for dinner.

For Mike, Gino's generosity provides not only a place to stay but also some employment in Gino's construction business. Mike is supplementing that income with a valet parking job at Mama's Fish House.

While Gino is often very generous, it comes at a price. We call him the Needler. He enjoys making snide remarks at the expense of others.

Mike says he's taking off again. He's been at the Needler's for a few months and it sounds like he's gotten tired of it. Last week at the beach Gino was cutting Mike down and I thought Mike would punch him but he just stared at him. I can dig it that he wants to move out, but I don't get it when he tells me and all of our surfing gang that he's going to California to sell Amway products.

"Hey," my brother says, "I'll be a natural."

It's been three days since Mike left. My phone rings and its Gino. He's going off on me about Mike.

"What are you talking about?"

"Yeah sure, Bill, just play dumb. How much was your cut?"

"Cut of what?"

"All you Boyums are alike. Blood is thicker than mud."

He hangs up on me and I hold the phone, confused.

I call Jeff, a mutual friend, to fill me in.

"Mike stole a bundle from Gino."

I try to let that compute in my brain.

"But Mike is in California. You took him to the airport, didn't you?"

"Yeah, but he doubled back. He was trying to fake us out."

"What?"

"Yeah, and it woulda been a clean alibi but by a fluke I ran into him at Ooka's Sporting Goods yesterday. Bill, I tried to talk to him but he was acting so weird and kept saying he couldn't get into it. I split but couldn't stop thinking about it. Ran into Gino when I went to Honolua for a surf. Told him Mike was back and how weird he was acting when I confronted him. Gino didn't tell me then but he sure figured it out quick 'cause he paddled in right away. The waves were good, too. Later he told me Mike had taken bolt cutters to his storage locker in Kahului and grabbed his shoebox with close to a million bucks in it."

"Jesus. Now he thinks I was in on it."

"You're not alone, pal. He thinks I'm in on it, too. He thinks we're all in on it. Paranoid fucker."

After the phone call I'm in shock. It stings that Gino has accused me of being part of my brother's conspiracy and that my friendship with him, however it has been defined, is over in an instant.

But the worst sting is that Mike has stolen a huge amount of cash from someone we all consider a pal. I know Mike felt he'd hit rock bottom when he returned from jail, but now he's found a way to extend that bottom into a deeper abyss.

The shit hit the fan four days ago. Mike phones me from Oahu.

"Mike, what the hell?"

"It's just pirate booty, Bill. Hopefully you'll understand one day."

The phone call is short and I feel empty when I hang up.

Where will he go? What will he do?

All I know is that he's disappeared.

The '80s are over and so is my second marriage. It's 1990 and Nat and

Cyrus are sixteen and fourteen. Our boys' club has moved to an apartment in Wailuku, close to where Cyrus does his swim practice.

The boys are discovering a passion for spear fishing as a pleasant contrast to their life at the local high school, where their ethnicity excludes them from mainstream social interaction. I continue to churn out days at the Hyatt as a massage therapist. In my discretionary time, I try to get in as much surfing and windsurfing as I can. Every day is jam-packed.

I have a break between appointments and I'm leafing through *Newsweek* when I find a follow-up article on Sean Flynn. After twenty years someone has finally been able to enter Cambodia and interview people involved with his capture.

Sean and a cameraman had gone beyond the front lines and were captured by the Khmer Rouge. I remember how he'd anticipated that scenario. They would get their story and be released to tell it.

But they weren't. According to this article they were towed around Cambodia for a few years in a situation where their captors didn't really know what to do with them. It finally got down to feeding foreigners or feeding their own. Ultimately Sean and his partner were taken to a ditch and executed with a shovel blade to the back of the neck.

It's overwhelming for me to find this out after all these years of holding out hope. For us, he had simply disappeared. We loved him. Sean had quickly become a brother to Mike and me. But everyone loved him. He had charisma. Why didn't I try harder to persuade him to cancel his trip to Vietnam? Because of the way he was, I always thought he would somehow show up one day and say, "Have I got a story for you."

When I think of Sean, it's a sad reminder of my past life. Mike got me into many close calls, but probably saved me from my youthful fantasy about serving in Vietnam. Because he led me on a different path, however rocky, I've been able to enjoy these years as a father, trying to make it all work. I smile inside when I think about my brother.

I slide the magazine aside and phone Nat.

"Put the noodles on and have Cy make some sauce."

For the last six years I've been training them to be self-sufficient in the kitchen.

"I did it all, Dad. Cy isn't home from swim practice yet."

"Thanks, Nat."

I buy noodles in bulk and have boxes of them piled up in the living

302 / JOURNALS FROM THE EDGE

room, ready to use as we need them. It's so easy not to have to attend to female sensitivities since Susie and I split up.

Nat is a great study in the kitchen but hasn't done as well in school. Cy isn't, either, but it appears he's paving his road with competitive swimming. The irony with Nat is that he's such a consummate reader. I figure he's wasting his talents and missing out on an avenue that includes higher education. My fear is that skipping college might limit my son's options in life. Ultimately I've learned that limited options can lead to criminal activity.

When I arrive at home Nat is reading the book, *Wounded Knee*. His mother's father has Native American blood and he loves to read about that part of his heritage.

I glance at him and am happy he hasn't turned into a TV junky like me. He had a great attention span as a young child when I read him the same books my grandfather had read to me. I hope it also means that perhaps he's applying himself in school.

"Required reading?"

Nat lifts his eyes to me and shoots me the stink eye. He almost spits his words.

"A school book? You gotta be kidding, Dad. This book is about the truth. All they teach you in school is the bullshit lies. They don't want us to know what really happened to the people who were in North America before the Europeans came. It's just like the deal here with the Hawaiians having their Kingdom stolen by the U.S., more lies."

I'm zoning out. Nat is right about lies.

This year, 1990, James Stockdale, my father's good friend from his days at Pax River, has just come out with a startling revelation.

In a media interview he said, "On August 4, 1964, I was squadron commander and one of the pilots flying overhead during the Gulf of Tonkin incident. I had the best seat in the house to watch that event, and I saw our destroyers shooting at phantom targets—there were no North Vietnamese PT boats there... There was nothing there but black water and American firepower."

Stockdale also said his superiors ordered him to keep quiet about what he'd witnessed. After the North Vietnamese shot him down and captured him a year later in 1965, this knowledge weighed heavy on him. He was concerned that his captors would eventually force him to reveal that he knew the most terrible secret about the Vietnam War—that there had been no 'incident' in the Gulf of Tonkin and the pretext for sending in active military combat troops for overt operations was a lie.

I'm looking at Nat. You think you're bitter about how those Indians and Hawaiians got screwed? Well, I'm bitter, too, son.

But this is no time to support Nat's arguments about not doing his schoolwork. I have many arguments for him to get involved in school, and I can see that he's formulating his own against ever doing so by throwing the baby out with the bath water. Nat is in his junior year and now it's time for him to show some promise if he ever hopes to get into college. Perhaps it's already too late.

"OK, here's the deal, if you don't go to college, then you have to start working when you graduate."

The thought occurs to me that my edict is a deferment of sorts—a work deferment. That's my version of tough love. I made an oath to steer away from any physical punishment when they were born. The alternative is to attempt to focus them on the consequences of their actions.

I'm worried Nat will finish high school and get caught up in the errant surf scene that is alive and well here. There would be plenty of opportunities for him to repeat a life of crime like Mike's. Many of Nat's friends are the thugs at the local surfing beach. Added to that, he's high strung like his uncle. The potential for a repetitive cycle is likely.

Nat doesn't back down on my threat of the dreaded four-letter word, 'work.'

"Maybe I'll be a cook."

Cyrus lumbers in the door from swim practice.

"I'm starving. Is dinner ready?"

Nat turns his anger towards his brother.

"Yeah, no thanks to you. Where've you been?"

Cyrus drops his swim gear on the floor by the door and I motion for him to pick it back up and get it to his room. He does and points his thumb at his brother.

"What's with him?"

Nat always gets pissed off when I pressure him about school. I don't think any further agitation will be productive and I always want things to be mellow around mealtime. He's within hearing range and has cooked our dinner so I don't answer Cy's question.

Cy flares at my silence.

"Are you pissed off, too?"

I pinch my fingers by my lips to give him the signal to cool it. Cyrus blows me off and retreats to his room.

At moments like these I remember Dad's prized Pachinko machine I broke as a kid. I realize parenting is a haphazard affair. How can I get all the balls in the buckets without breaking the glass?

Cy re-enters the living room after overhearing the TV news, which is giving the weather and surf report. Surfing has become a well-anticipated activity now that the weather guys can forecast a swell several days in advance. When I was young it was always a surprise. If you rallied quickly when you saw the whitewater, it meant you could usually paddle out before the crowd arrived. These days the crowd is there before the surf.

Cyrus is keen.

"Whoa. Look, Dad. It's going to be huge. I haven't surfed for weeks. Can I cut school?"

Despite my best efforts to keep school in the spotlight, I still want to surf myself. Every time it's shaping up to be this good, I still allow a surf day from school.

Cyrus's physical abilities are going to be his ticket in life; he has no interest in reading. It has worked for him so far. After six years of immersing himself in swimming, surfing and paddleboarding, fourteen-year-old Cyrus is becoming a jock stud. From the time when he was a skinny runt and got picked on after school, he took what I said about might making right and made it his mission never to be a skinny runt again. When he asks to go surfing, I respect his focused dedication.

"Yeah. We'll catch a few waves early, but I can't miss work tomorrow."

Nat laughs and scoffs at me from the kitchen.

"Yeah, I can see how school is real important."

Nat brings out three huge bowls of noodles and sauce and we dive into his food.

I ask Nat, "Gumbo? This is unreal."

Cyrus has his mouth within two inches of his food. His appreciation is obvious.

Nat smiles.

"See, I do have what it takes to make it on my own."

"I know you do," I reply with my mouth full.

Once Nat can see he has proved his point, his countenance changes. Both boys are always less edgy when they're eating. Nat pulls up a bundle of mail and shuffles through the stack.

"All bills except this one I found from the Philippines."

Philippines? Strange how just a word dredges up a memory that makes my heart race. Everything about that fiasco remains crisp; my trip with Mike to find a large-capacity cargo ship, the Kojakian Customs agent at the Manila airport, the wrong-way twist of the agent's wrist that was the only thing that prevented us from spending forever in a Philippine jail.

Nat looks at me and guesses I'm time traveling.

"Ya ditching us again for some kind of top-secret surf trip with Uncle Mikey?"

The sensitivity in Nat's voice about my on-and-off presence as a father during parts of their earlier years is obvious. Perhaps if he knew my experience with my own father, he wouldn't be in such a hurry to scratch open my old wounds about repeating history. I know Nat's dig, that my brother still has the power to call me away to join him, was born during those years. But times have changed and both boys are ready to go on a rugged trip.

"No," I snap. "We're all going to G-land this summer, together. From now on if I go, you go. Besides, I don't know anyone from the Philippines."

I cringe at the knee-jerk defensive reaction. It's my son, not the DEA. I'm mad at myself and grab the envelope.

Cautiously I examine the handwritten address and a stamp that reveals it's from General Luna. Funny name for a place. Manila is the only place in the Philippines I'm familiar with, so who could be writing to me? I re-examine the handwriting. Is it Mike's? No, it's too small and delicate. Perhaps it's a wrong address—there are many Filipinos on Maui. I put the letter aside.

The boys are voicing their various gripes about being teenagers at Maui High School while my thoughts drift to my brother as I finish my meal.

I haven't heard from him since he fled Maui two years ago.

I really miss Mike. After all the effort to spring him from jail, he only stayed on Maui for such a short time. Who knows when I'll see him again. Obviously he was desperate to take Gino's money, but my initial disgust with his heist has subsided. He had gone wrong so many times before, I'd become accustomed to it. Why do I want to have him by my side again? All I know is that I do.

Cyrus begins to slide my bowl of food to his place at the table. The noise of the bowl dragging on the table snaps me out of my trance.

"Hey, son. I'm not finished. Go get your own."

"Sorreee, Dad. You looked finished. What planet were you on?"

"None of your business, wiseass. Your business is to get your homework done before you fall asleep. Your last report card was pathetic."

Cyrus whips me the shaka hand sign.

"No sweat, Dad."

I clean up after dinner. Nat buries his face in a book he wants to read and Cyrus retires to a book he's supposed to read.

Nat grows excited.

"Check this out, Dad. These people moved around as much as we do."

I turn to listen to him and see that Cyrus is already asleep. Nat reads me a section of his book concerning how the American Indians migrated to more remote areas to escape the white onslaught. But I'm not listening.

If Mike were around now he could live with the kids and me. I wouldn't have to worry about female trinkets waiting in precarious spots, like windowsills, to be broken by rough-playing kids. It would be great fun in the boys' club. If...

It dawns on me that Mike wouldn't have written me in his own handwriting. He's on the run. Of course he would have someone else send his news. The Philippines? That qualifies as a pretty remote place to hide and is also within his usual theater of operations.

Is he there? Maybe this letter has the answer.

I finish up the dishes and rip the strange letter open. There is an answer but not what I expect. The first sentence has me spinning and I retreat to my bed.

"My name is Jaime Rusillion and I regret to inform you..."

Regret, the word that rocks me to the core. I know what's coming next. This is what it really means when you live life in Edge City.

"...that your brother John Michael Boyum perished on our island last June 1989. After examining his passport it is apparent that he passed away on his 43rd birthday. He had embarked on a lengthy fast and was found by Pastor Mozo, with whom he had arranged to bring him some fruits to begin eating again. Immediately after his death I sent the report to the U.S. State Department. But after all this time has gone by and no one has contacted me from his family, I thought it proper to send you this unfortunate news myself. I found your address in a light search of his belongings. I wrote to you because he told me himself that both of his parents had already passed on. Enclosed is his death certificate. I'm very sorry to give you this sad news. He has some minimal possessions and writings that he made while he was here. If you want to come and claim them, I would be happy to have you visit our island. At that time we can also determine a final resting place for your brother.

Respectfully yours, Jaime Rusillion, Mayor of General Luna, Siargao Island, Mindanao, Philippines."

I feel separate from my body but hear a howling moan roaring from my chest.

The kids run into my room.

"Dad?"

Chapter Nineteen

Leyte Gulf
1990

Black smoke surrounds us. Mikey disappears. I freeze and bend over, grabbing my stomach. A siren blares and my fingers plug my ears. I'm scared. Mikey appears out of nowhere in the dark smoke, grabs my hand and pulls me with him into the clear air.

The vision from that crash when we were boys is as graphic as it was that day. The image re-forms and as we emerge from the smoke, his hand slips from mine. The air show scene fades and is replaced by one from the late '70s. Mike had contracted malaria while we were in Java. He wasted away quickly to an emaciated one hundred twenty pounds and I decided to fly him to Singapore, where there would be much better medical care. I gazed into his shrunken face as I carried him onto that plane. Each fragile rib expanded in his fight for every breath. Death hovered over him.

Chug chug chug. Leaning against the rail of this ferry, I can feel the engine vibrate in my chest like a heartbeat that's waking me from a deep coma.

I have to shake my head to remember how I got here. Mimi sent me off from the airport in Kahului, tears in both our eyes. Then one foot in front of the other and the blur of air travel; Manila, Cebu and a puddle-jumper to Surigao City on the northeast tip of Mindanao. It's amazing how my empty shell can do all this movement with just a ticket and a passport.

They tried to send me off whole. My sons hugged me with all the strength they had, to radiate spirit back into my body, but the emptiness stayed after I said goodbye to them.

This ship is slow, and right now slow feels safe. Slow gives me the sensation of having more time—more time to come to grips.

Another journey. It's somehow comforting to remember all our surf trips to Southeast Asia over the years. When I've spoken to other well-traveled surfing pals, many have told me horror stories of their journeys in this part of the world. They ranged from food poisoning to being ripped off or getting in trouble with the local authorities. I'm forty years old and fancy myself as a veteran traveler, able to withstand any curveballs the Third World has to throw at me.

I shake my head again. I'm so full of shit. Mike always set everything up for me to be comfortable. He's the one who knew how to move through this part of the world. Even now that he's gone, I know where I'm going because he's been here before me.

A saltwater crocodile surfaces and reminds me that this isn't a surf trip. I try to amuse myself.

"Crocs don't surf."

A slight smile almost creeps across my face as I remember Robert Duvall's famous movie line in "Apocalypse Now": "Charley doesn't surf." My odyssey is like a Conrad journey into the heart of darkness, but I shake off any similarities. Hopefully I can make sense of it all—later.

For the moment, I'm trying to channel the mantra from a Ram Dass book Mike had when we were in Lahaina, *Be Here Now*. Vibrant scenery is pulling me back to the here and now. A windless haze hangs in the air over the shoreline of brilliant green coconut palms. Perfect waves peel from the ferry's wake on a glassy sea as we slip through narrow waterways between many small islands. It's gentle and warm for a moment.

That moment disappears. The haze turns ominous. The coconut trees become a prison of dark foreboding secrets, with trees packed so tightly that they deny entrance into whatever joys they might hold. When I see the ferry's wake cut clean lines behind the ship, I'm reminded of how far apart my brother and I had drifted these last few years.

Fear infects my mind. This ferry ride is the last leg to my destination. Siargao Island, for all I know, is beyond The Edge. Spasms of uncontrollable tremors grip my body. Why am I going there?

My fear is confirmed by a thundershower erupting into a quick deluge. All the outside passengers pull various forms of cover over their heads. I let it drench me, but the touch of the rain that always felt refreshing before now feels like tears. Everything is different and there's no escape from this heartache while I'm conscious.

I just want to relax like these other passengers who lay sleepily about the ship with food they've purchased from the open market in Surigao City. Their food reminds me that the mayor's letter mentioned Mike died forty-three days into a fast.

The warm sun returns. From a far corner of the ship, a Filipino with a rich tenor voice is singing "Some Enchanted Evening," backed up by a scratchy radio. His song is comforting and, along with the pulse of the engine, the effect allows me to embrace sleep. As I slip away I have a time-warp dream from 1959.

Mikey and I just saw the new movie "South Pacific" at the North Island base theater.

I tell Mikey, "I like the fighter planes from WWII, but all those songs were yuck."

"Yep. But how 'bout that place? Nice, huh?"

"Was that paradise, Mikey?"

"Sure. Bali Hai. I'd like to go there."

We get home and I tell Mom in front of Dad, "We saw 'South Pacific.'"

"Your dad was in that area during the war."

"It looked like a beautiful place. Mikey says it's paradise, like Maui."

Mom and I watch Dad storm out of the room.

Mom tells me, "For your dad, the war wasn't like that movie."

"Oh."

The ferry shudders to a stop and I jolt awake, soaked in sweat. We are at a dock on a beautiful, coconut-clustered island.

I question a mother and two kids as I point towards shore.

"Siargao?"

They smile and nod.

"Yes. Heneral Luna."

I remember the postmark General Luna but I don't see any buildings, only a pot-holed dirt track that leads into the thick coco palm forest.

I wonder if when Mike first saw this same scene whether he had any premonition that all his roads had been destined to lead him here. Could he have known that this road would be his last?

Everyone from the ferry piles into a large, brightly painted open-air bus. The only motor vehicle with four wheels on this island slowly bumps its way until we arrive at the ocean on the east side.

General Luna, General Santos… The Filipinos have a great affection for their generals; many towns are named after them. General Luna is only a small village but fortunately for me many people here speak English and, even though they have strong accents, I'm pleased to be understood.

A sweet older lady directs me to several clean but simple one-room bungalows on the beach. She holds my arm sympathetically and tears well up in her eyes. I only glance at her and can't bear her feminine sentiments. She has obviously met my brother. I remember how Mikey always brought out that tendency in Mom. Jeez, Mom died eleven years

312 / JOURNALS FROM THE EDGE

ago. My mind fills with sorrow and I realize that in death Mike has again become Mikey for me.

The whole village must know the purpose of my visit. Their quick peeks at me feel sympathetic. I drop my small bag on the floor of my bungalow. The physical part of my journey is over. Many questions have filled my head during this trip. Will this place give me the answers?

The bed looks minimally comfortable but I lay down to gather myself before I explore. Within two minutes I hear noises outside. When I sit up, my small window reveals a crowd of young children who begin to serenade me with a tender Filipino song. Their voices stir my heart and it's apparent that they are welcoming me in my time of grief.

After they finish I'm revitalized and go outside to take in the windless Pacific Ocean. I guess my height scares the children and most scatter. Two boys, oblivious to me, continue to play some sort of tag with each other. Their youth carries me back to mine. Details from after the air crash when I was a kid invade my memory.

I rip free of Mikey's arm and take off with my arms spread wide, weaving around the sky in my imaginary jet. Mikey chases and tackles me. He's trying to stick pieces of straw in my ears. We're both laughing.

"Where're your glasses, walleye? You can't fly if you're blind."

"I left 'em at home so I wouldn't lose 'em."

"Sir."

"Huh?"

"I'm the oldest so you need to always salute me and say 'sir.'"

"Dad's the oldest."

I turn my head back and forth to avoid the straw.

"We're on our own, so I'm the boss."

"No, Dad's the boss."

"But he's gone. Could be a year. Who knows? By then you'll be my slave."

I giggle.

"Never."

I escape and continue my flight home.

The present lurches back and realize I must be staring at the boys too long. They suddenly stop playing and see that I'm blocking the escape route used by the other children. The bigger boy shoves the smaller one behind his back and glares at me defiantly. I speculate for a moment that my far-off stare might be as intense and scary as Dad's used to be. Are they brothers? I step back and allow them to escape but immediately wish they hadn't left. I turn, slowly opening the screen door to my room. It squeaks and tears well up again. The past roars back to that same scene in 1956.

The screen door to our home on the Chesapeake Bay squeaked as Mikey shoved me inside. Our house was a mess; kitchen dishes piled in the sink, half-eaten food left on the table, clothes littering the hallway. I stumbled in backwards in order to keep my eyes on whatever torture he might attempt, still giggling when I crashed into a human wall. My giggling stopped and I didn't want to turn around when my hands felt strong legs. Mikey entered and his mischievous smile changed to terror when he saw Dad. My eyes remained glued on Mikey.

Dad was very fit, with dark eyes and hair cut in a no-nonsense flat top that looked like the deck of an aircraft carrier. He wore a brightly-colored aloha shirt that had Primo Hawaiian Beer in bold print surrounded by bright flowers.

His strong thumb pinned my forearm and spun me around so he could give me an ice-hard look.

"Both of you in your room. Now."

I looked at him with my mouth open.

Bam. He slapped me hard across the face.

"Close your damn trap. Are you catching flies?"

I pinched my mouth shut but it wasn't enough. He slapped me again.

"Look at me straight."

When I didn't wear my glasses, one of my eyes pointed in a different direction than the other.

I feel my cheek. That slap from so many years ago stung and tears flowed from my eyes just like they're doing now.

Mikey reached out and pulled me back out of Dad's range, where we both attempted to melt into the wall.

Dad yelled, "Move."

But we were frozen with fear. Dad dragged both of us to our room. The door slammed and he quickly withdrew his belt.

"I don't ask much of you little foul-ups."

His voice continued to rise until he sounded like Charlton Heston delivering the Ten Commandments.

"Make your bed, put away your clothes, empty the trash and wash the dishes."

Someone in this village is playing Elvis's "Love me Tender." In a blink, I'm back to the present, thinking I have the explanation for Dad's outrage when we were little boys. My sister had told me that Mom had grown up with house help because her father, Papa Bace, was a Naval officer stationed overseas. During my grandfather's career, Mom's childhood was spent in many poor countries where it was traditional to have servants. Maybe that's why Mom's homemaking skills were just about nil and her expectations of our doing anything around the house when Dad was at sea were about the same. When he returned, our house was usually a mess. Dad would flip out and beat the crap out of Mikey and me. I can almost understand it now. He couldn't hit Mom, so he took it out on us. Mikey often pulled me behind his back to protect me, like this boy just did.

Elvis takes me back to that same moment in time. I can't control this flashback.

Outside our door, our twelve-year-old sister heard Dad above her "Hound Dog" forty-five record. She screamed while beating on the door.

Mom rushed to join Mimi and yelled, "Stop it, Jack! Stop it! Stop it! You can't do this. You can't just be gone and then come home and belt them."

But the door was locked and he didn't stop.

Inside our room the belt had started flying immediately with no aim.

"This is a fact of life. You break the rules and you will get punished."

I covered my face with my hands, which bled when the buckle connected. Mikey stepped in front of me, getting the buckle across his face before he could cover it.

"Your rules? I hate you."

"You hate me? Yet every bit of food you eat comes from me."

Everything Dad said ended with a strike of the belt.

"I provide the house you sleep in." Crack! "I provide the clothes on your back." Crack! "Everything you have I give you!" Crack!

I watched in horror, powerless, while Mikey stood up to Dad and didn't flinch. When my eyes flew around the room I spotted Dad's flight helmet just underneath my bed. Sometimes I used it to pretend and if he saw that I've been playing with it...

Dad didn't see it and left us, broken in our room.

I lie down on my cot, grip my stomach and come back to 1990. But recalling this gut-wrenching memory jolts me into understanding how Mikey might have been motivated to steal Gino's money and end up here on this remote tropical paradise.

Our gang of friends had just emerged from the ocean at Hookipa Park on Maui and were gathered around our parked cars. We had been fantasizing about a surf trip when the topic of costs surfaced to challenge us.

Everyone knew Mike was the sage of surf fantasies.

"If you can pay for it with money, then it's cheap."

I remember thinking, there's that stupid cliché again.

Gino hissed with a venomous tone.

"Yeah, sure," he said. "Money is nothing when you get free rent and free food. You going to go traveling with all that extra dough you make parking cars, Mike?"

The tables had turned. Mike was destitute and it was humiliating for him to be parking cars at a restaurant where he would have been treating everyone to eat during his free-spending days. Gino, the Needler, got under everyone's skin—but Mike was obviously the most vulnerable.

Mike had turned red and taken a deep breath but didn't reply.

Gino said, "That's right, big spender. Everything you get is from me. You don't have any cool things to say now, do you?"

We knew Gino's generosity with Mike came packaged with a harsh edge. But why had he chosen to dress Mike down in front of all of us? We were pretty stoned and weren't able to digest the heavy vibes at that moment. But their clash threw a bucket of cold water on our surf fantasy.

Lying on this cot two years later, I become aware of the extra charge that Gino's tirade carried with it. He'd had no idea how we'd listened to that same rant from our dad. Of course Dad's sermon had a belt attached to it. I knew from the look on his face, though, that my brother had a tempest raging inside. Yet he remained silent in front of Gino.

After Mikey's heist, Gino's lovely wife told me what happened a week after the demeaning incident on the beach.

"Mike was doing some odds-and-ends type of chores with me. We were in our storage locker in Kahului and I was looking for something I needed. I told him, 'No Mike, it's not in there. That's where he keeps his cash.'"

I wasn't there but I can just imagine how Mike made a mental note of the loaded shoebox. God, I can just hear Mike say another cliché of his: "Revenge is a dish best served cold."

I'm feeling lonely and wondering how lonely Mikey felt out here by himself during his last days. In order to ward off sadness, I examine my immediate surroundings. The compound of bungalows is well swept, but there seems to be little activity. In contrast to the hum of the ferry, this village is quiet and serene.

No more memories. I'm ready for a walk. Behind me, I notice that the coconut trees are growing at many different angles. The small ones are straight up, while tall ones are leaning over, helter skelter. Some are just stumps. The effect is that the forest appears uninviting and dense, like a bamboo thicket. That leaves my path of least resistance along a wide white sand beach on the edge of clear calm water.

Mikey sure knew how to find a paradise.

A hundred yards later I chance upon a gazebo filled with older men who have been drinking and admiring the late-afternoon light. All of them are dressed simply, in tattered shorts and cast-off t-shirts that advertise logos from all over the world. This must be the end-point for relief clothes gathered in wealthy U.S. cities.

The one exception to this crowd is a middle-aged man who steps forward and extends his hand. He's dressed in nice slippers, long pants and a handsome aloha shirt.

"My name is Jaime Rusillion, I'm the mayor. We don't get very many tourists, so you must be Bill."

"I am. Nice to met you, Jaime."

He allows a hearty chuckle.

"Although you don't look like your brother. He had a very unique appearance and name."

"Mike is common in the U.S."

"Yes, I know—but he initially introduced himself as Max Walker. I had read the comic strip called 'The Phantom' and knew he was giving me an alias. My guess was that he was on the run."

Using yet another nom de guerre was not unusual for Mikey. I hadn't heard him use Max before, but it didn't surprise me that he did. It was one of our favorite comics.

The other men are passing around a jug and taking swigs. Finally it's handed to Jaime, who passes it on to me.

"This is tuba, from the sap of the coconut. It's sweet when we first start drinking. Then it slowly ferments and we never know how drunk we'll get."

I accept the jug and take a swig. It already tastes like moonshine and I wish I'd been there in the beginning when it was sweet. But I'm ready to shake my blues.

Soon the effect is noticeable and enjoyable. The men give me huge smiles while we trance out, and before long I feel like one of them. I smile back at Jaime and wave at all the men.

"Good vibes here."

"The people who live here stick very close to each other, especially in light of what happened."

"What happened?"

Jaime's eyes widen.

"A typhoon. I believe you call them hurricanes."

Jaime points at the coconut trees.

"It came ashore here at 220 miles an hour."

Jesus, I remember the angled coconut trees.

Jaime continues pointing and I gradually discern a roofless stone church, blackened with mildew.

"You see that? We all huddled inside that church and it saved our lives."

He chuckles again and points out a beautiful purple sea with red clouds above.

"Now we have moved our church out here by the water. Nice, yes?"

I nod drunkenly. It is nice and I don't feel so lonely anymore.

"But the next time a storm arrives, we'll hide behind those stone walls."

I contemplate this fragile gazebo which generates spirit, and the stone church that provides safety. A person needs both to survive. The opposing forces of freedom and security have been big issues in my life and I can relate to Jaime's metaphor.

When it's dark everyone lumbers away and I stumble back down the starlit beach to my room. A simple dinner of fish and rice awaits me. I eat and fall into a dreamless sleep.

I wake to find a pile of Mikey's possessions on my doorstep. There isn't much: a few clothes, a rice cooker, swim goggles and fins, some maps of the Philippines, a picture of me with my two sons and pictures of Mimi and her kids. There are more photos, but I'm drawn to a packet of letters—a diary written during his fast. I speed-read the first pages but slow down on Day 3, when he refers to a line from one of the Carlos Castaneda novels about victory being the loss of human form. As much as I enjoyed those novels, reading this quote in the context of my brother's death is unsettling.

Another paragraph draws me in.

This is the most time alone in my whole life- already exceeds all the previous times. Except for my day 6 hike for water I haven't been with anybody. It's difficult now, cuz I hurt and would like comfort and cuddling.

Jaime walks up and points at Mikey's stuff. I put the diary down, shattered by what I've just read.

"This was all he had."

He picks up one of Mikey's swim fins and directs my attention over the water to a distant speck of sand with one coconut palm.

"Your brother would swim to that small island every day. The water is shallow but the current is strong. That was his regimen. He was an odd fellow and kept to himself."

Jaime's testimony is adding to my picture of Mikey's isolation. My brother had always been the more gregarious of the two of us. Knowing he was by himself and in pain tears me up. The thought of him enduring loneliness at the end of his life is heartbreaking.

Jaime picks up a picture of Mikey with his swim goggles, swim cap and a Phantom t-shirt.

"You see. He was reincarnated as Max Walker."

The Phantom on the t-shirt has his arms crossed over his chest and is gripping two .45-caliber pistols, the same way Mikey is posing—except that my brother doesn't hold any pistols. The words on the t-shirt read, "The ghost who walks never sleeps."

Jaime sees that I'm spacing out on the picture and puts it down.

"I can see you need to be alone with all this. I'll check on you later."

I barely hear him speak or see him leave while I recall our childhood infatuation with this comic strip hero. But the memory also makes me cringe when I remember our grandfather's .45 pistol with all its history.

Wishing to escape, I put the pictures aside, but suicide and all its implications have already broken like an avalanche into my psyche.

Mikey had been alone and on the run. Was this his way out? More likely I can imagine him stepping up to the edge of the cliff to see if he was destined to go one way or the other. My grief doesn't allow me to methodically plow through everything he's written. I shuffle through his letters like a deck of cards and somehow gravitate to Day 29, where he wrote about that edge.

I realized my choices were there- successfully pull off a change-of-life pattern or adopt one of three forms of slow-motion suicide: drug addiction, alcoholism or gluttony—my natural forte. But that glorious balmy night, surveying the vast wreckage of my life I realized I could never go on continuing as high-powered Mike, capable of brilliance but just as capable of holocaust levels of needlessly excessive despair and pain.

Excessive despair and pain are all I can feel at this moment. I wish I could end this introspection because I don't feel emotionally strong enough to continue. However, it's beyond my control and this torturous train of thought doesn't let up.

In 1960 Mikey faced a crossroads with Papa Bace's .45 in his hand. Our grandmother had called Mikey a bad seed after our grandfather died. But a seed is something that is planted and cultivated. Maybe Mama Marcelle was taking a subtle swing at our father. Unfortunately, the vulnerable person at the time was Mikey. I begged and pleaded with him back then to give me the gun. He gave it to me and told me not to ever talk about it again. I thought everything was fixed—too young to realize how being labeled as a no-good would continue to eat away at my brother's self-worth. Life for both of us moved on. Now I realize he had just stuffed it inside, where guilt became his monster demon.

His belongings are talking to me. Here on this remote island Mikey faced yet another crossroads. Now it's eating me up that I'm too late to share my insights with him. Could they have made a difference and saved him from himself and his 'victory?' Looking out for each other had always been our unwritten contract. Even Mom sensed Mikey's vulnerability when we flew off to Central Asia in 1971. She told me to watch out for him. What a joke that was.

He was Jumpin' Jack Flash, after all.

Mikey introduced me to the Devil, or at least the incarnation of hell on earth, on that weird December night in Karachi. Between the cocaine and the lure of easy money, I didn't stand a chance of protecting Mikey from himself. Could it really have been possible to save my brother—or was it more likely that he would've taken me over the falls with him?

Mikey was so cool, but cool has a price. Cool. Cool. I'm slipping away, back to the moments just before the air show crash.

"Cool as what, Mikey?" I'd asked.

"Cool as—nothin'. Nothin' needs to come after 'cool as.' Those two words say it all. I heard one of Dad's pals say a pilot needs to be at two thousand feet before he can safely punch out. Nothing compares to that cool."

"Punch out?"

"Yank on an ejection handle when there's no hope left. Fires them out of the jet like a rocket."

"Oh. That sounds scary."

"Well, it's the only thing left to do if they want to live but, like I said, they need two thousand feet."

Mikey came up short on altitude here on this tropical island. I grit my teeth and decide it doesn't matter whether it was an intentional suicide or an unintended misfortune. There's nothing I could have done, but I'm amazed how susceptible I am to self-blame.

A return to Mikey's diary may offer me an escape from this inner inquisition. I need answers and quickly flip to the end. The last page shakes in my hands. It's titled Day 42. He wrote that the next day was the day he planned to start eating. Tears well up in my eyes again and his writing blurs. One line jumps out at me.

I've ridden this dead horse of a pen just about as far as it will go.

I can tell that he meant that literally since the ink fades in and out on the next lines, but the enormity of the metaphor is too much for me to handle. It's only partially comforting that he planned to eat again and live. Are there more answers in this diary? I stuff the letters back in the packet and decide to read them later, hopefully when I can handle the details of my brother's final hours.

The last item I examine is his passport. It reveals the last chapter of his travels in the South Pacific. He had stopped in Fiji, Australia, Vanuatu and the New Hebrides before ending up in this beautiful haven. I spend a long moment staring at his passport picture. This is my brother, Mikey. Now he's gone.

I begin packing his possessions for my return and realize I only want his diary. Everything else is just things, replaceable things. These things can't define a life, although his spartan belongings do make a statement.

Mikey's fins and goggles look back at me like old friends. I haven't come prepared for any exercise—but it dawns on me that now I can repeat the swim he took to the small island. The exertion will do me good and maybe I'll be able to find Mikey out there in the ocean. He had done it and so should I. Even in death our brotherly competition is still present. I'll wear his swim shorts to keep him close.

The water is warm and clear when I enter to prepare my goggles. A quick glance at the small island Jaime told me about tells me the tide is much lower than it was yesterday. Yesterday it looked like a speck; today it appears like a large ship. This adds to my sense of confidence and I settle into an easy rhythm.

Swimming was a gyroscope for Mikey and me throughout our lives. It was a fundamental exercise that prepared us for everything we did, from surfing to just feeling good. Swimming was our mantra.

I'm feeling good and the ocean off General Luna is like a waist-deep swimming pool. When it's like this, I feel like I can swim forever.

Suddenly little bits of seaweed are bent over at an extreme angle as if they're in a strong wind. The tide is flowing at an alarming rate and I remember Jaime's warning. The island no longer appears any closer when I lift my head to check. The tide must be advancing, which would explain the island's getting smaller and appearing further away. But that is really no relief since no matter which way the water flows, I'll be swept away from land towards open sea. Self-doubt enters my mind. What if I guess incorrectly about compensating for the current and end up drifting even more off-course? Sounds like the story of my life.

I decide not to dwell on that negative thought. As long as I can mark my progress by focusing on short-term targets of reaching this trumpet shell or that starfish, then I can reach my goal.

However, the water clarity begins to dim and along with it, my confidence. The strong current churns up sand and when I search for reference points, I'm lost in a storm of swirling sediment. This is vertigo like I used to experience flying through clouds with my hang glider.

As my equilibrium disintegrates, my history with Mikey surfaces in full focus. So many times his lack of proper planning and anticipation led to a string of disasters that he always explained were the nature of the business. I had strung along, disoriented, and every time I got burned I swore I didn't want to be a part of that nature.

The image is so clear—Mikey slamming Dad's ski boat throttle all the way forward, the boat leaping to full speed and my arms feeling like they were yanking out of my sockets. The rest of that memory played out like a die cast for our life—my wobbling skis, my frantic hand signals and Mikey, not looking back. After I'd hit a wake cockeyed and bounced across Chuckatuck Creek like a skipping stone, Mike pulled up next to me with the boat.

"Come on, no crying. Just stuff it in. You don't want anyone to think you're a baby, do you?"

Mikey grabbed me by the float ring and rolled me into the boat.

"Man, you looked like the human cannonball. Shoulda seen it. Kaboom!"

He was laughing and I started to laugh.

But I'm not laughing now. When I examine the results of his endeavors, I know I didn't have his level of faith. Why did I keep forgetting? That first bust in the L.A. airport? My God, he confided in a stewardess he'd never even met before. Manila, the Filipino Kojak and that stupid Right Guard stash can? Even the bust in New Caledonia, which he blamed on a snitch, was more likely the result of what I later learned was him snorting blow at a Noumea night club when he first arrived on the island. And what was he thinking that time he doubled back to grab Gino's money? Wasn't it obvious he would run into someone he knew on Maui? Ever since I've been living outside Mikey's world, I've come to see how his antics have stood out so blatantly among people who earned money the old-fashioned way.

In 1970, he'd thought he had it down. He knew back then that standing out in the straight world was dangerous and his solution was simple. I remember how he put down other smugglers living inside the U.S.

"They were dumb shits, Bill. They were living flamboyant lifestyles in plain sight. When you live outside U.S. laws, you have to live outside the U.S."

But he never anticipated that the straight world would soon find Bali and all the other out-of-the-way places he'd discovered. That's why we weren't invisible during our wild days together—yet Mikey went on thinking he was exempt from the laws that applied to everyone else. Living outside the law ended up making him stand out in exactly the same way he'd warned against in 1970. And his extremism in everything he did had fallout. A forty-three-day fast is a stunning example. Only this time he, not the people around him, got consumed in the process.

Many memories are flooding my mind from our time together, but suddenly I consider I might be sliding into yet another catastrophe. Where am I going to end up on this swim? I don't know these waters. The way Jaime spoke, the locals have a healthy respect for this current. When Jaime first informed me of its danger, I discounted it. Mike and I had often heard these types of warnings before embarking on what we considered to be standard-issue swims. We were powerful swimmers and reveled in fighting a current. The current would always let up eventually, allowing us to advance towards wherever we were heading. It was a psychological battle where we felt we could match the flow of the ocean. It ebbed until it advanced. The main thing was to hold our ground so we could be there to succeed when the current shifted. We could always make it, as long as we never gave up.

I flash that this is the same kind of forcefulness that made Mike think he could survive alone for forty-three days without food.

Jaime had been correct. This is an exceptionally strong current.

Where am I headed? To a small sand spit with one lone coconut palm? Or am I heading out to an unknown sea? Mikey is already in that sea. Am I ready to follow him there?

The water has become milky with sediment. I'm now swimming blind and need to make a commitment one way or the other. When I poke my head above water, forward progress to the small island has stopped. I glance back towards Siargao and realize that I'm being swept around to the west of the point.

Quitting has always been distasteful to me and I feel Mike urging me to continue. But I'm not going for it and I change course back to the island, just barely able to reach the shore around the point.

While trudging through a mucky mangrove shoreline, I'm startled when a bubble bursts to the surface. Is it from the suction of my foot lifting out of the mud? Or is it something else? The memory of the crocodiles on the ferry trip to this island invades my mind and quickly I pull myself up on a mangrove root. The roots are thick enough that I'm able to stretch from one to another until I make it back to the hospitable sand beach on the Pacific side of the island. Fear and fatigue have wiped me out. Dragging myself back to my room, I collapse for the rest of the day.

Jaime pokes his head in my door in the late afternoon and wakes me up.

"Do you want to see us tap the coconut tree tonight? This time you can start when it's sweet."

His eyes question the mangrove grime all over my legs.

"I went for a swim to the island."

He nods but seems unconvinced, so I confess.

"I didn't make it. The current was strong like you said. I guess my brother was lucky when he did it."

Knowing Mike, he hadn't planned ahead, so what else besides luck could explain his swimming success? I could blame my turning around on the hangover and jet lag, but why do I need to justify it? For a ghost? Somehow I need to justify my quitting to this total stranger. I figure Jaime qualifies because he's my only living connection to my brother's last days.

"When I swam back, the current swept me around the island, over to the mangroves."

He lifts his eyebrows.

"Well, you made it. Why don't you clean up and eat a little? Then if you want to have some company, come join us."

When I eat, I think about how satisfying it is and how Mikey had gone forty-three days without.

I clean up and return to my room, full from a satisfying meal. My cot is typical for a tropical climate. It isn't clean and smells of mildew, like our cots in the bamboo huts at our surf camp. We were able to escape our moldy sleeping quarters on some glorious nights at G-Land. The wind was sufficient to ward off the mosquitoes and a group of us used to hang out on hard bamboo planks in an open-air gazebo up on stilts. There we could soak in the fresh ocean air and smoke weed. The surf pounded like the Guns of Navarone while we absorbed the stars.

Last night at Jaime's gazebo, or church as he described it, had brought back those same sensations. The tuba had replaced cannabis as a vehicle to connect with the cosmos, God or any of the manifestations that make a man feel connected to the greater universe. Jaime's soothing effect on the other men made me feel relaxed; he had a gentle non-judgmental tone and was the kind of holy man I could open up to with my troubles.

The swim has perplexed me and I crave some balance so I stride off down the beach to take Jamie up on his invitation. The air by the water is that perfect temperature which is neither too hot nor too cool. It feels like a Samadhi tank, where sensory deprivation focuses all my attention to the night sky.

I arrive at the gazebo. The local men have taken their places and are embarking on another night of drinking tuba. This is my kind of spiritual communion.

Jaime smiles at me and clues me in on their current conversation.

"They're complaining that the government sent rotten dried fish in the relief effort after the hurricane. We already had plenty of fish. We needed rice. Many people went hungry here after the storm. Now the government wants labor to help with a military listening post. These men are not motivated to help them. They resent the government in Manila."

"It sounds like you're on your own out here."

"Yes. But this last year since the storm the rice crop has been good. These people have accomplished so much."

He puts his fingers to his lips.

"But don't tell anyone or they will tax us."

I know he's trying to be light, but I look away at the stars and contemplate a life of accomplishment. Jaime probably expects a chuckle or some response at his humor because he apologizes.

"Excuse me for burdening you with our problems. You've come from far away and may have many questions. I'm here to help if I can."

"No, it's OK. I was just sad I wasn't able to see my brother before he died to tell him how proud I was of what he accomplished. Eighteen years ago, I missed being there to tell our father that same thing because I was far from home when he died."

"What did your brother accomplish?"

"He manifested a dream we both had when he established a surf camp on Java. We got to enjoy it for many years." I pause. "Not enough years, of course, but we had it, right in the palm of our hands. It was a paradise, just like this, where we went surfing every day. So we were fortunate to have been able to enjoy that. It was the first of its kind and the obstacles were great. There are now many surf camps like it through-out the world. That was an accomplishment, to do it first. But it was also a drain of extravagant spending and somehow it all unraveled."

"Why?"

It's apparent to me that Jaime has served in some other capacity than just as mayor. His line of questioning is simple but leading. When I answer I try to grasp an overview while we stare into the timeless space of the night sky.

"I guess anyone who only knew Mike's life during the surf camp peri-od could point to events that occurred after he made that dream come true, but really the seeds of self-destruction were sown before, when we were young boys."

"Those seeds weren't planted too deep, were they? You've uprooted and traveled far from home to find a dream, a paradise as you say. But as you can see from our own troubles, that is only a matter of perspec-tive, is it not?"

"I realize that but for my brother and me, home and deep roots were not in our upbringing. Traveling and escaping to a dream was."

"Why was it that way?"

"Because our father was a Naval officer. We moved constantly. He was a hard man and it was rough, especially for my brother. We became masters of escape."

I have tears in my eyes and they must shine in the little light there is in the night sky because Jaime lays his arm over my shoulder in a com-forting manner.

"What would you have told your father if you had seen him before he died?"

"I don't know."

The mention of his death strangely makes me feel sympathetic to Dad. It brings back an image of his staring into space after Mom informed him of Mikey's discharge from the Navy. Now I can begin to see how the disappointments he encountered at the end of his career must have been so crushing.

Early in his career his performance as an aviator and ship captain had always been measured and evaluated. This worked for him. But those days had evaporated by the time he was working at the Pentagon. He must have experienced the ultimate frustration when he saw that politicians now controlled his performance. Their micro-management and wasteful spending resulted in what he viewed as a half-assed war campaign. But knowing Dad, he would have still held himself responsible for the failure in Vietnam.

This all happened while on the home front he was losing control of his oldest son. Mikey had stood toe to toe against Dad, threatening to fight back. This mutiny and then the disgrace of Mikey's general discharge must have cracked Dad's world view.

He finally broke a few years later when I had to talk him down from the curse of that god-damn pearl-handled .45. But Dad's rebound from the cane grass with Papa Bace's gun was only temporary. In three more years he was ravaged by cancer.

Dad's life always had uncanny parallels with the obsessed captain in the novel *Moby Dick*. I can understand how Ahab's thirst for revenge grew like a cancer. How could the captain of a ship deal with the trauma of a lost leg? Each step on the rolling deck would be a constant reminder of his impotence.

My silence has lasted too long. Jaime gives me a friendly touch and I turn to him.

"I wish I could've told him that I forgave him and that I finally understood the reason he was the way he was and not only that, I was proud of that reason. I realize now that in order to do his duty, his soul had been damaged. But Jaime, I didn't understand these things then and I wasn't ready to forgive him on his deathbed. I was only unexplainably sad at that point, like I had lost something I didn't know I had. It has taken me all these years since he died to gain the perspective I'm telling you now."

Before I left on this trip I read an article in a news magazine about a new term psychiatrists have coined for what happened to veterans from Vietnam: post-traumatic stress disorder. They have their term and I have my experience. As a boy, I was always enamored with the image of a fighter pilot—but back then the thick veneer of heroics and glamour surrounding the exhilarating test pilot days masked Dad's war trauma from me. If the term creates understanding, I wish I'd had it then. It had been so confusing not to understand the reason why Dad was so cruel.

"Damaged his soul? How was that?"

"War. His time in the Navy."

It's my best guess. Something traumatic must have happened to change him into the man Mom sometimes called Captain Bligh. His high stress level continued even after WWII. Until he stopped flying jets in 1959, he had been in "Cold War" readiness, shadowing the Soviets.

I'd tracked down Chuck Soderlund, Dad's wingman from their night fighter squadron on the USS Wasp. He was excited to hear my voice and said I sounded exactly like my father. That made me shudder. Chuck had Parkinson's disease and his wife translated his information for me.

"Even forty-five years later I can still feel that dull fatigue, a physical and spiritual fatigue, that I and many other pilots had reached by the time we were engaged at Leyte Gulf. Even though we knew the war was won, I assumed I would be killed any day. There was just no way that I could live through many more missions. This feeling didn't involve any gloom or fear—it was just a natural condition, like the weather. A fact of life."

Those were the four infamous words I had heard Dad speak so often when he lost control of his emotions. I didn't understand them back then, but now I can begin to appreciate their use by the hardened man who was my father.

Yet his softer side was still there. I occasionally witnessed his island-boy style resurface in brief moments, just as an amnesiac has fluttering memories of a former life. I was never able to enjoy those moments, though, for fear that the least provocation would trigger a return to his violent persona.

I glance at Jaime. He's still an island boy at the age of fifty-eight, full of love and understanding.

I attempt to explain my thoughts to him.

"Our father felt lucky to have the opportunity to chase his dream of going to sea. When he shipped off to the Naval Academy he didn't antic- ipate war, especially with the Japanese."

I drift off again in silence.

After a few moments Jaime offers, "Sometimes in life we have to face bad luck."

"Yes, the war was bad luck but you know, he had incredible good luck surviving."

"How was that?"

"He went to flight school just before his ship was deployed to Guadalcanal, where it was sunk soon after."

I'm not going to bother telling him about just missing the devastation at Pearl Harbor or meeting Mom.

"So he was a pilot?"

"Yes, a night fighter pilot."

"Where?"

"He was all over the Pacific on an aircraft carrier. He fought at night, and sometimes day, in the island-hopping campaign from 1944 to '45; Wake, The Marianas, Iwo Jima, Guam, Palau, Okinawa, Formosa and finally Leyte Gulf, where they annihilated the Japanese Navy."

I had studied Dad's WWII history in detail after he died and was very proud of his service. He had flown air cover in every amphibious landing and had watched Marines, affectionately called grunts, die by the thousands after landing on dangerous beachheads. Like an iron angel, Dad had tried to protect them, with varying degrees of success.

I remember him belting Mikey for using the word 'grunt' with a sneering tone. For Dad, grunt had more meaning than we would ever know.

Jaime snaps me out of my thoughts.

"Leyte? Bill, do you know where you are?"

"Well, we're off of Mindanao on this small island. How do you say it? Schar-gow?"

"Yes, that's it."

Jaime points to some lights on a distant island to the north. The tropical haze has prevented me from seeing it during the daytime.

"Can you see that island? Its name is Leyte. Between this island and Leyte is Leyte Gulf. Your father fought in the sky right over this beach in WWII. If he flew at night he flew under these stars. Perhaps I saw him."

My mouth drops open.

"Yes. My friends and I observed that air battle from this same beach when we were twelve-year-old boys. When white streaks filled the sky, we thought it was entertainment for our pleasure until we saw the explosions. Then we knew it was serious and that men were dying."

It dawns on me that Jaime had been through the same air show trauma that Mikey and I had experienced. This is stunning information and I thirst for more.

"Were there Japanese on this island?"

"Oh, yes."

"Were they cruel?"

I had learned that the occupation of the Philippines had been harsh. Then there were the atrocities of the Bataan Death March and the slaughter of one hundred thousand civilian Filipinos during the fall of Manila. The Japanese had a reputation for cold-blooded brutality, so I wanted to know how that played out here on this remote island. Had Jaime experienced abuse under their control?

"No, they weren't. When they came here, they put down their guns and lived agreeably with us until the day of that battle."

His response surprises me. Had all the gentle soldiers in the Japanese Imperial Army been stationed on this island? It didn't seem likely. I become intrigued with the idea that this paradise had perhaps tamed a small segment of their cruel army. Were they gentle warriors, part of an unknown story?

"What happened then?"

"Many of them tried to escape this island in a small ship. An American fighter plane swooped in and blew it up, killing most of them."

The thought occurs to me that Dad might have been one of those American pilots unfortunately strafing those humane Japanese. I try to imagine how he must have had to cut off any sensitivity to his emotions in order to do his duty. They say the soul is shaped by the fond memories of our upbringing. For Dad, those memories included many Japanese chums and classmates growing up on Maui.

Jaime grimaces.

"The crocodiles ate the ones who survived. They were in that same area where you swam today."

I shudder at Jaime's reminder. What a horrible fate, to be a victim of those primordial creatures. Too bad those escaping Japanese soldiers had been the kind ones.

Jaime notices me shiver.

"Yes, you were lucky today. The next time you swim, go farther south towards Tuazon Point. The water is clear and excellent there. But it has ghosts."

This catches me off guard as I haven't taken Jaime for the superstitious type.

"Ghosts?"

"Well, yes. The story goes on. The remaining Japanese soldiers fled to a cave at Tuazon Point. A few weeks after they began hiding there, the entrance of the cave collapsed after a severe rain. Those soldiers' voices could be heard for weeks afterwards—then silence. Since that time Tuazon Point has been considered haunted. Only a few will even set foot there. I believe that is why your brother decided on that place to conduct his fast."

"Wow. He went to a haunted place. Why?"

"As you can see, these people are poor. But when your brother attempted to fast earlier in your same bungalow, people from the village would bring him food. They would never allow a person to starve in their village. It's just not in their nature. That's why he had a gazebo built out at Tuazon point where he could fast without temptation. I can have Officer Magdalena take you out there tomorrow. He has the only motorcycle on the island and isn't afraid of ghosts."

"I'd like that."

When I search the stars again I think of how Dad and I admired the night sky together over Papa Bace's pier in 1964. He had reminisced with me about how he used to navigate back to his carrier, his home.

I whisper, "My God, these are the stars."

"Yes, they are."

Jaime is contemplative for a moment.

"Your brother was born in 1946—so it appears your father left this place and returned to America to give life to Mike. Forty-three years later your brother came to rest here. Perhaps this was his home all along?"

He's right. When the war was finished, Dad returned and fathered a true 'victory' baby, Mikey, who was born when they moved to Key West, where Dad trained with the first jets.

There's a symmetry to it that's heartening.

"Yes. Perhaps he is home."

Officer Magdalena revs his motorbike. He's a grim-faced contrast to almost everyone else in General Luna and maybe that's why he was designated as the only policeman on the island. He's also one of the few who dares go out to Tuazon Point. Another brave soul is Mikey's friend Pastor Mozo, who was designated to bring him fruit to break his fast.

I figure someone either needs a gun or God or perhaps the memories of a dead brother to set foot in that place.

Magdalena has seen too many American cop movies and is showing off his gun to me.

"Like Dirty Harry, yes?"

I nod.

He has no idea how guns keep haunting me. He's wrapped up in the infatuation of violence just like many people in the world outside of utopias like General Luna. It feels like a sacrilege to have him accompany me to the sacred site of my brother's last days. But what choice do I have? I jump onto the back of the bike.

We arrive at a breathtaking spot. Coconut trees rustle their fronds together and a small, perfectly shaped wave peels off the reef a short distance from a pearl-white sand beach. As Jaime reported, no one is around.

Magdalena ghoulishly shows me the cave where the Japanese were trapped at the end of the war. It's much more interesting to him than where Mikey's gazebo used to be. The platform for the gazebo has already been dismantled and only the four posts remain. I tell Magdalena I want to be alone for a while and sit within the perimeter of the site while he examines the sealed tomb of the cave entrance.

I remove the diary from the envelope and read to myself.

On his last page Mikey wrote:

"It is only a few yards to a beautiful moonlit beach. I wish I possessed the strength to get that far. To be able to swim in this water is so revitalizing. Pastor Mozo comes tomorrow and after I have the fruit I told him to bring, I should be able to reach the water."

His writings make it clear that Mikey had considered this last fast a continuation of his effort to cleanse his soul. He recalls how pot and LSD provided temporary relief from the tortuous assaults on his self-worth growing up. Cocaine and heroin had brought many of those undesirable past manifestations to the surface. This fast was an attempt at a final exorcism of the psychological demons that he knew he needed to eliminate if he were to move on and redirect his life.

He went on to write that some very uncomfortable sores were erupting from his body on day 15, and yet he persisted in continuing his fast, thinking it would heal all.

It didn't work. Maybe there was too much to cleanse and the toxins came roaring out of his body like demons, consuming him in the process.

My thoughts return to Dad. He was so much a part of Mikey's unraveling. Once he lost his military grip on life after his breakdown, had his demons done the same thing? This inner battle concerns me. Is it a genetic thing? How can I deal with the rest of my life in a manner that will free me from these tormenting emotions and ultimate physical collapse?

Even Officer Magdalena seems able to feel my sadness and doesn't interrupt my silent communion with my brother and father.

When I return to General Luna, I go with Jaime to the place where they have buried my brother.

"It is a nice spot, yes?"

We're gazing out over Leyte Gulf and inside my head I'm seeing and hearing the Navy Hymn play while flag-covered bodies slide into the ocean. "Eternal Father, strong to save, whose arm hath bound the restless wave."

The battle is over.

That hymn always brought tears of pride to my eyes when I was a kid watching "Navy Log" on TV. When I think about it now, it still does.

"Yes, it is a wonderful spot."

"A stone for his grave?"

For me, the body and a burial place are not the person. The limitless drops of the ocean and infinite stars in the sky instead contain that person for me. I'm thinking about all those sailors whose bodies slid into the unmarked ocean.

"No burial stone, please. My memory is here."

I place my hand over my broken heart and Jaime and I drift away on the silence. Melville's perfect passage on death comes back to me.

"Yes, there is death in this business of whaling—a speechlessly quick chaotic bundling of man into Eternity. But what then? Methinks we have hugely mistaken this matter of Life and Death. Methinks that what they call my shadow here on earth is my true substance. Methinks that in looking at things spiritual, we are too much like oysters observing the sun through the water, and thinking that thick water the thinnest of air. Methinks my body is but the less of my better being. In fact take my body who will, take it I say, it is not me."

Jaime lays his hand on my shoulder and breaks our silence.

"I understand. How was your trip to Tuazon Point?"

He has been so understanding and gentle; he epitomizes the feeling I'm receiving from this trip to General Luna.

"It was revealing, Jaime," I say, and thank him for what he did to make the trip possible. And there is so much more I want to say about Mike and what he'd written and how I believed he hadn't planned on dying.

But we don't get to choose when, do we? I'm sure it was so easy to slip away when he was that close to the edge. Forty-three is young, but at least it's older than those soldiers who were forced to starve inside that cave. At least my brother did what he did by choice and had the luxury of plenty of fresh water and open sky. Even though he may not have been aware of it, he chose to be in a place that Jamie has suggested may have been his real home considering the chain of events with our father's history in this place. According to what Jamie has told me, this island may have tamed its Japanese occupiers, and I have no doubt after reading Mike's diary that this place also touched his soul. I can only imagine that his last days were peaceful. We have so few choices where death is concerned. It seems to me he had more choices than most people.

Jamie nods. "You're welcome. I'm glad to have been of help, and to know the stars your father used to find his way in the night sky are now your brother's to behold."

I tell him how much I appreciate that beautiful thought. "Yet the part that hurts," I add, "is being left behind." It's like a stab in the heart, not just because I lost a brother who means so much to me, but because I've lost a potential future with him.

That's it. From now on I will have to carve out my own path without hope of ever having grand dreams with Mikey again. If I get into trouble in life, I will have to solve it on my own. I'm already doing that now but when Mikey was alive and in my heart, he was the captain of our ship. He always had been.

Jaime shakes my hand and wishes me farewell.

"Your brother told me he left some belongings and money in Davao City. I can give you the address but I must warn you, Catobato Province isn't like here. Islamic separatists operate there and have recently kidnapped Western visitors for ransom. If you go, watch yourself."

Maybe some of Mikey's pirate booty is there but in the frame of mind I have, the booty perhaps possesses some unwanted karma attached to it. I've ignored Jaime's warning once before and am not going to do it again. Everything I need for closure is in my heart.

"I think I'll just go on home."

I'm home on Maui and crying the tears that have built up over a long time. Despite all that happened with the camp, our split and his jail time in New Caledonia, I had always presumed things would eventually come together for my brother and me.

Now he's gone, and I know I'm finally on my own. The enormity of it is overwhelming. While Mikey always represented a wonderful fantasy of the future for me, I realize that any fires for those fantasies with him are now extinguished. But I can't stop thinking about the past. I gaze out over the pulsing green cane fields and glide back to 1956.

I'm lying in bed one morning, still knotted up from the belting Mikey and I had yesterday.

I hear Dad order Mom to have me report for breakfast.

Dad is at the head of the table and has his newspaper in front of his face. I attempt to pull my chair out as softly as I can. Maybe he won't notice me. I don't want breakfast and can't wait until I'm safe at school. Mikey sits across from me, staring lifelessly down at his eggs with dark blue and red patches on his cheeks, nose and arms. Mimi is staring blankly at Mikey's face. Mom is scraping eggs onto my plate. Her concerned expression tells me something is wrong. Like Mikey, I stare at my food, hunched over my plate.

Dad snaps his paper closed. I peek up and can see his scowl. His eyes drop to an envelope in front of his plate and he removes a sheet of paper with black holes burned on it.

He works his jaw into a tighter clench and finally speaks in a low tone.

"Do you want to explain this?"

I'm frozen.

"Your teacher has written that you have used your glasses to burn holes in this assignment."

He holds up the incriminating sheet of paper.

Mimi looks over at Dad.

"Oh, come on!"

He glares at her and she knocks her chair over and runs from the room.

I rub my sore hands from blocking yesterday's buckle. Mom is giving Dad her pained face that begs him to be calm.

I keep my eyes on Mom while I answer Dad.

"I wa-wanted to see how a magnifying glass worked."

He yells, "You what?"

I inch my chair back.

Mom and Mikey have tears in their eyes, yet I can see Mikey is also angry.

"You have abused the gift of your glasses to misuse them as a tool to waste school property."

My mouth hangs open but when I spot Mikey stretching his mouth open wider than looks normal, I quickly shut mine tight. I get Mikey's message that if Dad has the range, he'll slap me.

Dad points to our bedroom. I get up from the table and see Mikey's tears.

Dad follows me. When we're alone in the bedroom, he continues.

"Don't you realize what it is to have the opportunity to improve your vision with the money I provide?"

The belt hits my chest hard before I have a chance to turn away from him.

"When are you going to understand the value of hard work?"

This time the belt has a direct hit in the center of my back.

Dad stops while I stand there, empty and exhausted.

"Don't leave this room today."

His black look crushes me.

"I'm only finished for now."

Mikey almost falls into our room when Dad opens the door to leave and squeezes by him to get his school books.

The door shuts and Mikey drapes his arm over me.

"You know, I've been here so many times."

He shifts his eyes to our window.

I hug him and lean over the ledge, inspecting the drop.

Mikey says, "It's not so far anymore, is it?"

I'm sobbing. I spot Dad's flight helmet and pull it out from under my bed. When Mikey sees me admiring it, he comes over and pulls it gently from my hands and slips it over my head. He has that fearless grin I love and now he's rubbing my back. My sobs go away when he salutes me.

A wild reaction surges through my body and I jump out of the window, like the human cannonball, and tumble onto the sandy ground. When I glance back up, Mikey is still smiling, waving me on to get going.

I start running—and keep running. I don't know where. The helmet is rattling around my head and my brains feel like they're coming loose.

There it is—the front gate of the Naval Air Station. The MP's spot me but don't move from their post. I salute them like everyone else I have seen enter the base and climb up and into the cockpit of the out-of-service Super Sabre F-86.

I speak into my imaginary microphone, "Squadron Leader, Squadron Leader. I'm flying over the Yalu River—Mig Alley, keeping my eyes peeled for bogeys."

The MP's are walking over to me. I'm crying and my hand yanks on the ejection handle over and over again until the MP's wrestle me from the jet.

336 / Journals from the Edge

My hand is still clenched from the grip on that ejection handle so many years ago. Anger surges up inside of me at the thought of that vulnerable little boy, but the words Mikey said to me before he left Lahaina for the South Pacific in 1967 surface to soothe the wound.

"All that stuff that happened in the past, you gotta let go of it. You can't be pissed off at Dad. He's the result of his own exposure to a reality he couldn't handle. Leave the judgment behind, otherwise it'll keep you from being in the here and now."

I open my eyes to see the cane grass still pulsing in the wind, like a green ocean. I'm struggling to make sense of it all. Like Ishmael, I claw towards the surface of a stormy sea of words, my lungs exploding with emotion, grasping for Queequeg's metaphorical coffin to burst forth from the maelstrom.

I hear my heavy-footed sons at the front door and jolt back to the present. My hand opens from its tight clench, wipes the tears from my eyes and prepares for the hug I need to give them.

The End

20447855R00207

Made in the USA
San Bernardino, CA
11 April 2015